iPad® for the Older and Wiser

Get Up and Running with Your iPad or iPad mini

3rd Edition

Sean McManus
with Rosemary Hattersley

This edition first published 2013
© 2013 Sean McManus

Registered office
John Wiley & Sons Ltd, The Atrium, Southern Gate, Chichester, West Sussex, PO19 8SQ, United Kingdom

For details of our global editorial offices, for customer services and for information about how to apply for permission to reuse the copyright material in this book please see our website at www.wiley.com.

A catalogue record for this book is available from the British Library.

ISBN 978-1-118-63501-8 (paperback); ISBN 978-1-118-63498-1 (e-mobi); 978-1-118-63499-8 (e-PDF); 978-1-118-63500-1 (e-pub)

Set in 11/13 Optima LT Std Roman by Wiley Indianapolis Composition Services

Printed in the United Kingdom by Bell & Bain

Dedication from Sean McManus

To Karen

About the authors

Sean McManus is an expert technology and business author. His other books include *Microsoft Office for the Older and Wiser*, *Social Networking for the Older and Wiser*, *Web Design in Easy Steps* and *Raspberry Pi For Dummies*. His tutorials and articles have appeared in magazines including *Internet Magazine*, *Internet Works*, *Business 2.0*, *Making Music* and *Personal Computer World*. His personal website is at **www.sean.co.uk**

Rosemary Hattersley has been writing about consumer technology for more than a decade. Most of her work can be found in *PC Advisor, Macworld* and *iPad & iPhone User*. She's written for and edited *The Complete Guide to The iPhone 5,* in addition to guides for the iPad mini, Android and Windows 7 and 8. She's also a knitting geek. Her marriage to *Macworld*'s editor mended a schism in the Mac/PC divide. Then along came Android to rain on the iPad's parade. As if!

Publishers Acknowledgements

Some of the people who helped bring this book to market include the following:

Editorial and Production
VP Consumer and Technology Publishing Director: Michelle Leete
Associate Director – Book Content Management: Martin Tribe
Associate Publisher: Chris Webb
Assistant Editor: Ellie Scott
Editorial Manager and Project Editor: Jodi Jensen
Copyeditor: Kathy Simpson
Editorial Assistant: Annie Sullivan
Technical Editor: Mark L. Chambers
U3A Reviewer: Jean Judge

Marketing
Associate Marketing Director: Louise Breinholt
Marketing Manager: Lorna Mein
Marketing Assistant: Tash Lee

Composition Services
Compositor: Jennifer Henry
Proofreader: Linda Seifert
Indexer: Potomac Indexing, LLC

Acknowledgements

Thank you, as always, to my wife, Karen, for all her support while I was writing all editions of this book.

I've had the support of a great team at Wiley on all editions of this book, including Sara Shlaer, Jodi Jensen, Kathy Simpson, Grace Fairley, Mark Chambers, Ellie Scott, Birgit Gruber, Chris Webb, Kate Parrett, Steve Long, and Jennifer Henry. Jean Judge gave valuable feedback on behalf of the U3A.

For help with research, testing things and mocking up screenshots, thanks also to Kim Gilmour, Mark Turner, Kieran McManus, Peter Döring, Annie Alexander, Neil Cossar, Wylda Holland, Marcus Dawson, Mark Young, Robert Kealey, Wendy White, Annemarie O'Brien and Mark Bennett.   —Sean McManus

Thank you to Mark Hattersley and the entire Wiley team for checking through my work and offering additional tips.   —Rosemary Hattersley

The Third Age Trust

The Third Age Trust is the body which represents all U3As in the UK. The U3A movement is made up of over 800 self-governing groups of older men and women who organise for themselves activities which may be educational, recreational or social in kind. Calling on their own experience and knowledge they demand no qualifications nor do they offer any. The movement has grown at a remarkable pace and offers opportunities to thousands of people to demonstrate their own worth to one another and to the community. Their interests are astonishingly varied but the members all value the opportunity to share experiences and learning with like-minded people. The Third Age Trust's endorsement of the Older and Wiser series hints at some of that width of interest.

Contents

Chapter 3 – Getting connected · 33

Chapter 4 – Keeping notes on your iPad · 55

PART II – Using your iPad for communications

81

Chapter 5 – Managing your address book and birthday list

83

Chapter 6 – Keeping in touch by email

93

Contents

Icons used in this book

Throughout this book, we've used icons to help focus your attention on certain information. This is what they mean:

Equipment needed — Lets you know in advance the equipment you will need to hand as you progress through the chapter.

Skills needed — Placed at the beginning to help identify the skills you'll need for the chapter ahead.

Tip — Tips and suggestions to help make life easier.

Note — Take note of these little extras to avoid confusion.

Warning — Read carefully; a few things could go wrong at this point.

Try It — Go on, enjoy yourself; you won't break it.

Trivia — A little bit of fun to bring a smile to your face.

Summary — A short recap at the end of each chapter.

Brain Training — Test what you've learned from the chapter.

PRACTICE MAKES
PERFECT

To build upon the lessons learnt in this book, visit www.pcwisdom.co.uk

- **More training tutorials**

- **Links to resources**

- **Advice through frequently asked questions**

- **Social networking tips**

- **Videos and podcasts from the author**

- **Author blogs**

Introduction

Equipment needed: Just this book and your iPad.

Skills needed: Some curiosity about the iPad and what it can do for you.

What is the iPad?

The Apple iPad (see Figure 0.1) is a lightweight portable computer. It's hugely successful with people of all ages and has found plenty of fans among older computer users, many of whom may have shied away from using computers, email and the Internet in the past.

The iPad is based on a touchscreen. This means that the screen can detect when you're touching it, so you don't need any other input device. Instead of using a mouse to move a cursor around, you use your finger to select what you want on the display screen. Rather than typing on a separate keyboard, you touch the keys on a picture of a keyboard on the screen. You slide your fingers across the screen to move items around and use a host of other *gestures,* or finger movements, to issue commands. It's a completely different way of working and having fun. Like driving a car, it takes a little time to learn the controls; but before long you're able to control the device without even thinking about it.

Why you might want an iPad

The iPad is ideal for older and wiser computer users for a few reasons:

- It includes all the software you need for using the web, keeping in touch with friends, browsing photos, watching videos, listening to music, reading books, managing your address book, taking notes and viewing maps. In fact, it can do pretty much everything you're likely to want to do with a computer.

- It's extremely lightweight, so you can use it comfortably anywhere.

Figure 0.1

- The screen is easy to see, and you can magnify websites and photos to get a clearer view.

- The size of the screen also means that the icons are well spaced, so it's easy to control the device by touch.

- You can enhance your iPad by adding free or inexpensive software *apps* (applications) that cover virtually any hobby or interest you have. Apple makes it easy for you to find and install these apps too, as you'll see in Chapter 14.

- The iPad is ideal for relaxing on the sofa or for taking out and about with you. Its large screen is ideal for watching programmes using the free BBC iPlayer catch-up TV service or for viewing your photos as a slideshow.

You may be worried that the iPad is completely different from what you're used to. The good news is that the iPad is much simpler to use than a desktop computer. Apple has a reputation for creating products that users find quick to master and intuitive to use, and this book introduces you to the important features so that you can get started quickly.

You'll soon love the flexibility and immediacy of the iPad. It can be taken anywhere, and it wakes up from its sleep mode immediately so you can use it on impulse when you think of something you want to email, Google or watch. Most of the time, you'll find that the iPad does exactly what you want with much less fuss than the typical computer.

iPad models

The iPad is one of many touchscreen devices known as *tablet computers*. Its slick design and intuitive controls helped it capture the tablet market quickly. When the iPad was launched in April 2010, it took just one month to sell 1 million of the devices and 12 million programs (called *apps)* to run on them. In October 2012, Apple launched a fourth version of the iPad, as well as a smaller, cheaper model called the iPad mini.

You can now choose an iPad in either of two sizes. The iPad that's been around for a while has a 9.7-inch screen (measured on the diagonal) and is about 9.5 inches long by 7.5 inches wide. The new, more compact model — the iPad mini — has a 7.9-inch screen, and measures 7.87 inches long by just under 5.5 inches wide. Either model fits easily into your bag. Depending on what you're doing with it, you can use the iPad for up to ten hours before you need to plug it in and recharge its battery.

Apps and services

Apple supports the iPad with a variety of services, including the iTunes Store, which sells music and video; the iBookstore, which sells books and magazines that you can read on your iPad; and the App Store, which sells software for your iPad. More than 300,000 apps are available for the iPad, and you can choose among 1.5 billion books in the iBookstore and more than 26 million tracks in the iTunes Store. There's also a vast amount of free content to enjoy. Of particular note are the iTunes U video lectures from the world's best-known universities, and the thousands of *podcasts*. Podcasts are audio and video programmes on particular topics, as well as on-demand versions of recent radio shows. Avid readers, meanwhile, can choose from thousands of free books. Conveniently, many of these can be found in the same iBookstore where you can buy bestsellers and magazine subscriptions using your iTunes account.

Although not a phone, the iPad has similar software to the iPhone and offers lots of communication options. However, you can make only Skype or Internet calls on the iPad. The iPad also has excellent music-playing options.

How this book is structured

This book takes you through the whole process of discovering the iPad. It's divided into four parts:

- Part I helps you get started with your iPad. You find out about the different iPad versions, as well as how to set up your iPad, get connected to the Internet, and create notes.

- Part II is all about using your iPad for communication. The iPad is ideal for activities such as web browsing and emailing; it also has a great address book and calendar function. In this part, you find out how to exchange instant messages with friends who have compatible Apple devices, and, if you have an iPad with built-in cameras, you see how to conduct video calls using FaceTime.

- Part III gets into the really fun stuff: adding music to your iPad and taking and viewing videos and photos. You see how to buy music and videos from the Apple iTunes Store, watch films, listen to music and copy your music CDs onto your iPad. In this part, you also discover how to create playlists of your favourite songs and hook up your iPad to speakers.

- Part IV shows you how to expand your iPad by adding new software from the App Store. This part focuses on helping you get familiar with the iPad's location tools and Maps app, as well as buying books and subscribing to digital magazines.

- Appendix A offers some basic tips to help you troubleshoot when your iPad doesn't behave quite as you expect it to. And Appendix B, the glossary, provides a handy reference when you need to refresh your memory about an iPad term.

As you work through the book, you build on some of the skills that you develop along the way. You might want to read the book in the order in which it was written, but we provide reminders and cross-references as appropriate, should you prefer to jump around among the chapters.

Visit **www.pcwisdom.co.uk** for bonus content and additional information.

PART I
Getting started with your iPad

Writing notes on this is a piece of cake.
—All you need is a fine magic marker.

Choosing an iPad

1

Equipment needed: A credit card – if you haven't yet purchased your iPad!

Skills needed: None, but computer-buying experience – or a solid idea of how you want to use your iPad – might make this easier.

Once you've decided to buy an iPad, you have a few more decisions to make because several versions of the iPad are available. The easiest decision is probably whether you want a standard-size iPad with a 9.7-inch screen or the new iPad mini, which has a smaller screen and is slightly cheaper. As you can see in Figure 1.1, you can easily hold the iPad mini in your hand, so it is a fair bit smaller than its big brother. But the screens on both are generous.

The iPad mini has a 7.9-inch screen (measured across the diagonal, which is how computer displays and TV screens are usually described), and the viewable screen area is roughly the size of a Penguin paperback novel. The standard iPad has a 9.7-inch screen, and the viewable screen area is roughly 7.5 by 5.5 inches.

The other way the standard-size iPad differs from the mini is that the screen is not as detailed or sharp on the smaller model. You're more likely to notice the comparison when looking at the two iPads side by side, however, than you are to notice the less-detailed resolution of the iPad mini. The iPad mini has at least as good a display as most other tablets on the market and a better one than some laptops. Its 1024×768 pixel resolution is the same as that of the original iPad, which launched in 2010.

Figure 1.1

Both the latest-generation full-size iPad and the new iPad mini come with iOS6, the latest version of the iPad software. This software includes everything you're likely to need at first, from a web browser and email to a calendar and note taker; a camera; and photo, music and video libraries. For details on what's new in iOS6, see Chapter 3.

How much storage space do you need?

You can't add extra storage space to your iPad later, so you have to decide upfront how much space you're going to need. You have the choice of iPad models that offer 16GB, 32GB or 64GB of space.

⚠️ Apple uses some of the iPad's storage space for its own software and memory, so you actually have less space to use than the advertised capacity. A 16GB iPad, for example, has only 14GB that you can use. Don't buy an iPad with just enough space. Leave room for Apple's software – and room for your music or photo collection to grow.

To put these figures in perspective, 1GB is enough to store about 10 hours of music or 1 hour of film (half that much for high definition). If you take 600 photos with the third-generation iPad's 5-megapixel camera, you use up about 1GB of storage space. Apps also use space. Some apps are negligibly small; others that are rich in sound and images may take up to about one-third of a gigabyte. If you want to put your own documents on your iPad, these documents will draw on the same pool of storage space.

As you can tell, how much storage you need on your iPad depends on what you want to use it for. Consider, too, that if you have a laptop or desktop computer, you'll be able to store nonessential items there, so you don't need to buy the most expensive iPad model. But if you want to store thousands of photos, music and lots of video clips on your iPad, you may quickly run out of space on the 16GB model.

You can change the music, videos, apps and photos on your iPad regularly. You might delete films or TV programmes from your iPad after you've watched them, or put new music on and take some old music off when you fancy a change. Apple's iCloud service enables you to download music, videos and apps again if you delete them from your iPad. You can also use your computer to store content and then copy it to your iPad when you want to use it. We look at how this process works in Chapter 3.

Which generation of iPad to choose

Although Apple launched a new version of the iPad in October 2012 – the fourth-generation iPad – it's still possible to buy the largely similar third-generation iPad and the iPad 2. All three versions have cameras on the front and back, but the cameras on the iPad 2 aren't as good as the ones on the third- or fourth-generation iPad. Along with the camera improvements came support for dictation by means of a digital assistant known as Siri. Siri can be useful for making voice memos or helping you find information on the Internet, but this feature can be frustrating to use because because Siri doesn't always understand what you want or what you're saying. See Chapter 4 for details of how to use Siri.

The extremely sharp screen resolution (2048×1536) known as the *Retina display*, was introduced with the third-generation device and continues on the newest iPad. Text and images are much sharper, and high-definition videos can be played at their full quality with the improved screen resolution.

There is little to distinguish the third-generation iPad from the newest iPad aside from the way the latter connects to speakers and other accessories. The software that runs the iPad, known as iOS, was updated just before the fourth-generation iPad and iPad mini were launched in late 2012. Both of these iPads come with the latest software version available (iOS6) already installed. You can update an iPad 2 or a third-generation iPad to this version of the software very easily. In fact, when you connect your iPad to your computer to back up or synchronise, it will probably offer to perform the update for you. Therefore, updated iPad software isn't a reason to choose the very latest iPad device over the earlier versions.

When Apple releases a new iPad, it often adds some new software features. You can add some of these features to older iPads for free by updating your software. See Chapter 3 for details about updating to iOS6.

Connecting to the Internet: Wi-Fi or 4G/3G?

The iPad can support two types of Internet connections: Wi-Fi and mobile communications.

All iPads, including the iPad mini, can use Wi-Fi to connect to the Internet wirelessly. A Wi-Fi connection works well in a small area, such as in an Internet café or hotel lobby, or in your own home if you have a Wi-Fi router for your broadband connection. It's usually free for you to connect to public Wi-Fi, but places like hotels sometimes charge for access. Wi-Fi has the advantage of being faster than mobile communications networks, but it has the drawback of being available only in some areas and in a fairly small radius within those areas.

For every generation of the iPad, a more expensive version of the device is available that can also use mobile communications. This type of iPad works a bit like a mobile phone in that you can connect anywhere you can get a mobile signal. But you have to buy a data plan (basically, a contract) from a mobile-phone company to be allowed to use its network. Although you buy your data plan from a mobile-phone company, the iPad isn't designed to support voice calling. You can, however, use FaceTime for video calling (see Chapter 7) and you can add a Skype app for communications (see Chapter 14 for advice on adding apps).

The original iPad, iPad 2 and third-generation iPad support a type of mobile communications called *3G,* short for *third-generation mobile communications,* which is widely used in the United Kingdom. The fourth-generation iPad 4 is the only model available in the UK that supports 4G – the fastest and most expensive way to connect to the Internet. In the United States, 4G availability is more widespread, so Apple offers a 4G version of the third-generation iPad that can take advantage of the faster network. If you don't have 4G in your area, the iPad will use the best available alternative (typically, 3G). Many people, however, have iPads that simply connect to the Internet over Wi-Fi, without the 3G or 4G option.

Unlike with a mobile phone, you don't need a long-term contract for 3G or 4G access on your iPad. Although many of the contracts rebill automatically at the end of each month, typically you can cancel at any time and start up again later (a 30-day notice period is usually required). You may want to buy just a month's network access for your summer holiday, for example, and cancel it when you return. Daily and weekly contracts are also available, so you don't have to buy a full month's worth of access.

The contract allows you to download a certain amount of data over the network within a certain time frame. O2, for example, offers a contract that gives you 1GB of data to download within 30 days, which amounts to about 200 songs, 2 hours of video or 10,000 web pages (according to O2's own estimates).

Remember that your 3G or 4G data use counts against the monthly data limit you agreed to with your provider. Try to use your 3G access sparingly. If you go over the data limit for the month, your bill could be substantially higher than you anticipated. Use Wi-Fi whenever you can, because it isn't subject to such limits.

Data just means information. It includes maps, web-page content, music, videos and anything else you get from the Internet.

The 3G and 4G iPads also have GPS, a positioning system that uses a network of satellites to work out where you are. If you want to use Maps extensively, GPS can be extremely useful, although the Wi-Fi-only iPad also has some positioning features that are more basic (and less accurate).

The 3G/4G iPad is the natural choice for somebody who travels a lot, especially within the UK, or for someone who wants to make extensive use of the Maps feature on the road. It can be very expensive to use 3G or 4G when you're roaming abroad, however, even if you have a data plan for the country you're visiting. It's easy to burn through your data allowance on mobile communications, especially if you have access to a superfast 4G network. You can turn off mobile communications until you need it (see Chapter 15), however, to make sure that you're using your data allowance only when you choose to.

If you opt for a 3G or 4G iPad, it will use Wi-Fi instead wherever Wi-Fi is available to save you from using up your data allowance unnecessarily.

When you buy an iPad from a shop, you'll usually be sold the latest version. However, it's also possible to buy older iPads from the Refurb store on the Apple website (**www.apple.com**) or even eBay. Alternatively, you can get an iPad 2 or third-generation iPad on contract when buying through a mobile phone operator. This can help spread the cost but isn't cheaper overall.

For purposes of this book, we assume that you've chosen – and probably already have – your iPad and are mainly interested in learning what it can do and finding out how to achieve specific tasks. Where there's a difference between the latest iPad model and the older versions, we'll make the difference clear.

Summary

- There are four generations of iPads to date, plus the new iPad mini. The iPad 2 introduced two cameras, and the third- and fourth-generation iPads have a much higher screen resolution than previous iPads. The newest iPad and the iPad mini are the latest models, released in late 2012. Both come with iOS6, the latest version of Apple's iPad software.

- The iPad is available with storage capacities of 16GB, 32GB and 64GB.

- You can't upgrade the memory of your iPad later, so make sure you pick one that'll be big enough.

- You can add, delete and then reinstate music, photos, videos and other files you store on your iPad easily, so it doesn't matter if they don't all fit at the same time.

- All iPads can use free Wi-Fi to connect to the Internet, including through your wireless router at home, if you have one.

- Some iPads also enable 3G or 4G communications. You have to pay more to buy one of these devices, and you also have to pay for a data plan to take advantage of the 3G or 4G mobile communications network.

- Wi-Fi offers a connection within a small area, such as in a café or in your home. 3G or 4G is more like the connection for a mobile phone, and you can use it wherever you can get a 3G or 4G signal.

- You can buy your iPad direct from Apple, on contract from a mobile communications phone operator company or from a consumer electronics store. When buying outright, Apple sets the price.

Brain training

At the end of each chapter in this book, there's a short quiz to refresh the points covered and give you a break before the next chapter. Sometimes, a question has more than one right answer.

1. Wi-Fi is:

(a) A wireless Internet connection

(b) A companion for Hus-Bandi

(c) A type of mobile phone

(d) A high-tech way to order coffee

2. A 4G iPad is:

(a) One that is moving incredibly fast

(b) One that costs £4,000

(c) One that can use a mobile communications network to access the Internet

(d) One that weighs the same as a few paper clips

3. To store the most films, music, photos and apps on your iPad, you need one with this capacity:

(a) 16GB

(b) 32GB

(c) 64GB

(d) 4G

4. The best iPad for using maps is:

(a) The 3G or 4G version

(b) The Wi-Fi–only version

(c) The iPad mini

(d) The third-generation iPad

5. The iPad mini differs from other iPads because:

(a) It's smaller.

(b) It's cheaper.

(c) It comes only as a Wi-Fi version.

(d) Its screen isn't as sharp as that of other iPads.

Answers

Q1 – a   **Q2** – c   **Q3** – c

Q4 – a. (Both third- and fourth-generation iPads have GPS built in.)

Q5 – a and b. (Third- and fourth-generation iPads have better screen resolution than the mini, but the original iPad doesn't.)

Getting your iPad up and running

2

Equipment needed: An iPad; ideally, a broadband Internet connection and a Wi-Fi router set up (note that for the best performance, an 802.11n router is preferable).

Skills needed: None, but experience installing software is helpful.

You've ripped open the packaging and admired the shiny screen, and now you want to start playing with your iPad. The bad news is that you need to spend a little bit of time setting it up before you can do anything with it. The good news is that – if your experience is anything like ours – it's easier to set up your iPad than it was to get it out of the shrink-wrap.

In this chapter, we guide you through the process of setting up your iPad. We give you a first glimpse at how it works and show you how to configure it so that it's as easy to use as possible. We also show you how you can copy information between your computer and iPad by using the iCloud service or the iTunes software on your computer.

Setting up your iPad

Your iPad should arrive at least partially charged, so you can start setting it up straight away. If you can't get a response out of your iPad, or it shows you a dead-battery image, jump ahead to the instructions on charging your iPad later in this chapter and then double back here to continue setting up. The iPad uses its touch-screen for almost all of its controls, so there are very few buttons on it, as you can see in Figures 2.1 and 2.2.

Copyright © Apple Inc.

Figure 2.1

Because of the bevelled edge, most of the buttons aren't visible from the front, so we've flipped the iPad over to show where they are. The top figure shows the buttons on the top edge; the bottom figure shows the buttons on and bottom edge. You can use them all while still looking at the screen.

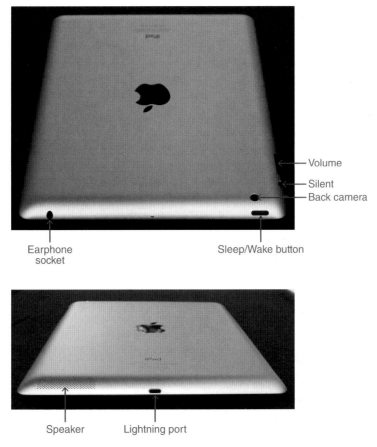

Figure 2.2

Turning the iPad on and off

To turn your iPad on for the first time, you press the Sleep/Wake button at the top edge of the iPad (refer to Figure 2.2, top). Most times, though, you will simply be rousing it from or putting it into locked or sleep mode. This state might be a bit surprising if you aren't expecting it, but after two minutes of inactivity, the iPad locks itself to save power. You can also force it to lock straight away by pressing the Sleep/Wake button. A locked iPad can still play music and respond to volume controls, but the screen is switched off and won't respond to your touch. This can be useful if you're taking your iPad out and about, as the battery won't drain while it's tucked away in your bag. To unlock the iPad, press the Home button and then use the slider. Alternatively, if you have a Smart Cover on your iPad (not available for the first-generation iPad), just open the cover. An iPad can be unlocked almost instantly.

The other state that your iPad can be in is fully switched off. You can switch off your iPad at the end of the day (although people often just leave the iPad locked so that it starts more quickly the next time they need it). To turn your iPad off, press and hold the Sleep/Wake button and then drag the red slider to turn it off. You turn it on again by pressing and holding the Sleep/Wake button.

The iPad remembers what you were doing before it was locked or switched off, so all your apps will be exactly where you left them. If you're halfway through an email when your plane is called for boarding, lock your iPad so you can stash it in your bag for now and continue writing later.

It usually doesn't matter which way up you use your iPad, but to set it up, you need to hold it so that the round button on its front surface (the Home button) is at the bottom. On the top-right edge of the iPad when you look at the screen, you can find the Sleep/Wake button. Press and hold the Sleep/Wake button, and you see the word *iPad* on the screen.

Toward the bottom of the screen is the first touchscreen control you'll use: the slider (see Figure 2.3). Beside it are instructions that cycle through lots of different languages. Put your finger on the arrow and move your finger to the right, keeping it in contact with the glass all the time. As you move your finger, the arrow moves with it. When the arrow reaches the right edge of its box, release your finger, and your iPad is unlocked. Use this swipe-to-unlock motion to bring your iPad out of its locked-screen standby mode whenever you want to use it.

For the next step, you need one of the simple gestures used to control the iPad: the tap. On a touchscreen, tapping something is a bit like clicking it with a mouse on a desktop computer. To tap something, you just touch it briefly and then lift your finger from the iPad. You'll often use this gesture to select things or to push buttons on the screen; these buttons are just symbols or words that do something when you touch them.

Figure 2.3

Use the skin of your fingers, not your fingernails. It's easiest if you use the part of your fingertips where your fingerprints are. You don't have to press the screen. Just touch it. Something to keep in mind: The touchscreen normally won't work through gloves.

The first thing you'll select by tapping is the language. If you're happy with the language selected and shown at the bottom of the screen, tap the blue arrow in the top-right corner to confirm. If you're not happy, tap the arrow at the bottom of the screen to see a list of available languages. You can scroll through this list by putting your finger on it and dragging your fingertip up and down the screen without lifting your finger. When you find your preferred language, tap it; then tap the blue arrow in the top-right corner. Setting your language takes a moment. You use a similar process to choose your country or region in the next step, tapping Next in the top-right corner after you've chosen your country.

Next, you're asked whether the iPad should enable Location Services. If you enable Location Services, you allow some of the software on your iPad to know your iPad's approximate location. This feature is a big help when you're using Maps (see Chapter 14) or taking photographs (see Chapter 13). We recommend that you enable Location Services. Tap Next again afterward.

Confirming setup over Wi-Fi

The next step is connecting your iPad to your Wi-Fi connection so that you can send the iPad's setup information to Apple. (Wi-Fi is a way of wirelessly connecting computers and other devices to the Internet and to each other.) If you don't have a Wi-Fi network at home, you can set up your iPad by using a friend's network or a public Wi-Fi network in a café or library.

You can also set up your iPad by plugging it into your computer. Tap Connect to iTunes; then tap Continue, and follow the instructions in the section 'Connecting your iPad to your computer' in Chapter 3. After you've given your iPad a name and answered the questions that appear on your computer screen, return to this page of the book to continue setting up your iPad.

To set up a Wi-Fi connection on your iPad, you need the name of the Wi-Fi network and its password. If you're using your own router, you can find out or change the password by checking your router settings. If you're using public Wi-Fi, you're usually given the network name and password together.

If a Wi-Fi network is in your vicinity, you'll be asked to select it and then enter its password. If several networks are nearby, you may have to choose your network from among them. Choose a network to connect to by tapping its name.

> You may see available Wi-Fi connections listed that don't require passwords. Avoid these, as they may connect you to a rogue network. For more on security matters, see Appendix A at the back of this book.

A keyboard appears on the touchscreen (see Figure 2.4) so you can enter the password for the Wi-Fi network by tapping the keys on the screen. When you type a password, you can see only the latest character entered for a moment, so keep an eye on the characters as you type to make sure you don't make any errors. To enter a number or symbol, tap the key labelled .?123. If you hide the keyboard by tapping the key in its bottom-right corner (the one showing a picture of a keyboard), you can bring it back by tapping the password box. You find out much more about using the keyboard in Chapter 4.

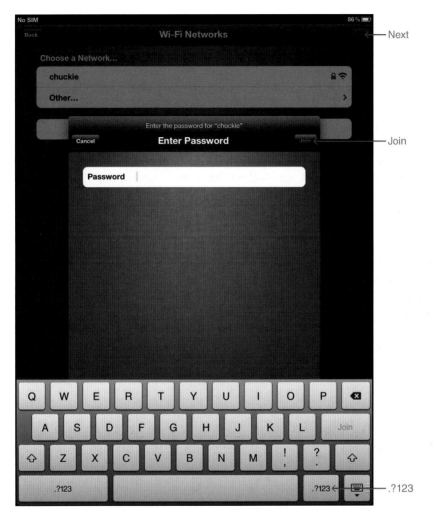

Figure 2.4

When you type a password on a computer, it usually shows up as a line of dots onscreen. On the iPad, however, each character appears on the screen for a moment to allow you to make sure that it's correct. Whenever you enter a password on your iPad, you should ensure that nobody with sharp eyes is reading it over your shoulder.

When you've finished entering the password, tap Join (refer to Figure 2.4). You should see a tick beside your chosen Wi-Fi network, showing that it's been set up correctly. Then you can tap Next in the top-right corner.

When Wi-Fi has been set up or you've completed setup by using your computer, you'll be asked to choose to set up your iPad as a new iPad or restore it from a backup that you made previously. (You see more about backing up your iPad in Chapter 3.) If this iPad is your first one, or if you don't have a backup of your old iPad, you can just tap Next in the top-right corner. Otherwise, choose the source of your backup (iCloud or iTunes) to copy your backed-up apps and data to this iPad; then tap Next.

Creating an Apple ID

To use many of the features of your iPad, you need an *Apple ID:* a combination of your email address and a password that you make up yourself. You use your Apple ID when you use FaceTime (see Chapter 7) and instant messaging (see Chapter 8); you also use it to buy books, music, films and apps. Apple asks you to create an Apple ID and enter credit card details or the number of a gift certificate, which you can buy from many high-street shops. The iTunes Store uses a secure connection, so your credit card details are safe and can't be stolen by anyone as they are sent over the Internet.

You can skip the step of setting up your Apple ID and/or your email address for now, if you prefer. However, you will need it sooner or later, even if just for backing up your iPad using the iCloud service.

> Apple asks for your birthday for two reasons: to shield you from buying content that you're not old enough to see (not likely to be an issue if you're reading an *Older and Wiser* book!) and to help you recover your Apple ID password if you forget it.

You also have to accept the iPad software licence agreement. This agreement is mainly about the copyright in the content you download to the iPad, such as maps; it also includes clauses about what data Apple collects about you and how it uses it. You can tap each section and scroll through its terms and conditions to read them, but you have to accept the terms to be able to use your iPad. (As you discover new features in this book, we'll flag up anything you should be aware of with respect to privacy.) When you're happy that you're not signing your soul away, tap Agree in the bottom-right corner. Don't worry, Apple won't send you a deluge of spam emails; but Apple will send you receipts and let you know of any unusual activity going on with your Apple ID account.

Enabling useful features

Your new iPad includes 30 built-in apps that allow you to browse the web; send and receive email; view your digital photos, books and videos; and find directions. There are also several optional features that allow you to synchronise the contents of your iPad with your computer or to back it up without having to remember to do so. Along the way you'll be asked to agree to a range of terms and conditions relating to your use of some of these features. We detail each of them in the following sections.

iCloud

During setup, you'll be asked whether you want to use iCloud. This service uses the Internet to back up your iPad and to share its content with other devices you own. When you use iCloud, your files are copied to a private part of the Internet. Only your other devices (such as your iPhone or your computer) can copy your files from there. This means that you can back up your iPad and copy files between your computer and your iPad without having to connect them.

We cover iCloud in more detail in Chapter 3. If you choose not to use iCloud for now, you can easily enable it later; but we recommend that you choose to use iCloud and also use iCloud to back up your iPad over Wi-Fi. As noted above, although the basic service is free, there's an option to upgrade to more storage later. Because of this, you need an Apple ID to use iCloud.

Find My iPad

Apple's free Find My iPad service helps you recover your iPad if it's ever lost or stolen. It enables you to log in to a web browser to see where your iPad is on a map, to send a message on the iPad screen to whoever found it, and even to set a passcode remotely or delete the iPad's contents to stop someone else from getting your sensitive data. We recommend that you enable this feature. If you also have an iPhone or a Mac, you can use those devices to find your missing iPad, too. There are also third-party apps that offer similar features.

When your iPad is up and running, you can test it by visiting **www.icloud.com** on a web browser and logging in with your Apple ID. Later in this chapter, you find out how to change your iPad settings. You can turn Find My iPad on or off by going into your iCloud settings.

Dictation

Another useful feature is Dictation, which enables you to speak to your iPad instead of typing on its keyboard. The Dictation feature is available on all iPads except the original, although on the iPad 2 it appears only in certain scenarios. We recommend enabling this feature when you're asked about it. We explain in Chapter 4 how useful Dictation can be to you.

Information collection

In the Diagnostics section, Apple asks whether it can collect information about how you use your iPad to help Apple improve its products. You may prefer to decline permission if you prefer to have control of what data about you is being sent, and when.

Registration

You can choose to register your device to your Apple ID, which means that Apple will make a note that you own this iPad. Registration speeds any support requests you have and enables Apple to send you relevant product information.

Navigating the Home screen

When you've finished setting up your iPad, Apple confirms that the device is ready to use. Tap Start Using iPad and the Home screen appears, showing several icons (see Figure 2.5).

Figure 2.5

Each activity on the iPad takes place within a software application called an *app*. On the Home screen, you can see icons for the apps that come installed on your iPad: Messages, FaceTime, Photos, Camera, Maps, Clock, Photo Booth, Calendar, Contacts, Notes, Reminders, Newsstand, iTunes, App Store, Games Center and Settings. Note that if you're using a first-generation iPad, you won't see the Camera or Photo Booth icons as there's no built-in camera. At the bottom of the screen, on a shelf called the *Dock*, are icons for Safari (the web browser), Mail, Videos and Music.

> Don't hold your finger on an icon for too long; if you do, you'll go into the mode for arranging icons (see Chapter 14). If the icons start jiggling, press the Home button on the front of your iPad to make them stop.

To launch an app, just tap its icon. Try starting some apps to see what they look like. Without any content on your iPad, some of them won't do much; but you can take a quick peek and practice using the touchscreen. When you finish exploring an app, or if you get lost, press the Home button to go back to the Home screen, where you can select another app.

Changing the iPad orientation

You can use the iPad any way around. Rotate it, and the screen contents rotate too, so that you're always looking at them the right way up. Refer to Figure 2.5 to see the iPad in portrait orientation (taller than wide); Figure 2.6 shows the iPad in landscape orientation (wider than tall).

Figure 2.6

As you try different activities with the iPad, you'll find that some work more naturally in one orientation than the other. When you're writing notes or emails, for example, landscape orientation is easier because the keys on the keyboard are larger for easier typing. You can also rotate the iPad to match the shape of photos (portrait or landscape) so that you can view them at their maximum size (see Chapter 13).

Making your iPad easier to use

For those who have impaired vision or hearing, several settings make the iPad easier to use. You can find the following settings by opening the Settings app from the Home screen, tapping General on the left side of the screen and then tapping Accessibility:

● **VoiceOver:** This feature reads the iPad screen aloud for the benefit of people who can't see the screen. It also enables a comprehensive set of gestures for navigating content and entering information. When you're using the keyboard, for example, you can flick left or right to advance through the keys and have the iPad read them aloud. A double tap enters the character chosen.

VoiceOver completely changes the way that the iPad is used. We won't be covering it further in this book, but if you believe that you might benefit from it, the iPad manual provides comprehensive guidance. (Go to **http://support. apple.com/manuals** and choose the iPad manual you want to view.)

- **Zoom:** If you have impaired vision, you can use the Zoom feature to magnify the iPad screen. When this feature is switched on, you zoom in by tapping the screen twice in quick succession, using three fingers both times. To change which bit of the screen you're looking at, touch the screen with three fingers and then move them in any direction on the glass surface. To increase or decrease the magnification, tap with three fingers; then quickly tap again with those fingers, keeping them on the glass. Move your fingers up the glass to zoom in and down to zoom out. The process sounds complicated, but you can practise on the screen for zoom settings. You can use any combination of fingers and thumbs on both hands. You don't have to use three adjacent fingers if that feels awkward, for example.

  This feature is for those with impaired vision who need to enlarge everything on the iPad's screen, including its buttons. In Chapter 9, you discover the pinch gesture, which is an easy way for everyone to magnify web pages and photos.

- **Large Text:** This feature increases the size of the text in emails and notes. You can use Large Text in combination with the Zoom feature, which helps you see the other elements of those apps.

- **White on Black:** This feature reverses the colour scheme so that the text is white on a black background. The feature has a side effect, though: Icons and images also have their colours reversed, so they look like negatives.

- **Speak Auto-Text:** If you turn this feature on, the iPad speaks its text corrections as you type. This feature is useful for everyone and works independently of VoiceOver. You see more about it in Chapter 4.

- **Speak Selection:** In Chapter 4, you find out how to select text. If you switch on Speak Selection, you can choose to have selected text read aloud to you.

- **Mono Audio:** Stereo audio works by delivering different parts of the sound to different ears. Those with poor hearing in one ear might miss part of the sound, so the mono audio setting enables you to hear the complete soundtrack in each ear.

- **Assistive Touch:** This feature enables you to carry out complex gestures and activate the iPad's physical buttons by using a menu. Assistive Touch enables you to use the iPad together with a joystick or to carry out gestures that are too difficult for you otherwise.

● **Triple-Click Home:** This is a shortcut for managing VoiceOver, Zoom, Assistive Touch and White on Black. When this feature is activated, you can press the Home button three times in quick succession to turn all four features on or off.

Adjusting other iPad settings

The iPad is a sophisticated device and has many settings that you can adjust. Fortunately, you can ignore the vast majority of these settings, but here are a few that you may want to know about:

● **Brightness:** To change the screen brightness, go into Settings, and tap Brightness & Wallpaper. Touch the round button, and slide it right or left to increase or decrease brightness. The Auto-Brightness setting adjusts the brightness automatically, depending on how much light there is in the room.

● **Wallpaper:** The *wallpaper* is the image in the background of your iPad's locked and Home screens. To change it, go into your Brightness & Wallpaper settings and then tap the iPad picture. You can choose from among more than 30 images provided by Apple or select any of your own photos on the iPad.

● **Sounds:** To turn off the sounds when you type on the keyboard, or when you lock the iPad, unlock the iPad, or get email, go into your General Settings and then choose Sounds.

● **Volume:** The easiest way to change the volume is to hold the iPad with the Home button at the bottom and find the rocker switch toward the top-right edge (refer to Figure 2.2, earlier in this chapter). This switch clicks in two directions to turn the sound up or down. A side switch near the volume control silences sound effects and alerts but not any music or programmes that are playing. When you use these controls, the iPad screen shows you the volume change or mute status in the middle of the screen.

● **Reset:** To reset some or all of your settings, go into your General Settings and then tap Reset. The resulting screen gives you several options. If you choose Reset All Settings, the iPad's settings will be set to their factory defaults, but your information on the device (including your contacts and music) will be unaffected. If you choose Erase All Content and Settings, your data will be deleted from the iPad, and the iPad's settings will all be set to their factory defaults. You can also reset the network settings (including for Wi-Fi networks), reset the dictionary (used for Auto-text, which we cover in Chapter 4), reset the Home screen layout and reset location warnings (which normally are presented once for each app that tries to use your location; if you reset the warnings, you'll be asked again for each app).

You can configure the side switch so that it locks the iPad orientation instead of muting your iPad. That means that when you turn the device, the screen contents don't rotate as they usually do. This feature can be handy if you're reading or watching TV at an angle in bed. Go into the Settings app, tap General, and then change the option Side Switch to Lock Rotation. You can change it back again at any time.

Charging your iPad

At the top of your iPad screen is the *status bar,* which includes information about your iPad and the current time. In the top-right corner, you can see the battery indicator, which shows (as a percentage) how charged your battery is. Your iPad warns you when the battery gets low.

You can charge your iPad by connecting it to your computer. For this method to work, the iPad needs to be in sleep mode, and the computer needs to be switched on. Older computers may not be able to provide enough power to charge in this way, though, and even if they can, the process is relatively slow. So the best method is to plug your iPad into the wall. In the box that your iPad came in, you'll find two parts that slot together to create a standard electrical plug.

The cable provided with the iPad, which you can also use to connect your iPad to your computer, connects the plug to your iPad. The USB connector slots into the hole on the back of the plug. The other connector slots into the dock connector on your iPad. Note that the latest iPad models, launched in October 2012, provide a new connector type, known as a *Lightning* connector. You can't use a connector from an older iPad to charge one of the latest models.

When the battery is charging, the battery icon shows a lightning bolt.

A fully charged battery has enough juice for most journeys, and you may need to charge your iPad only every few days if you use it around the home. Apple claims that the battery will last for up to ten hours while you're using Wi-Fi, watching videos or listening to music. If you use 4G/3G to connect to the Internet, the battery life is cut back to up to nine hours.

You can take a few steps to prolong your battery life:

- Don't leave your iPad in a hot car and keep it out of the sun (not exactly an issue during the average British summer). Apple says that heat degrades battery performance more than anything else.

- Adjust the brightness to the minimum comfortable level (refer to 'Adjusting other iPad settings', earlier in this chapter).

- Every month, go through at least one charge cycle, charging the battery to 100% and then running it down completely.

- If your iPad gets hot when charging, and you've bought a protective case for it, remove it from its case.

- Keep your iPad software updated. Software updates might include features that help optimise battery use.

- Turn off Wi-Fi and/or 4G/3G when you won't be using them (see Chapter 3). See Appendix A at the back of this book for more power-saving advice.

- Minimise the use of Location Services, such as Maps. (You can turn off Location Services in the Settings app.)

- Download new emails and other regular updates less frequently. Check fewer email accounts automatically, and turn off features to push email to your iPad (see Chapter 6).

Because the battery wears out over time and can be replaced only by Apple, these tips will also help you prolong the life of your whole iPad. Apple estimates that you can fully charge and discharge your iPad 1,000 times before the battery performance falls below 80% of what it should be. Even if you managed to exhaust your iPad every day, that would give you nearly three years of life, so your iPad is designed to last many years.

You can charge your iPad abroad by using the power adapter. You need to plug the electrical plug into a travel plug adapter that fits the wall socket in the country you're visiting.

Summary

- To turn on your iPad, press and hold the Sleep/Wake button.

- Use the skin of your fingers on the touchscreen, not your fingernails.

- You can use the iPad any way up, and the screen display will rotate so that it's always the right way up for you.

- iPad activities take place within software applications, called *apps*.

- You can find icons for your apps on the Home screen.

- Touch an app's icon to start the app.

- The Settings app is used to set up your Wi-Fi connection, 4G/3G connection, passcodes and features to improve ease of use.

- To slide a switch on the screen, touch it and move your finger across the iPad screen, or simply tap it.

- The iPad has a keyboard that appears onscreen when you need to type something, such as a password. To hide it again, tap the button in the bottom-right corner of the keyboard.

- You need access to a Wi-Fi network or a computer to set up your iPad.

- Accessibility settings allow you to adjust screen colours, use an external joystick and use voice controls.

- The best way to charge your iPad is to charge it from the mains.

Brain training

Now that your iPad is set up, you're ready to begin using it. You can refer to this chapter if you need to change your settings in future, but for now, take a quick quiz to refresh your memory. Keep in mind that a question may have more than one right answer.

1. You can charge your iPad by:

(a) Connecting it to a power socket

(b) Connecting it to a computer, with the computer in sleep mode and the iPad switched on

(c) Connecting it to a computer, with the computer switched on and the iPad in sleep mode

(d) Connecting it to your computer keyboard

2. You can use your iPad:

(a) In landscape orientation

(b) In portrait orientation

(c) With the Home button at the top

(d) Back to front

3. If you hold your finger on an app for too long:

(a) The app will launch.

(b) The app will be deleted.

(c) All the apps onscreen will jiggle around, and you might accidentally rearrange things.

(d) You can cancel the action by pressing the Home button.

4. To prolong your iPad's battery between charges, you can

(a) Delete its contents

(b) Turn off the Wi-Fi or 4G/3G

(c) Check your email less frequently

(d) Keep it cool

5. To silence the locking sound on your iPad:

(a) Push the Sleep/Wake button really gently.

(b) Slide the slider on the side of your iPad.

(c) Adjust your sound settings.

(d) Put your iPad in a case.

Answers

Q1 – a and c   **Q2** – a, b or c   **Q3** – c and d   **Q4** – b, c and d   **Q5** – b and c

Getting connected

3

Equipment needed: Your iPad and access to a broadband Internet connection or wireless network; a micro SIM card if you have a 4G or 3G iPad.

Skills needed: Knowledge of how to connect other computing equipment to your PC and network is helpful, but we'll explain everything as we go.

As we note in Chapter 2, you have to get online to send setup information to Apple just to get your iPad up and running. But connecting to the Internet also allows you to get the most from your iPad. When you're online, you can send and receive emails, surf the web for information and entertainment, and download music and apps. In this chapter, we show you all you need to know to connect your iPad to the Internet.

Setting up your Internet connection

In this section, we look at how to set up a new Internet connection. You'll need your Wi-Fi network name and password and your micro SIM from your 4G/3G data provider if you have a 4G/3G iPad. After you've set up your web connection, see how it works by checking out Chapter 9 on browsing the web or Chapter 15 on Maps.

Setting up a secure Wi-Fi connection

If you followed the steps in Chapter 2 to set up your iPad using Wi-Fi, you already have a Wi-Fi connection. But you may need to set up others from time to time, such as when you visit a hotel or a friend's house and want to use the Wi-Fi there.

> After you've joined a particular Wi-Fi network for the first time, your iPad will join it automatically in future without asking you for the password. That means your web browsing should be seamless from then on while you're using the same Wi-Fi network (unless the password for the network changes, in which case you'll be asked to enter it).

To set up a Wi-Fi connection, you need to use the Settings app, which is the engine room of the iPad. It's where you can change lots of different aspects of how the iPad is set up and how you use it. Go to the Settings app (the cog wheels icon) by tapping it on the Home screen. On the left, you can see the different settings you can change. Tap Wi-Fi, and the Wi-Fi settings appear on the right, as shown in Figure 3.1.

Make sure the switch in the top-right corner says that Wi-Fi is on. You can touch this switch and slide it left or right to turn Wi-Fi on or off. When you see switches like this, you can just tap them to switch them on or off.

Look through the list of Wi-Fi networks for one with a padlock symbol next to a black fan. The fan indicates the strength of the wireless network. Ideally, you want to connect to a network with three stripes. Choose the network by tapping its name and then entering its password, as described in the section on setting up your iPad in Chaper 2. Tap Join, and you should see a tick appear beside the Wi-Fi network's name to indicate you are connected to it. Even when using a Wi-Fi connection at a friend's house, a secure network with password protection is preferable.

If you see a network that doesn't have a padlock next to it showing that a password is required – especially if you are at an Internet café or coffee shop that offers free Wi-Fi – don't join it. Unsecured wireless networks can be dangerous. Snoops may try and connect to your iPad and read your email or glean information about you that they can exploit.

Figure 3.1

Never enter your credit card or bank details, check your bank balance online, or carry out any online shopping at a Wi-Fi hotspot. This applies whether or not the network you've just connected to requires a password to access it. The padlock sign provides reassurance that the connection is secure and that information you send is encrypted, but there's always a chance of someone peering over your shoulder and noting what you type. For more on security and privacy, see the advice in Appendix A.

If you're not connected to Wi-Fi, your iPad will tell you if it comes across other Wi-Fi networks you might be able to join. Just because the iPad identifies them, however, doesn't mean you can join them. They might belong to your neighbours or to nearby businesses. And if there's a padlock beside the network name, it means you need a password to use it. You can stop your iPad from telling you about networks it finds by turning off the switch beside Ask to Join Networks in the Wi-Fi settings.

Setting up a 4G/3G connection

You can use mobile communications on your iPad if you have a model that supports 3G or 4G. To start using 4G/3G, you need to have a micro SIM card from your data plan provider. iPad mini users need a nano SIM card. If you buy direct from Apple, the company can install the necessary SIM card for you. If you buy your data plan at a mobile phone shop, they might install your SIM card for you there, too. Otherwise, you'll need to phone or register with a 4G/3G provider online to get them to send you a SIM. If you receive your micro SIM or nano SIM by post, these are the steps you need to follow:

1. Your micro SIM card will probably come in a piece of plastic the size of a credit card. You need to snap the SIM card out of it to fit it into your iPad. Keep a note of its mobile broadband number, which will look like a mobile phone number.

2. Use the special SIM eject tool that came with your iPad to open the SIM tray on your iPad (indicated in Figure 3.2). When you hold the iPad with the Home button at the bottom, there is a tiny round hole on the left edge. On the original iPad, it's towards the bottom; on later iPads, it's near the top. Insert the tool (a paper clip will also work) in the hole, and the tray will spring out. Figure 3.2 shows the eject tool being used to open the SIM tray in the side of the iPad.

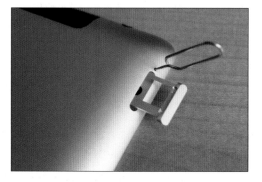

Figure 3.2

3. Remove the tray completely from the iPad and place the micro SIM card into the tray. It will only go in one way around. If it's too big, check whether there is any more plastic on it that is designed to be snapped off. Remember you can use only a micro SIM card, not a standard mobile phone SIM card.

4. Carefully replace the tray the right way up. The metallic side of the SIM card that looks like a circuit board should be facing down, towards the bottom side of the device, away from the iPad's touchscreen.

5. When you turn the iPad on, you'll see a message telling you the iPad is waiting for the SIM to be activated.

What you do next depends on which communications provider you use. For O2, which enables you to sign up on the iPad itself, follow these steps:

1. Ensure that you are using the latest version of the iPad software. (See the section 'Updating your iPad software', later in this chapter for instructions on updating your iPad software.)

2. Go into your iPad settings by tapping the Settings icon on the Home screen.

3. Tap Mobile Data on the left and then tap View Account on the right.

4. Touch each box in turn on the form (see Figure 3.3), and the keyboard will appear so you can enter the information required. Enter your first and last names. The telephone box, confusingly, is not for your phone number. It's for the mobile broadband number that came with your SIM card. You also need to invent a password and enter it twice (to make sure you type it correctly). When you finish entering information in one box, tap the next box on the screen. To scroll the form, touch it and drag your finger up the touchscreen. Touch the data plan (or package) you require, and tap the Next button at the bottom of the form.

5. Enter your payment information and address.

6. Read and agree to the terms and conditions. You can scroll the terms and conditions by touching and dragging them.

7. You will see a summary confirming your package and pricing, and when you tap the Submit button, the data plan will be activated.

8. To see how much of your data allowance is still available, go into Settings, Mobile Data, and then tap View Account. Note that your remaining data might be shown in MB – 1GB is equal to 1024MB.

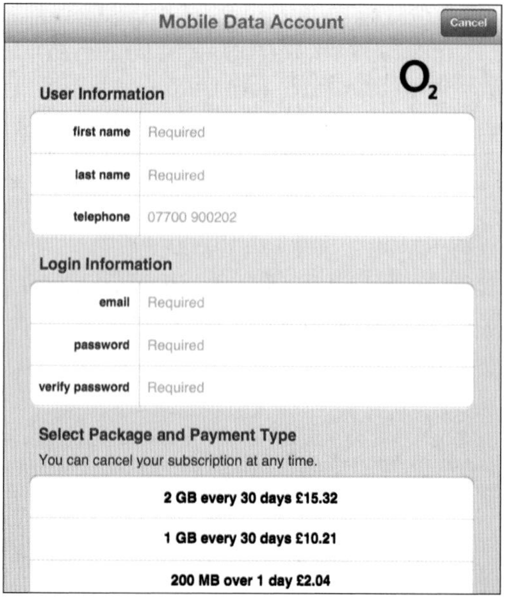

Mobile Data Account	Cancel

O₂

User Information

first name	Required
last name	Required
telephone	07700 900202

Login Information

email	Required
password	Required
verify password	Required

Select Package and Payment Type
You can cancel your subscription at any time.

2 GB every 30 days £15.32
1 GB every 30 days £10.21
200 MB over 1 day £2.04

Figure 3.3

If you want to use your iPad on a plane, go into the Settings app and turn on Airplane Mode (it's the first option in the top left). You just slide its switch to On. This will turn off the radio transmitters and Internet connections so you can use your iPad without interfering with aviation systems.

Understanding your Internet connection

In the status bar in the top-left corner of your iPad, you can see some icons representing the status of your Internet connection. Much of the time when you're using the Internet, you'll see a fan symbol, which shows that Wi-Fi is working (see Figure 3.4). The more lines showing on the fan, the stronger the Wi-Fi signal is.

Figure 3.4

If you have an iPad with mobile communications, you will also see a bar graph indicating the strength of the mobile communications network and the name of your mobile operator. Your iPad will use Wi-Fi whenever it's available and will automatically switch to the mobile network when it's not.

Your iPad will use the best-quality mobile network connection available, and you will see a symbol in the status bar to indicate which type of connection you're using. In order of quality, from fastest to slowest, the symbols are LTE, 4G, 3G, E (EDGE network) and a round circle (GPRS data network). The LTE and 4G connections are available only on third- and fourth-generation iPads and the iPad mini, so those symbols will appear only in areas where those networks exist. If your iPad can't connect to a 4G or 3G network, it may try to connect to the slower EDGE or GPRS data network.

When you see those symbols, you're using up your data plan, so don't go crazy downloading movies. To stop the mobile communications network from being used, go into the Settings menu, tap Mobile Data or Cellular Data and then switch it off.

If you're somewhere that your 3G or 4G mobile communications provider doesn't cover, the data roaming feature might still enable you to get a connection through another provider. It can be expensive, though, so we recommend you turn roaming off. You'll find it in the Settings app, under Mobile Data.

Remember that if you're using mobile communications and have a limited data allowance, any web pages, maps, apps, music or videos you download will eat into that data allowance. It's cheaper, and faster, to use Wi-Fi where available.

Securing your iPad

There are a number of settings you can use to protect your iPad from loss or unauthorised use. Even if you don't have any valuable data on your iPad, these settings can help protect younger family members from content they shouldn't see online – and to protect your wallet from the risk of them accidentally buying hundreds of apps on your account!

Adjusting the Parental Controls (Restrictions)

To restrict the content that can be viewed on your iPad, go into Settings, tap General and then tap Restrictions. Tap Enable Restrictions at the top of the screen, and you will be prompted to enter a four-digit passcode, twice, just to make sure that it's entered correctly.

Restrictions let you restrict access to video conferencing (FaceTime), the web (Safari), iBookStore and Apple's music store (iTunes). They also let you prevent users from installing or deleting apps. You can decide whether to allow the iPad's location to be detected in Maps and whether email accounts can be changed. In-App Purchases enables people to buy content from within an app, and you can restrict explicit music, films with certain certificates, and TV shows and apps unsuitable for younger audiences. There are also settings to stop users from playing multiplayer games and adding friends in Game Center, which is an app that comes with the iPad to help you play games with your friends.

To change or disable Restrictions, you need your Parental Controls passcode, so don't forget it. If you do forget your PIN, you have to 'restore' your iPad to its factory settings – not something we recommend.

Setting a passcode for your iPad

You can protect your iPad from unauthorised access by adding a passcode lock. To do this, go into your General settings again, tap Passcode Lock and then tap Turn Passcode On. As with the passcode for restrictions, the iPad will ask you to enter it twice to make sure you don't mistype it.

If you turn off the Simple Passcode, you can have a longer password using a combination of letters and numbers. The passcode is normally required immediately, but you can set it to be requested after 1 minute, 5 minutes, 15 minutes, 1 hour or 4 hours. Allowing a pause of a few minutes lets you pop into your iPad to quickly look something up without having to enter the passcode.

You can also set the switch so that all the iPad's content is erased after someone enters the passcode incorrectly ten times. This helps protect your data if your iPad is lost or stolen but isn't recommended for anyone who's ever forgotten a password and has had to keep trying different possibilities!

Using the iTunes software on your computer

You might already have a computer that you've been using for photos, music, email, contacts and the web. Apple provides two different approaches for copying information from your computer to your iPad. Most obviously, you can connect your iPad to your computer using the USB cable provided. Apple provides free software called iTunes for managing the content on your iPad. If you can't find a Wi-Fi connection to set up your iPad initially, you'll need to use iTunes on your computer to set up your iPad.

Alternatively, you can use the iCloud service, which copies information between your computer and your iPad using the Internet. It does so automatically, which saves you having to remember to synchronise content. You need your iPad to be connected to the same Wi-Fi network as your computer for it to work. The iCloud service is very convenient, but if you use a Windows computer, you might find it can't yet do everything you need. We cover iCloud later in this chapter, but we recommend that you learn about what iTunes can do for you, too.

Installing iTunes on your computer

Apple installs iTunes for you on its computers, so this section applies only if you have a Windows computer. The iPad doesn't come with a software disc, so you need to download iTunes from Apple's website and then install it.

If you're not comfortable with downloading and installing software, you might want to invite a friend to help with this part. To get the software, you need to use a web browser on your computer, such as Internet Explorer, to visit **www.itunes. com/download**. When you get to the site, complete the form and click the Download Now button. When you're asked whether to Save or Run, choose Run. (You may also need to tell Windows to go ahead and install the software if the overzealous User Account Control screen comes up and warns you that you've tried to do something.)

During installation, you must decide whether to add shortcuts to your desktop (recommended) and whether to allow Apple to update the software automatically (recommended for security reasons). You can also choose whether to make iTunes the default for playing music on your computer. We recommend that you try iTunes first and decide later whether you'd like to use it all the time. You can change this setting on the iTunes Preferences menu. Unless you want to change something, it's okay to leave the default settings unchanged during installation.

During installation, you'll see a green progress bar go from left to right many times. When the installation is complete, iTunes will tell you, and you will need to restart your computer.

Connecting your iPad to your computer

Now that you have the iTunes software installed on your computer, you can connect your iPad to it.

The charging cable for the iPad has a flat USB connection at one end. This end goes into your computer or laptop. It doesn't matter which USB port you connect it to. The same USB connector is used for charging the iPad from the mains. When doing so, it's easier to insert the USB connection into the adapter first (as shown in Figure 3.5 – top), rather than trying to do so when the plug is already in the wall socket. You need to have the 'prong' image facing you. Don't try and force the connector in the other way round.

The tiny Lightning connector at the other end of the cable connects to the Lightning port (see Figure 3.5 – bottom) of fourth-generation iPads or the iPad mini. (Earlier iPad models have a larger 30-pin dock connector socket). It plugs in just beneath the Home button at the bottom of the iPad. It doesn't matter which side up you plug this in for the Lightning port, but the 30-pin connector can go into the socket only one way.

If you've got an iPad that uses a flat, wide 30-pin connector, you'll find this will go in only one way round. If you can't get it to fit easily, try turning it over. Don't force it, or you might damage the cable or the socket.

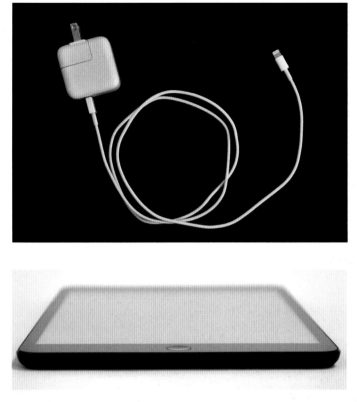

Figure 3.5

When you connect your iPad to your PC for the first time, a box pops up on your PC screen to say that a device driver is being installed. When the box confirms that your device is ready, you can click the button with the red cross in its top-right corner to close the box. An Autoplay box opens, asking what you want to do with this device. You can ignore this box and just close it in the same way without taking any other action for now.

The iTunes software then starts on your PC. This can take a moment or two, so be patient if it doesn't appear instantly.

If you close iTunes by mistake or it doesn't open for some reason, you can restart it like any other program. If you made no changes to the default options when installing iTunes, you will have an icon on your desktop, which you can double-click. Alternatively, put your mouse cursor over the Start button in the bottom-left corner of your computer screen, click it, click All Programs, click the iTunes folder and then click the iTunes icon. If your computer runs Windows 8, iTunes will instead be one of the many 'tiles' covering your Start screen; click to launch it.

Synchronising your iPad with your computer

When you connect your iPad to your computer, the iTunes software synchronises them. That means updates are copied between them so that new contacts from your computer are added to your iPad and new photos from your iPad are copied to your PC, for example. If you delete contacts or photos on one device, they might also be removed from the other.

When you connect your iPad to iTunes, you'll see the summary pane, as shown in Figure 3.6.

The central box at the top in Figure 3.6 shows the status of iTunes and will show you when files are being copied across. Underneath that, you can see buttons that go to the settings for Info, Apps, Music, Movies, TV Shows, Podcasts, Books and Photos.

If you don't see the settings for your device in iTunes, tap the button labelled On This iPad in the toolbar across the top, as you can see in Figure 3.6.

The settings give you a lot of control over which files are copied across. In the music settings, for example, you can choose to copy across all your music, or particular artists, albums or genres. You can also create playlists (which are lists of songs) and choose to synchronise just some of those so that you have your favourite songs on the iPad, for example, or the songs you've selected for a special occasion. Similarly, if you download podcasts (regular free radio or video shows) on your computer, you can pick individual episodes or choose to copy a certain number of unplayed episodes to your iPad. Under the Photos settings, you can choose to synchronise selected folders from your computer or choose to synchronise with your photo library in a program like Adobe Photoshop Elements. In the Info section, you can synchronise browser bookmarks or contacts from Windows Contacts, Google Contacts or your Yahoo! address book by clicking Info.

If you change any of the settings, you'll need to click the Apply button in the bottom-right corner to make your iPad synchronise with those new settings. If you change your mind, click the Revert button in the bottom-right corner, and iTunes will ignore your changes. These buttons appear only when you change settings.

If you don't want your iPad to synchronise when you connect it to the computer, connect the iPad and then hold down the Shift and Control keys on your PC keyboard (or Command and Option on the Mac) until the iPad appears in iTunes.

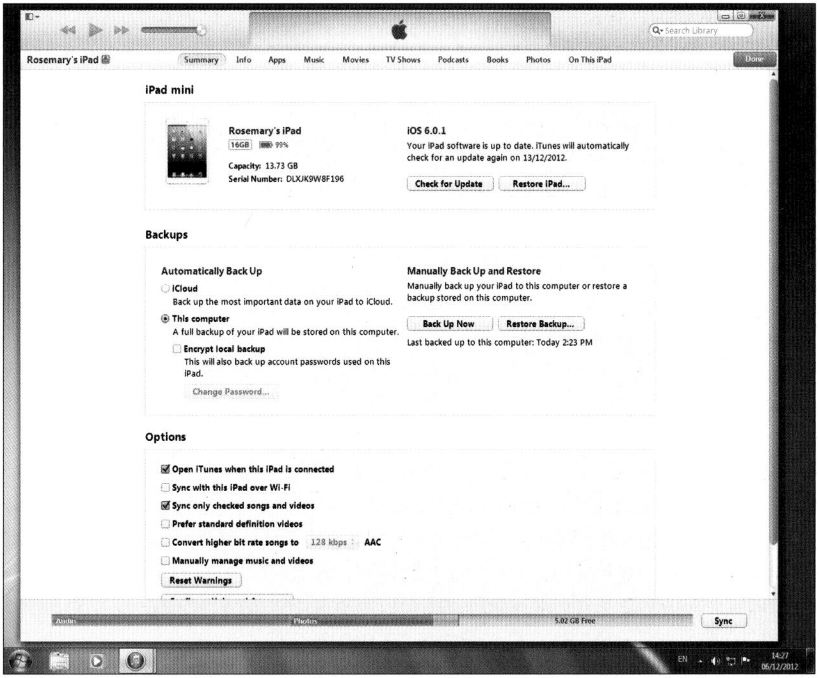

Figure 3.6

If you've ever spent time trying to work out how on earth you've managed to fill up your computer's hard disk, you'll love this next feature. At the very bottom of the screen (refer to Figure 3.6), you can see a Capacity bar that shows (by the length of each coloured section of the bar) how much space is taken up by each content type and how much total space is left on your iPad.

If you have a lot of music on your computer, there is an alternative to synchronising, called iTunes Match. It's a service that charges an annual fee, but it gives you access to all your music on the iPad. See Chapter 10 for more information.

Using Wi-Fi to synchronise your iPad with your computer

You can also synchronise your iPad with your computer over Wi-Fi, so you don't need to connect them physically. You'll need to have a computer that's part of a wired or wireless network. In practice, you should be able to connect any modern Windows or Apple Macintosh computer to a network that the iPad can also join. To enable Wi-Fi synchronisation, connect your iPad to your computer using the cable and then tick the box for Sync over Wi-Fi Connection in the Summary list in iTunes. You will need to scroll the screen to find it. Your iPad will then synchronise with your computer automatically once a day, provided that the iPad is connected to a power source, the computer and iPad are both on the same Wi-Fi network, and iTunes is running on your computer.

Backing up your iPad using iTunes

If anything should happen to your iPad, it's a good idea to have a copy of the information it contains so that you don't lose that too. It's one thing to lose your favourite gadget, but it can be heartbreaking to lose its photos and all your work.

You can keep a backup copy of your iPad's data on your computer. In the Summary list in iTunes you'll see a Backups section. Choose the option to create a full backup of your iPad on your computer. When you synchronise your iPad with your computer, iTunes will copy all the information from your iPad so that if something should go wrong with it, you can recover all your data by resetting the iPad or copying your backup copy from your computer to a new iPad. A further option is to use iCloud for backup.

Introducing iCloud

Apple iCloud enables content to be automatically copied between your iPad and other devices without you connecting them.

When you use iCloud, your files are copied to a private part of the Internet, and your other devices (such as your iPhone or computer) can copy your files from there. This means you can synchronise much of the content on your iPad with your computer without having to connect them.

Enabling iCloud on your iPad

You're invited to turn on iCloud when you set up your iPad, but you can change your settings at any time in the Settings app. Go into your Settings and then tap iCloud on the left. Figure 3.7 shows the iCloud settings.

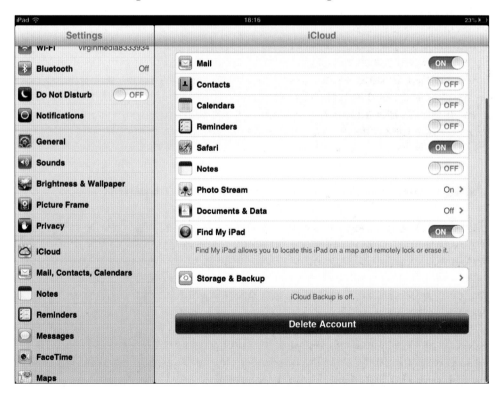

Figure 3.7

You can choose which files you would like to synchronise with your other devices, including Mail, Contacts, Calendars, Reminders, Bookmarks, Notes, Photo Stream and Documents & Data. The Documents & Data category includes any information created or stored in apps you add to your iPad that are designed to work with iCloud. If you want to synchronise emails and notes, you need to register with Apple for a free iCloud.com account (see Chapter 6).

When you use Photo Stream (see Chapter 13), any photos you take on your iPad are copied to iCloud and can be automatically downloaded on your computer. You can also upload images from your computer to your iPad automatically. Your photos appear in the Pictures folder on a Windows computer or in iPhoto or Aperture on a Mac. If you use the same Apple ID on multiple Macs and iOS devices, Photo Stream will beam your snaps to all of them that run at least iOS5. Bear this in mind if you have used your own Apple ID to set up a younger family member's Apple device.

Photos are stored in iCloud for only 30 days, so make sure you switch on your computer once in a while to download the photos from your iPad. The iPad, iPhone and iPod touch keep only the last 1000 photos from iCloud, To ensure that a photo is saved forever, go into the Photos app, tap Photo Stream at the top, tap the photo, tap Use Photo in the top-right corner and then tap Save to Camera Roll.

Using iCloud to synchronise with your computer

You can use iCloud to synchronise your iPad with another iPad, an iPhone, an iPod touch, a Mac or a Windows computer. Not all versions of the iPhone and iPod touch are compatible with iCloud, though, and older devices will need to have their software updated to version iOS5 or later. There isn't space to cover this here, but you can find out how to update your iPhone or iPod software at Apple's website.

If you have a Mac, you need to update your computer to use OS X Lion v.10.7.2 (or later) and turn on iCloud in your System Preferences. You also need to enable the Photo Stream feature in iPhoto or Aperture.

If you use Windows, you need to have Windows Vista (Service Pack 2) or Windows 7 or 8. We're sorry, but if you are still using Windows XP, you won't be able to use iCloud on your computer. To use iCloud on a Windows computer, you need to download and install some free software for your computer from Apple. You can find it at **www.apple.com/icloud/get-started/**. Follow the instructions there to enable automatic downloads so that any content you buy from Apple using your iPad (such as books, apps and music) is also downloaded to your computer automatically.

> To enable content bought on your computer (or other devices) to automatically download to your iPad, go into the Settings app, tap Store on the left, and switch on automatic downloads for music, apps and/or books.

Figure 3.8 shows the iCloud Control Panel on a Windows computer. You can find it at any time by going through your Windows Start menu or the Start screen in Windows 8. If you click Photo Stream Options, you can choose where you would like photos coming from your iPad to be stored on your computer. You can also designate an upload folder. Any photos you put into that folder will be copied to your iPad automatically over iCloud. There's no longer any need to mess around with cables to copy photos between your iPad and your computer! You can only copy contacts, mail and calendars, though, if you use the relatively expensive Outlook software on your PC, so you might choose to use the cable to synchronise your contacts from time to time anyway.

Figure 3.8

Using iCloud Backup

If you want to back up your iPad using iCloud, you get 5GB of storage for free and then you can pay a subscription fee to upgrade. Photos in your Photo Stream and content you buy from Apple, such as music, apps and books, don't eat into your 5GB allowance. Any music you didn't buy from Apple that you add to your iPad isn't backed up, so keep a copy of that on your computer, using the iTunes software.

To switch on iCloud Backup, go into the Settings app, tap iCloud and then tap Storage & Backup. The Storage & Backup screen shows how much storage space you have available and how much of it is still free. Note that 5GB isn't that much (you can fit it on a USB key), so you can rent extra storage space if you need it. It costs £14 ($20) per year for an extra 10GB of storage, £28 ($40) for 20GB or £70 ($100) for 50GB. The maximum available space is 55GB (your free 5GB plus a 50GB subscription). We've not found a need to purchase extra storage. However, should you find yourself eating into your storage space, see Chapter 14 on apps for details on how to ensure you manage app storage and keep costs down.

If you use iCloud Backup, your iPad won't back up to your computer when you synchronise it. Instead, when your iPad is plugged in to a power source, locked and connected to Wi-Fi, your data will be backed up over the Internet to Apple's computers in Maiden, North Carolina. You can also tell your iPad to make a backup at any time by going into the Settings app, tapping iCloud, tapping Storage & Backup and then tapping Back Up Now.

Updating your iPad software

From time to time, Apple releases a new version of the software on the iPad, which usually improves the iPad's reliability and introduces some new features. Messages and Reminders apps were introduced as free upgrades for all iPad owners in October 2011, when Apple released new iPad software called iOS5. Owners of the latest fourth-generation iPad and the iPad mini will find even newer software, iOS6, on their devices. If you have an earlier iPad model (except for the original iPad), you can upgrade to iOS6 for free. Some of the apps and features described in this book are available only to those who have this latest version of the iPad software.

You can update the software on your iPad without affecting any of the information, apps, music or other files stored on it, and the update is a free service. There's usually a lot of press coverage about a significant update, so you can easily find out what you can expect from a particular software update.

There are two ways you can update the software on your iPad:

- Connect your iPad to your computer and then click the Check for Update button in the iTunes software. When iTunes knows an update is available, this button is instead labelled Update.
- On your iPad, go into the Settings app and tap Software Update.

Because Apple updates its software from time to time, you might spot differences between what your iPad does and the behaviour described in this book. Previous updates have tended to introduce new features without dramatically affecting existing ones, though, so any changes are likely to be minor.

You can also update the iTunes software running on your computer. Apple regularly introduces new features and fixes bugs that come to light, especially when it launches a new iPad, iPod or iPhone. In the iTunes software, click Help at the top and then click Check for Updates.

Apple iOS6: the latest iPad software

Apple regularly updates the software for the iPad. Updates are free. iOS6, introduced in late 2012, added improvements in several areas but made one less successful change. With iOS6, Apple replaced the established Google Maps service with its own Apple Maps, which is something of a work in progress. There have been many complaints about out-of-date mapping and mislabeled places and streets. A red-faced Apple is working furiously to address this and will no doubt offer a far better version very soon.

Many of the improvements offered in iOS6 see better integration between the core features that the iPad comes with. Integration with the Facebook social network includes adding friends' birthdays to your iPad calendar and posting photos to your Facebook account. Enhancements to the Siri voice controls let you launch apps via voice commands, set reminders, send emails and (on GPS-enabled iPads with satnav software running) get turn-by-turn navigation directions. In Chapter 4 we look at how to use Siri's voice-recognition capability to dictate a memo, for example.

The latest iPad software also offers shared Photo Streams. Here, images you save on your iPad automatically appear on your Mac or PC (or in the Photo library of your iPhone, if you have one). However, your photos can also be shared with other iOS6 users – handy if your relatives and friends are also iPad users. Messaging is also improved with a VIP inbox feature so you can more easily see email messages from your friends and family that might otherwise get lost amid the deluge of junk mail.

Another enhancement in iOS6 sees the Safari web browser synchronising with its equivalent on your home computer, so you can quickly access sites you frequently visit or pages you've recently browsed, regardless of whether you did so on your iPad or your computer.

We also welcome the addition of Guided Access – settings that offer ways to control the iPad if you have hearing or visual impairments or need particular assistance using technology. You can apply suitable settings by going into Settings, tapping Accessibility and choosing Guided Access.

We look in more detail at some of these features throughout the book. First, though, you need to install iOS6. Updating your iPad to the latest version of its software is straightforward. When you connect your iPad to your computer, you get a message stating that new software is available for it. Allow your iPad to complete a full backup – as described in the earlier section 'Backing up your iPad using iTunes' – and then choose Install to start the upgrade process.

> Over time, Apple Maps is sure to be improved. But if you've got an iPad that runs iOS5 (tap the Settings app, tap General, tap About and look under Version to find out), you may prefer to stick with it for now so you can continue using Google Maps.

Summary

- To use 3G or 4G on your iPad (also known as mobile broadband) you need the right SIM card. For standard-size iPads, this is a micro SIM; for the iPad mini, you need a nano SIM.

- The Settings app is used to set up your Wi-Fi connection, 4G/3G connection, passcodes and features to improve ease of use.

- iTunes is free software for your computer that is used to manage the content on your iPad.

- You can also use the iCloud service to copy content between your iPad and other devices without connecting them.

- You can use iCloud or the iTunes software to back up your iPad.

- You can get free new features on your iPad by updating the iPad iOS software; if a new version is available, you'll see a prompt when you plug your iPad into your computer.

Brain training

Now that you know how to use your iPad, get online and synchronise its content, you're ready to start creating and saving content to it. First, we check that you really know how to keep track of all your iPad music, photos and documents. There may be more than one right answer to some questions.

1. You can access the Internet on your iPad for free:

(a) By connecting to your home Wi-Fi network

(b) By logging on to a free Wi-Fi hotspot or one that your mobile operator includes in your monthly contract

(c) By using the 3G or 4G connection on your iPad

(d) At many public institutions, such as libraries and museums

2. You can back up your iPad:

(a) To your home computer over Wi-Fi

(b) By using iTunes, but only music, books and movies will be stored

(c) Online, using a service called iCloud

(d) Over a 3G connection

3. When you see an *E* in the top-left corner of your iPad, it means:

(a) An entertainment app is running.

(b) You're connected to the mobile network on an iPad.

(c) You're connected to Wi-Fi.

(d) That's today's letter on *Sesame Street.*

4. You might not want to install iOS6 iPad software if:

(a) You aren't confident about performing an update.

(b) You're not sure whether your iPad's contents will be safe.

(c) You've got the very first model of iPad, which can't use the latest features.

(d) You prefer to stick with Google Maps.

5. Apple offers new iPad software:

(a) Only on new iPads

(b) As a free update for all iPad users (though the oldest iPads may not be able to use it)

(c) As a simple update when you plug your iPad into your computer

(d) You have to buy a new iPad to get the latest software and features.

Answers

Q1 – a, b and d (3G and 4G Internet access are included in your monthly contract, but check your allowance so you don't incur extra charges)

Q2 – a and c **Q3** – b

Q4 – a, c and d **Q5** – b and c

Keeping notes on your iPad

4

Equipment needed: An iPad that is ready to use, and reasonably clean fingers!

Skills needed: Knowledge of how to start apps.

Now that you have your iPad set up and know how to navigate its apps, it's time to start using them. In this chapter, you find out how to jot down ideas and memos on your iPad. You start by using the Notes app, one of the simplest apps that comes with your iPad, inspired by a humble pad of paper. Whether you're writing a shopping list, a song or a story, Notes is there in an instant to capture your ideas before they drift away. When you need to refer to a note, the search function makes it easy to find.

At the end of this chapter, we also take a look at the Reminders app, a sophisticated to-do list that includes alerts to make sure you don't forget anything important. Although you can email your notes to people, the Notes app is not intended for creating polished final documents for sharing. There are no features for bold text, underlining, different fonts or any other changes in formatting that you might be used to from a word processing package. That might sound like a limitation, but it's actually a strength. There is nothing distracting or unnecessary on the screen, so you can focus on what you're writing. If you're one of those people who has to fiddle with 15 fonts before you start writing, you're all out of excuses. You don't even have to save your work. Notes takes care of that for you automatically.

You've already seen the keyboard when you were entering passwords to set up your Internet connection. In this chapter, you have an opportunity to practice using it, and you see how the iPad's predictive text feature (called Auto-text) can help you write more quickly.

To start the Notes app, tap the Notes icon on the Home screen.

You can't change the text style used for individual notes, but you can change the appearance that all notes share. Go into the Settings app and then tap Notes. You can choose Noteworthy (default), Helvetica or Marker Felt text style. You can enlarge the text size of your notes to make the text easier to read and select. Go into the Settings app, tap General, tap Accessibility and then choose Large Text. See Chapter 2 for more details on the Accessibility options.

Understanding the Notes screen

Notes is a good example of an app that adapts to the orientation of your iPad to make the best use of the screen space. Figure 4.1 shows Notes in portrait mode, where the screen is filled with blank paper. To see a list of your notes or to search them, you need to tap the Notes button in the top-left corner, as we have in Figure 4.1.

Figure 4.2 shows what Notes looks like in landscape mode. You can see less of each note at a time, but there is a permanent pane on the left that lists your notes and enables you to search them. We prefer landscape mode because it provides a bigger keyboard, so typing is easier and more accurate. Use whichever orientation suits you better.

When using apps, it's worth rotating the screen to see if it declutters the screen or makes additional features easier to find and use.

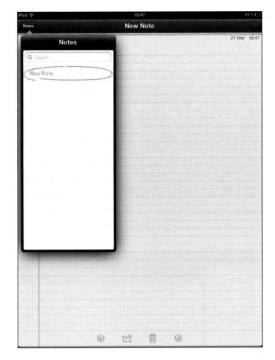

Figure 4.1

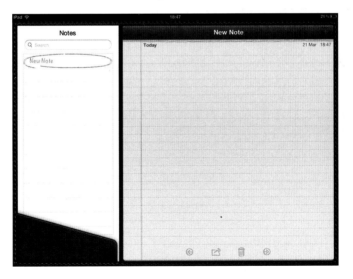

Figure 4.2

Writing your first note

When Notes opens for the first time, it shows what looks like a blank piece of yellow ruled paper. Tap this 'paper' and the keyboard appears so that you can start typing.

Choose your first words carefully: there are no filenames in Notes because your work is saved automatically, without any intervention from you. Instead, the first few words you write in a note are used to refer to it in the list of notes. If you start your note with a short title such as Lasagne Recipe, your notes will be easier to navigate. If your first line reads, 'My note about the way to make lasagne', all you'll see in the list of notes is an unhelpful 'My note about the way...' (see Figure 4.3).

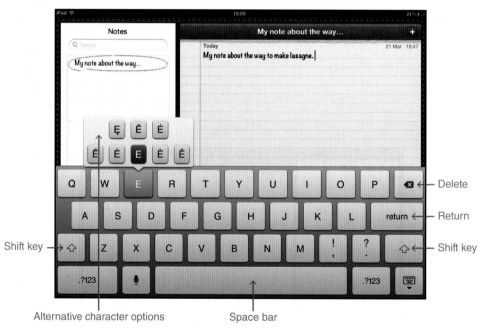

Figure 4.3

If you want to retitle a note, you can edit the first line or insert a new line at the start. You see how to edit what you've written later in this chapter.

Using the iPad keyboard

Some of the keys on the iPad keyboard are set out in the same way as those on a normal keyboard. The spacebar runs along the bottom in the middle, and the standard QWERTYUIOP layout for letters is present and correct.

In the top-right corner, you can see the Delete key (refer to Figure 4.3). Tap this key to remove a character or keep your finger on the key to keep deleting, first a character at a time and then a word at a time.

There are two Shift keys, but they work a bit differently to a normal keyboard. You can hold down the Shift key while you tap a letter key to type a capital letter as you would on a normal keyboard, but it might feel a bit awkward. Instead, you can tap a Shift key and then tap a letter. When the Shift key has been activated, the arrow in it turns blue. After you tap a letter, the Shift key is deactivated again.

To speed up your typing, the iPad helps you start a new sentence with a capital letter. When you finish a sentence with a full stop and a space, the keyboard automatically turns the Shift key on for the next letter. If you forget about this and tap the Shift key, you'll turn it off again, so your sentence will start with a lowercase letter instead.

The iPad keyboard has no separate Caps Lock key, but if you tap a Shift key twice in quick succession, caps lock is switched on (assuming it has been activated in the Settings, General, Keyboard options). If the whole of the Shift key except the arrow is blue, it means that caps lock is on and any letters typed will be capitalised until you tap Shift again.

If you tap something twice quickly, it's called a double tap, a bit like an iPad version of the double click you might use on a computer mouse. If the gap between your taps is too long, the iPad might think you made two separate single taps instead, so keep it snappy!

As with a normal keyboard, you can use the Shift key to get different symbols from some other keys. Using Shift with the comma key enters an exclamation mark, for example.

When you reach the end of a line, keep typing, and you will automatically be moved to the start of the next line. To start a new line at any time, tap the Return key. You can tap it twice to leave a blank line, to make it easier to see the gaps between paragraphs. When you start a new line, the Shift key is activated so that the first letter will be capitalised. If you don't want that, tap the Shift key to turn it off before you type your first letter.

Don't worry about running out of space on the screen: A note is like a never-ending sheet of paper. You can write as much or as little on it as you want, although you might find it easier to use lots of short notes rather than a few long ones. If your note is too long for it all to fit on the screen at the same time, you can scroll it up or down by touching the note and dragging your finger up or down the screen. The iPad is smart enough to know that if you drag your finger, you didn't intend to tap or select anything on the screen.

You can tap the spacebar twice quickly at the end of a sentence to enter a full stop and a space.

Entering special characters

Using the simple keyboard, you should be able to type shopping lists and simple notes. But what happens when you want to jot down a recipe with all the quantities of ingredients or need to complete your Spanish homework with all its accents? For situations like these, you need to know about the more advanced features of the iPad keyboard.

The iPad makes it very easy to enter accents (more so than on other keyboards we've used). To enter an accented character, just tap the letter key and hold your finger on it. A bubble appears above the key, showing the letter with different accents applied (refer to the E key in Figure 4.3). Without removing your finger from the touchscreen, slide it to the version of the letter you want. When you release your finger, the letter with the accent will be added to your note.

Even if you don't use any foreign languages, this is a useful technique to know. You can use it on the full-stop key to type speech marks, and you can use it on the comma key to enter an apostrophe or single quote mark. As you see in Chapter 9, it can also help you enter website addresses more quickly.

The iPad provides two special keyboards that you can use to enter numbers and symbols. Tap the .?123 key, and the keys change to the keyboard shown in Figure 4.4. This keyboard shows the numbers and most frequently used punctuation symbols. It also has an Undo key you can use if you make a mistake when deleting or typing text.

Do you remember the Etch-a-Sketch toy that was about the same size as an iPad and enabled you to draw pictures by using two dials and then delete the pictures by shaking the device? Perhaps as a tribute to that classic toy, you can also undo by shaking the iPad, although it's easier to tap the Undo key.

Figure 4.4

As with the letters keyboard, some of the keys on the numbers keyboard have additional symbols you can access by pressing and holding a key. The £ key, for example, provides quick access to other currency symbols. The apostrophe and speech-mark keys provide several different styles (including proper 66- and 99-shaped quotation marks). To enter a bullet point, press and hold the dash key until that symbol appears. The full-stop key can also be used to enter an ellipsis (three dots in a row).

If you just want to type one character from this keyboard, here's a shortcut. Touch the .?123 key and keep your finger on the screen when the keyboard changes. Slide your finger to the key you want to use and then release your finger. Your chosen symbol is entered, and the keyboard reverts to the standard ABC format.

From the numbers keyboard, you can access a third keyboard that offers a range of less frequently used symbols, such as square and curly brackets, the percent sign, and currency symbols (see Figure 4.5). It also offers a Redo key that allows you to reinstate something you undo without meaning to. To show this keyboard, press the #+= key that replaces the Shift key on the numbers keyboard.

Hide Keyboard

Figure 4.5

To go back to the letters keyboard from either of the other keyboards, tap the ABC key. To help you type fluently, the iPad automatically switches to the letter keyboard after you type a space or apostrophe. All three keyboard layouts offer dictation mode, which we discuss shortly.

Hiding the keyboard

The only problem with the keyboard is that it gets in the way of the note itself, which can make it hard to re-read your note. At any time, you can hide the keyboard by tapping the Hide Keyboard key in the bottom-right corner of the keyboard (refer to Figure 4.5). It's on every version of the keyboard. You can bring the keyboard back again simply by tapping the note to start typing. Elsewhere on the iPad, tapping within a text field brings up the keyboard so you can start typing.

Although it takes a little time to adjust to the feel of the onscreen keyboard, it is possible to type quickly. Notes provides the ideal place to practice your typing. Give it a go!

Dictating notes to your iPad

The third-generation iPad introduced a new feature that can speed up your writing: dictation. You can speak to your iPad and have your words (or, more usually, a close approximation of them) appear on your iPad's screen. If your iPad uses iOS5 or iOS6, you can also dictate memos to your iPad using Siri. (See the following section, 'Dictating notes with Siri'.)

When you use the dictation feature, your speech is sent to Apple, together with your name and information about your contacts and the songs in your music collection. It's best, then, not to dictate any deep, dark secrets to your iPad. Apple's central computers use this information to turn the things you say into the words on your screen. You can turn off the dictation feature in the Settings app (tap General on the left and then Keyboard on the right).

To use the dictation feature, tap the dictation key to the left of the spacebar, which has a microphone on it (refer to Figure 4.6). Because the dictation service requires the Internet, the dictation key won't appear on the keyboard when you have no Internet connection.

When you tap the dictation key, it pops out and shows a noise meter inside the microphone so you can see how well the iPad can hear you. Speak your words of wisdom, and when you've finished, tap the dictation key again to end. It takes several seconds for the iPad to work out what you've said, and then your words appear in your note. More likely than not, you'll need to edit your text to correct any words the iPad couldn't correctly make out. Shortly, you see how to do just that.

Figure 4.6

Dictating notes with Siri

Siri is the name of a digital assistant built into the iPad that recognises your voice. It can be found on the iPad mini and the third- and fourth-generation iPad models. You invoke Siri by pressing and holding down the Home button. Siri pops up as a captioned microphone next to the Home button. Start talking, and Siri listens to what you say. Once you stop speaking, Siri analyses the sentence and both shows and speaks what it thinks you've asked of it. To get Siri to take a memo say "Take a note, Siri". Siri will ask what you want to make a note of and then show you the new note. Press the Home button again to switch Siri off.

You can also use Siri to create and send emails, check the weather and start apps on your iPad. In addition, Siri is the navigator in Apple Maps when you use your iPhone or iPad with Wi-Fi + Cellular to get directions.

Using Auto-text to speed up your writing

You already know about some of the amazing things the iPad can do, but did you know it can predict the future? Okay, so maybe that's stretching it a bit. But it gives it a good go. Try writing the word *elephant*. You need to tap only four characters before the iPad guesses what you're intending to type and shows it in a small bubble below your typing (see Figure 4.7).

Figure 4.7

What you're seeing is the Auto-text feature, and you might already have noticed it working while you were entering text before. It's like a cross between the predictive text feature of a mobile phone and the automatic spelling correction feature of a word processor. It aims to enable you to type more quickly and accurately, but if you're not careful, the iPad can change words you don't want it to.

To accept the iPad's suggestion, just tap the spacebar. It doesn't matter how far into the word you are. If the iPad can guess it in four characters, you don't have to type any more.

If the iPad makes an incorrect suggestion, keep typing your word; the iPad keeps trying to guess it. Whenever the correct word appears, tap the spacebar.

The problem comes when you get to the end of the word and the iPad thinks you're midway through typing something else or thinks you've misspelled something you haven't. Try typing the word *ill,* for example. When you tap the spacebar, the iPad replaces your correct and complete word with *I'll,* which is used more often but which makes no sense in your sentence. To stop this happening, touch the iPad's suggested word on the screen, and it goes away. This feels a bit counterintuitive; usually you touch things to select them. But touching an Auto-text suggestion dismisses it. That's why there's a cross to the right of the Auto-text suggestion: When you touch it, you close it.

If Auto-text makes a change you don't want, use the Delete key to go back to the end of the word. A new bubble appears above the word, showing what you originally typed together with any other suggestions for what you might have been trying to type. Touch one of these options, and your chosen text replaces the Auto-text. The iPad is programmed to learn from you over time so that it can improve its suggestions to you.

In the Accessibility settings of your iPad (see Chapter 2), you can set the iPad to speak Auto-text suggestions out loud, even if you don't use VoiceOver. This can be a good way to make sure you notice the suggestions when you're typing quickly or looking at the keyboard. If you can't hear the suggestions, check that your iPad's volume is turned up.

Creating your own shortcuts

If you find that you often type the same long word or phrase, you can speed up your typing by entering an abbreviation that the iPad will automatically expand for you every time you use it.

To configure any abbreviations you want to use, go into the Settings app, tap General, tap Keyboard and then tap Add New Shortcut at the bottom of the screen. In the Phrase box, enter the full phrase you want to abbreviate. In the Shortcut box, type the short form you want to use. When you type this shortcut in a note, message, email or form box on a website, the iPad suggests the long phrase using Auto-text. You just need to tap the spacebar to accept the suggestion.

To delete any of your Auto-text additions, go into the Settings app, tap General, tap Keyboard and then tap Edit in the top-right corner. You see a list of your shortcuts, with a Delete button beside each one (a round red sign with a white bar). Tap the Delete button beside the shortcut you'd like to remove and then tap the Delete button that appears on the right to confirm. Tap anywhere else if you change your mind and don't want to delete.

Shortcuts can be real time-savers. You can use a three-letter sequence to stand in for your full email address, for example, so you can enter it quickly when you want to log in to a website.

Editing your text

Sometimes, you want to change what you've written in a note. You might spot a mistake you made when you first typed it, need to update it with new information or find that the iPad's dictation feature has already scrambled the eggs on your shopping list. The editing features of the iPad have some similarities with those of other computers, but the iPad also introduces some new ideas.

Positioning the insertion point

The *insertion point* is what Apple calls the cursor. It's the vertical flashing line that indicates where characters will be added when you type. As with a word processor, when you press the Backspace key, characters to the left of the insertion point are removed.

To reposition the insertion point, just tap your note in the place you want the insertion point to appear, and it jumps to the end of the nearest word.

You can't put the insertion point in the middle of an empty space on the page. If you tap the space after the last piece of text in your note, the insertion point goes to the end of your text. To create blank space between bits of text, add some blank lines by tapping the Return key.

If you want to move to the middle of a word, tap the word and hold your finger on the screen. You might find it easier to do this accurately if you make the text larger, using the Accessibility options in the Settings app (see Chapter 2).

A magnifying glass appears above the insertion point (see Figure 4.8) to show you where the insertion point is in your word, which gets around the problem of your finger's obscuring your view. As you move your finger left or right, the insertion point moves through the word, and you can see it in the magnifying glass. When you remove your finger, the insertion point stays where you moved it with the magnifying glass.

Once you have positioned your insertion point, you can add or delete characters using the keyboard.

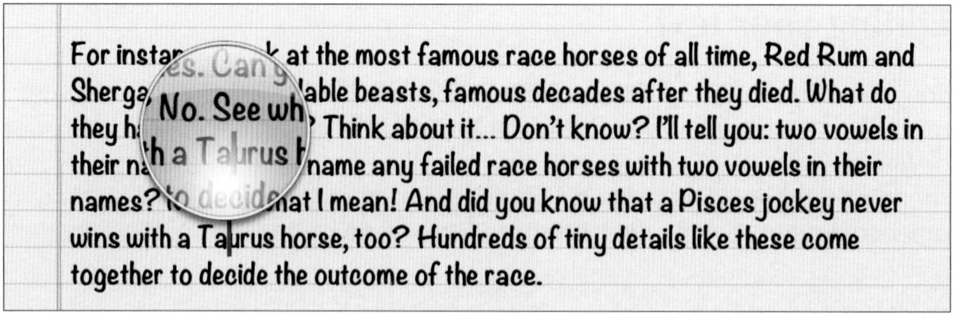

For instance, look at the most famous race horses of all time, Red Rum and Sherga, memorable beasts, famous decades after they died. What do they have... *No. See what a Taurus ... to decide* Think about it... Don't know? I'll tell you: two vowels in their names... name any failed race horses with two vowels in their names? *what I mean!* And did you know that a Pisces jockey never wins with a Taurus horse, too? Hundreds of tiny details like these come together to decide the outcome of the race.

Figure 4.8

Using cut, copy and paste

Sometimes, you want to move a chunk of text around and perhaps even move it from one application to another. You may want to copy something from a web page into a note, for example, or put part of a note in an email you're writing. The Notes app enables you to select chunks of text so that you can move them around within Notes or between applications.

The first step is to select the piece of text you want to use. There are three ways to do this in the Notes app:

- Tap the insertion point. A menu appears, with the options Select and Select All. Tap Select, and the nearest word is selected. Tap Select All, and all the content of the note is selected.

- Tap and hold your finger on a word anywhere in your note. The magnifying glass appears so you can position your insertion point. When you lift your finger, the menu appears, with the options Select and Select All. Tap Select to select the word or Select All to select your entire note.

- Double-tap a word to select it.

You can tell what text has been selected because it's highlighted in blue. There's also a menu above it, which we come to in a moment. First, take a look at the vertical lines at the start and end of the selected text (see Figure 4.9). The end of each line has a bobble called a *grab point*. To increase or decrease the area selected, you touch a grab point and move your finger across the screen. A rectangular magnifier helps you see what you're selecting. This is how you select a few words, sentences or paragraphs, or even just a few characters.

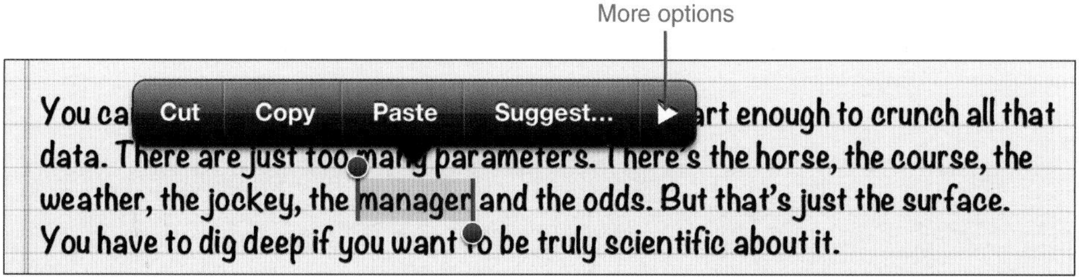

More options

You ca| Cut | Copy | Paste | Suggest... | ▶ |rt enough to crunch all that data. There are just too many parameters. There's the horse, the course, the weather, the jockey, the manager and the odds. But that's just the surface. You have to dig deep if you want to be truly scientific about it.

Figure 4.9

Spend a few minutes practicing selecting text, including sentences and paragraphs. It doesn't take long to get the hang of it, but it's one of the more fiddly techniques to figure out on the iPad.

The menu above your selected text shows you some or all of the following options (refer to Figure 4.9):

- **Cut:** If you cut a piece of text, it is removed from your note but temporarily kept in the iPad's memory. You can then insert your text into a different place in your note by pasting it there.

- **Copy:** If you copy a piece of text, it's left where it is now, but a temporary copy of it is made so that you can paste it (insert it) somewhere else in your note as well.

- **Paste:** If you select some text on screen and then choose Paste, the iPad deletes the text you have selected and pastes the last piece of text you cut or copied in its place.

To select one of the menu options (Cut, Copy or Paste), just tap it. To change your mind and do nothing, tap the selected text, or tap somewhere else in the note. When you're moving text around in your note, most of the time you just need to select the text, copy or cut it, move the insertion point where you want to paste it back in, and then tap the insertion point. If some text has been cut or copied, there will be a Paste option you can tap to insert it into your note.

⚠️ The iPad can 'remember' only one chunk of text at a time, so be careful, in particular when cutting text. When you cut a piece of text, it's removed from your note but kept in the iPad's memory. If you cut or copy another piece of text before pasting the first one, the iPad forgets your first piece of text, and you can't get it back.

If you want to delete a section of text, select it in the same way and then tap the Delete key on the keyboard. If you've hidden the keyboard, tap the note to show it again. If you select text and then type something, your new text replaces the selected words.

Fixing your spelling

The iPad gives you a helping hand and fixes some of your spelling as you type. You may even find yourself depending on some of its suggestions to speed up your typing. There's no need to tap Shift before the letter *I* if you're talking about yourself, because the iPad changes *i* to *I*; and if you type **ive**, it automatically changes that entry to *I've*.

The iPad is less confident about correcting other spellings. But if a word isn't in the dictionary, the iPad underlines it with red dots (see *scienc* in the first line of Figure 4.10). When you tap the word, suggestions for the correct spelling appear from the dictionary (see *wil* later in Figure 4.10). You can tap one of these suggestions to replace your original word with it.

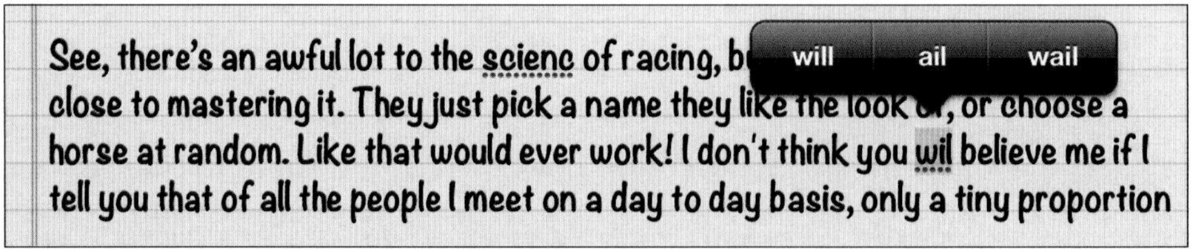

> See, there's an awful lot to the scienc of racing, b[will   ail   wail]
> close to mastering it. They just pick a name they like the look of, or choose a
> horse at random. Like that would ever work! I don't think you wil believe me if I
> tell you that of all the people I meet on a day to day basis, only a tiny proportion

Figure 4.10

This works when the iPad spots the mistake, but sometimes you pick up on mistakes that the iPad won't notice. If you wrote *Germany,* the iPad wouldn't dare question your judgement, even if you should have written *German*. In that case, you can try some additional options that appear in the menu above the selected text:

● **Suggest:** If you select a word and choose Suggest (refer to Figure 4.9), the spellchecker suggests alternative words to replace the one you've selected. When you tap one of the suggestions, the spellchecker replaces the original word with your new selected word. Like a computer spellchecker, this feature can't always correctly identify what you intended to write.

● **Define:** If you're not sure you've used a word correctly, you can use the iPad's dictionary to check. It includes detailed definitions and a mini encyclopaedia. When you tap Define, a bubble opens, showing the definition of your selected text (see Figure 4.11). This bubble is quite small, so if the definition is too long to fit in the bubble, drag its text up to read more. If Define isn't available as an option, the word isn't in the dictionary. Note that the first time you use this feature, you may need to download the dictionary.

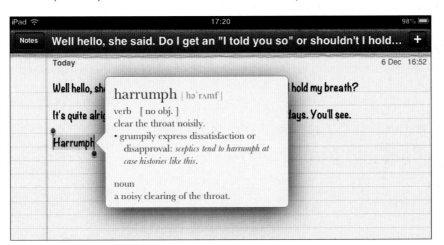

Figure 4.11

If there are too many options to fit in the menu above your selected text at the same time, tap the arrows on the right and/or the left of the menu to move between the different sets of options (refer to Figure 4.9).

If a word isn't in the dictionary, you can correct the mistake yourself by repositioning the insertion arrow and using the keyboard to add or delete characters.

Adding and deleting notes

When you started Notes for the first time, it opened with a blank note. When you want to write additional notes, you need to tap the Add Note button – the one with the plus sign in the top-right corner (refer to Figure 4.11). A new blank page opens, but your previous note remains in the Notes app for you to refer to at any time.

You can also delete notes by going to a note and then tapping the bin icon at the bottom of it (see Figure 4.12). A red box appears, titled Delete Note. Tap that box to get rid of your note, or tap somewhere else to keep your note.

You can browse through your notes by tapping the Previous Note and Next Note icons.

There's no undo for deleting notes, so don't delete something you might need later.

Emailing and printing notes

At the bottom of each note is an icon that looks like an arrow jumping out of a box (refer to Figure 4.12). You can tap this icon to email a note to someone. We look at how to set up your email in Chapter 6. When your email is set up, you can send your note just by tapping the arrow icon and selecting an email address.

You can also find an option for printing notes behind this icon. Apple uses a wireless technology that it calls AirPrint, which enables your iPad to send documents to a compatible printer without physically connecting to it. If you don't already have an AirPrint-compatible printer, look out for one the next time you want to upgrade your printer.

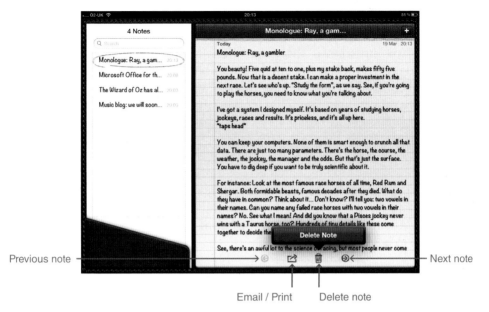

Previous note

Next note

Email / Print   Delete note

Figure 4.12

Searching your notes

Unlike with paper notebooks, you don't need to spend ages thumbing through your iPad looking for notes you made several weeks or months ago. The iPad saves you that kind of hassle because it has a search capability built in. Depending on what you use Notes for, this can be a powerful tool. If you keep recipes in Notes, for example, you can search by ingredient to see what you can concoct from what's left in the fridge. If you're using Notes to keep track of DIY jobs, you can search by room or by tool to help you plan your weekend.

When writing notes, think about the kinds of words you might want to use so you can find them again. You could add a few keywords to the end of a note to make it easy to find later.

Using the search in Notes

The search pane in Notes is shown on the left side of the screen in landscape mode; it also pops up when you tap the Notes button in portrait mode. It lists your most recently updated notes, with the latest at the top of the list, and a snippet of the first few words to help you tell the notes apart. The note currently on view is circled in crayon (refer to Figure 4.12). You can choose any of the others by tapping it in the list.

To search your notes, tap the search box at the top of the search pane (see Figure 4.13). Then use the keyboard to enter a word or phrase from the note. The word or phrase doesn't have to be from the beginning; it doesn't even have to be a complete word. Anything you can remember from the note, you can type into the search pane to help you locate the note.

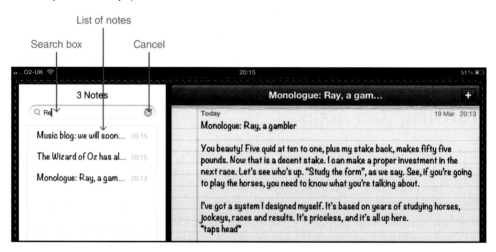

Figure 4.13

As you type, the iPad searches through your notes and narrows the list of notes below the search box to those that feature the word or phrase you're looking for. When you've found the note you need, tap it in the list to open it.

While you're typing in the search box, an X in a circle appears to the right of the search box. Tap this X to cancel what you've entered. You'll see this feature used in lots of other apps.

Using the iPad's Spotlight search

There is another way to search Notes and other content on your iPad. Spotlight search rummages through all the built-in apps to find a note, photo, song, email address or phone number or any other file you're looking for. It can also find apps by name and provides a shortcut for searching the Internet or for searching the online encyclopaedia Wikipedia.

To use Spotlight search, press the Home button to return to the Home screen and place your finger somewhere in the middle of the iPad's screen. Move your finger quickly to the right and then lift it. This gesture is called a *flick*. The Spotlight search screen rolls into view from the left. To go back again, you can put your finger in the middle of the search screen (above the keyboard) and flick it to the left. It doesn't matter if you touch an icon when you flick. As long as your finger moves, the iPad will work out that you intended to flick the screen, not tap the icon.

The Spotlight search looks like Figure 4.14. When you've added songs, films, contacts and calendar entries to your iPad, Spotlight can help you find what you're looking for amidst all this content. It can also help you find notes and apps on the device.

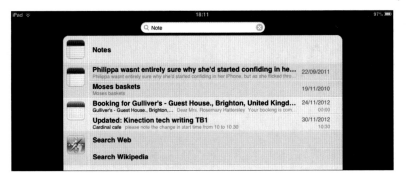

Figure 4.14

When Spotlight search appears, type what you're searching for in the search bar at the top of the screen. As with the search feature in the Notes app, the search results update as you type. Your notes appear in the search results, with an excerpt from the start of the note. Tap a note extract to go straight to that note. If you can't find what you're looking for, tap the Cancel button in the right corner of the search box to start again.

When you install your own apps later, Spotlight can save you a lot of time hunting around for the icons. If you want to try starting apps by using Spotlight, try searching for 'calendar', 'notes' and 'maps'.

Practice the technique of moving between the Home screen and the Spotlight search screen by using the flick gesture. The flick gesture is used in many apps, including Notes, to scroll rapidly through content. If you have a long note, try flicking up on it to scroll through it quickly.

As you install your own apps, more Home screens are added, and you use the flick to move among them too. From the Home screen, flicking right takes you to Spotlight search, and flicking left takes you to the next Home screen full of apps. If you try flicking left from the Home screen now, you see the icons move a little and then bounce back, because there isn't another screen of apps to go to.

You can also use the Home button to move between the Spotlight search screen and the Home screen. If you press the Home button when you're on the Home screen, you go to Spotlight search. If you press the Home button from the search screen, you go back to the Home screen. But where's the fun in that?

Using the Reminders app

The Notes app is great for capturing lists and ideas, but for notes that have a deadline or date associated with them, there's an even better app: Reminders. The Reminders app is a simple to-do list manager that ensures that you don't forget anything important. To start the app, tap its icon on the Home screen.

If you don't have the Reminders app on your iPad, see Chapter 3 for advice on upgrading your iPad's iOS software.

The Reminders app looks like Figure 4.15. On the right, there's a page where you can jot down a list of things you need to do. Tap the next blank line on this page, and the keyboard appears so you can type a short description of whatever you need to remember. To add another item, tap the Return key.

Figure 4.15

If you want to add extra information to an item, tap the description you've entered for it, and a small box appears on the left. A Delete button and a Show More button enable you to add notes or set a priority. If you want to be reminded when you need to complete this task, tap Remind Me and then tap the switch labelled On a Day. Tap the date and time, and a box with a 'barrel roll' control opens (refer to Figure 4.15). This control moves a bit like a fruit machine or slot machine. It has 'barrels' for the date, hour and minutes, which you can change by touching them and moving your finger up or down. You can also flick them to make them move quickly. When you've set the alert time, tap Done. You can set your alerts to repeat. So if you have a task you carry out each day, week, fortnight, month or year, you can enter it once, and the iPad will remind you each time it's due. If you have the Wi-Fi + Cellular version of either the latest iPad or the iPad mini, there's even the option to have your iPad remind you of a task you need to do once you reach a specific location. For example, 'Turn on the oven to 160 degrees when you get to Mum's'. Enter the address when you create the reminder, or use your Contacts list to import the address information to the reminder list.

When you complete a task, tap the tickbox beside it to remove it from your Reminders list. You can switch between viewing your completed and outstanding reminders by tapping Completed or Reminders on the left. If you tick a task as completed by accident, you can find it in the Completed list and tap its tickbox again to return it to its original list.

To browse your tasks by the dates when they are due, tap Date in the top-left corner to reveal a calendar. Drag it up and down to browse through the months, and tap any day to see the tasks that are due on it. Today's date is marked in red. Tap List in the top-left corner to return to list view again.

If you want to create new lists for your reminders or delete any of your existing lists, tap Edit in the top-left corner. Tap Create New List and then enter the name of the list to create it. The way you delete a list is similar to the way you delete your Auto-text additions, covered earlier in this chapter.

To change the sound used to alert you to a reminder, go into the Settings app, and choose Sound. The alert makes a sound when your reminder is due and also displays a message on your Home screen so you notice it when you come back to the iPad, even if you're not there when the alert sounds. You can change how your iPad reminds you by using the Notification Centre, which is covered in Chapter 8.

Summary

- Notes is an app that is used for writing, reading and searching text, from shopping lists to stories.

- You can't change the formatting of individual notes, but you can change the appearance of all notes.

- You can use Notes in portrait or landscape orientation. The keyboard is bigger if you choose landscape.

- Touch a note to make the keyboard appear.

- You can tap the Shift key and then press a letter to enter a capital letter. Double-tap Shift to switch caps lock on.

- There are two special keyboards for numbers and symbols.

- If you press and hold some keys, additional options appear, such as accented letters.

- You can undo by tapping the Undo button on the numbers keyboard or by shaking the iPad, which is more therapeutic.

- Auto-text tries to predict what you're typing. To accept a suggestion, tap the spacebar. To reject it, tap the suggested word on the screen or just type the rest of your word.

- To use the dictation feature, you need an Internet connection and a third-generation or newer iPad or an iPad mini.

- Tap your note to position the insertion point. To position it more precisely, tap and hold until the magnifying glass appears and then move your finger left or right.

- There are several ways to select your text. Use the grab points to increase or decrease the area selected.

- You can cut, copy and paste text.

- To see suggested spellings, tap a word that's underlined with red dots.

- You can search your notes within the Notes app, or you can use Spotlight search, which searches all the content on the built-in apps on your iPad.

- The Reminders app is used to keep to-do lists. You can set your iPad to remind you when a particular task is due.

Brain training

Congratulations – you've mastered your first iPad apps! Before we move on to explore how you can use the iPad for communications, take a moment to try this quick quiz.

1. To make it easy to find notes again later, it's a good idea to:

(a) Put a simple title in the first few words of the note.

(b) At the end of the note, add a few words that you may want to search for later.

(c) Use as many obscure words as possible.

(d) Check that your spelling is correct to ensure that any words you search for can be found in the note.

2. To enter quote marks in your note, you can:

(a) Go to the numbers keyboard.

(b) Go to the special-symbols keyboard.

(c) Tap and hold the full-stop key on the letters keyboard.

(d) Tap the spacebar twice.

3. If Auto-text correctly guesses a word you're typing, you should:

(a) Tap the suggestion to accept it.

(b) Tap the spacebar.

(c) Keep typing your word.

(d) Tap Delete.

4. To position the insertion point in the middle of a word:

(a) Tap the word.

(b) Double-tap the word.

(c) Tap and hold the word, and then move the insertion point when the magnifying glass appears.

(d) Tap the middle of your note.

5. To go to Spotlight search, you can:

(a) Go to the Home screen, and tap the Home button.

(b) Tap the search box in the top-left corner of the Notes app.

(c) Go to the Home screen, and flick right.

(d) Go to the Home screen, and flick left.

Answers

Q1 – a, b, and d   **Q2** – a, b, or c   **Q3** – b   **Q4** – c   **Q5** – a and c

PART II
Using your iPad for communications

I've just emailed all our friends, to tell them what losers they are for using clunky, old-fashioned laptops and desktops.

Managing your address book and birthday list

5

Equipment needed: Your iPad and your address book (whether it's on your computer or scrawled in a beaten-up old paper notebook).

Skills needed: Experience starting apps and using the iPad keyboard (see Chapter 4).

One of the most useful pieces of information you can carry with you is your address book. If you remember a birthday at the last minute and have to write out a card in the shop, or just want to phone a friend for advice or a chat, you'll be pleased to have your addresses and phone numbers at the tip of your fingers.

The iPad comes with an app called Contacts, which is designed to help you manage your address book. It's a simple app, but it's powerful because it's integrated with many other apps. When you're sending email, you can use the details in your address book to save yourself from having to remember or type somebody's email address, for example, and the Maps app enables you to find directions to and from your friends' houses quickly.

In this chapter, we show you how to manage your contacts on your iPad and how to use the Calendar app to view your friends' birthdays month by month. Note that to make the most of the features that we outline here and in other parts of this book, we recommend updating to the latest available version of iOS (the software the iPad and other Apple mobile devices use), as well as using the same Apple ID and enabling iCloud. For example, if you want to import contacts from your iPhone, Mac or iPod touch, you'll need both that device and your iPad to be running iOS5 or iOS6 and be logged in to the same Apple ID account.

Browsing your contacts

You can copy contacts from your computer or other devices (see Chapter 3), but if you haven't done that, your address book will be empty. So it won't be easy to visualise how it will look when it's finished. Take a look at Figure 5.1, which shows a page from an address book, to help you get your bearings.

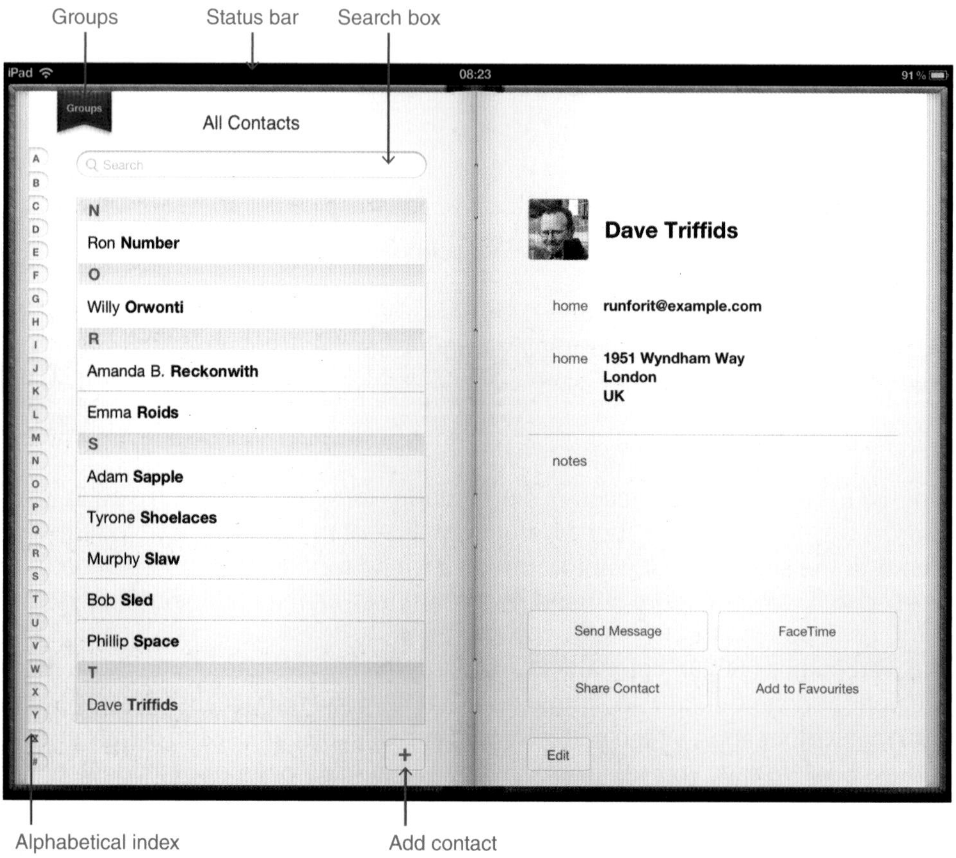

Groups   Status bar   Search box

iPad 🛜   08:23   91 % 🔋

Groups

All Contacts

Q Search

N
Ron **Number**

O
Willy **Orwonti**

R
Amanda B. **Reckonwith**

Emma **Roids**

S
Adam **Sapple**

Tyrone **Shoelaces**

Murphy **Slaw**

Bob **Sled**

Phillip **Space**

T
Dave **Triffids**

Dave Triffids

home **runforit@example.com**

home **1951 Wyndham Way**
        London
        UK

notes

Send Message   FaceTime

Share Contact   Add to Favourites

+   Edit

Alphabetical index   Add contact

Figure 5.1

On the left, you can see the list of contacts, grouped by the initial letters of their last names, which are shown in bold. The contacts are sorted by second name, but shown with first name first. You can change both the order of sorting and the order in which the first and second names are displayed by going into the Settings app; tapping Mail, Contacts, Calendars; and dragging the screen up to reveal the Contacts settings.

💡 If you have organised your contacts in groups using your computer, you can see these groups on your iPad by tapping Groups in the top-left corner of the Contacts app. To see all your contacts, tap Groups again, and choose All Contacts. You can also choose to view your contacts from your computer, from your other devices synchronised with iCloud (see Chapter 3), or all your contacts at once. You can't create or edit groups of contacts using the Contacts app, but if you add a new contact while you're looking at a group, the new contact will join that group.

To scroll the list of contacts, put your finger in the middle of it, and drag your finger up or down. You can also flick the list to move rapidly or tap the status bar above the list of contacts to jump to the first contact.

If you touch one of the letters in the alphabetical index on the left, you jump to people whose last names begin with that letter. You can also move your finger up and down this index to scroll rapidly through the address-book entries.

When you tap somebody's name, his details appear on the right. You can scroll the contact page on the right up and down, too, if it won't all fit in at once.

If you tap the Notes area, you can add comments to the person's details, such as a reminder of where you met her.

To send your contact an instant message (see Chapter 8), tap Send Message. On iPads with cameras, you can tap the FaceTime button on a contact's page to start a video call with her (see Chapter 7). If it's someone you might want to talk to often, tap Add to Favourites so you can find her more easily in the FaceTime app.

💡 To quickly start a new email to a friend, tap his email address. Tap his real-world address to see his home in the Maps app. When the iPad with an integrated teleporter eventually ships, we're sure you'll be able to materialise there in a single tap, too.

To send a contact's details to somebody else, tap the Share Contact button (refer to Figure 5.1) at the bottom of the contact's details. Then you can choose to share by email (see Chapter 6) or by instant message (see Chapter 8). To remove any information that's out of date, such as an address or phone number, swipe across it to reveal a Delete button. If somebody moves house, you can update your address book by tapping the Edit button while that person's details are onscreen. The process for editing a contact is similar to the process for adding one, which we look at next.

Adding contacts to your iPad

Now that you've seen how the app is laid out, it's time to start adding contacts. Start by tapping the Add Contact button. This button is a plus sign (+) at the bottom of your contacts page.

A new page in the contacts book opens, with a form for you to complete (shown in Figure 5.2). Because the keyboard pops up so you can enter contact information, you need to scroll up and down to see the full form.

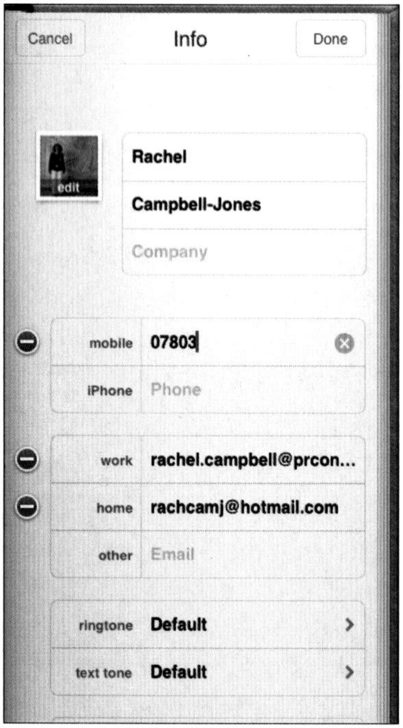

Figure 5.2

The cursor starts in the box marked First, which is for the person's first name. When you've finished filling in a box, either tap Return on the keyboard to advance to the next box down or tap the box you'd like to go to next. To add an address, tap Add New Address; the form expands with space for you to enter a street, city, county, postcode and country. When you've added one address, you can add another if you want to.

If your iPad has cameras, you can choose a ringtone for this person. This ringtone will be used to alert you when she requests a FaceTime call with you (see Chapter 7). You can also choose a text tone, which is used to let you know when somebody sends you an instant message (see Chapter 8).

It's easy to customise an entry to include all the information you want it to include. If you tap a label beside a box, such as Mobile, you can change it to something else, such as Home Fax. You can also change the descriptions of the different addresses belonging to a particular person (to indicate a home or work address, for example). There's a Notes box, which you can fill with any information you like, and you can scroll the form up and tap Add Field at the bottom to create extra boxes that you can label yourself.

Pay attention when you're typing details, because the keyboard layout changes depending on what you're entering. The keyboard you're shown prioritises the symbols you need most for a particular entry, such as numbers in the mobile box and the @ sign in the email box.

You can ignore any of the boxes that you don't want to use. When you look at somebody's details later, any sections you left empty won't be shown, which minimises the amount of scrolling you need to do to see all the contact's information. Many of your friends may not have a personal website or home page, for example, so you may skip that box. But you could link to the person's Facebook page, blog or company website.

The Contacts app uses some conventions you've seen in other parts of the iPad, including the way you delete something in a form. If you make a mistake and want to clear a box completely, tap the box to select it and then tap the round X button inside it on the right.

> You can delete unwanted sections of your contact pages, such as extra address lines. When you're editing a contact, a round red sign with a white bar appears beside any sections you can delete. Tap this sign, and a red Delete button appears. Tap that button to confirm the deletion, or tap elsewhere on the page to change your mind.

If you have a photo of someone on your iPad (see Chapter 13), you can append it to that person's contact page. Tap Add Photo to get started. You can even take a photo of the person with your iPad, unless you have the original iPad (see Chapter 13 for advice on taking photos). Select a photo from your iPad's Photo gallery. You can drag the photo to centre it and use the pinch gesture to resize it so that it best fits the square space available.

When you've finished adding or updating a contact, tap Done in the top-right corner of the contact form. To discard all your changes, tap Cancel in the top-left corner.

> To delete all of a contact's information, tap the Delete Contact button, which appears at the bottom of a contact's details when you edit them.

Adding birthdays and anniversaries

The iPad can help you keep track of your friends' birthdays. If you add the dates to your address book, you can use the Calendar app to see them organised in a list, or by month or week.

You can add a birthday to a contact's details when you're entering the contact for the first time, or you can add it later by viewing that person's details and then tapping the Edit button.

To add a birthday, tap Add Field and then tap Birthday. A box with a 'barrel roll' control opens, similar to the one for setting reminder times (see Chapter 4). You can roll the barrels to choose the date, month and year of your friend's birthday. The iPad's smart enough to know that birthdays happen every year, so enter the year your friend was born, if you know it. You can choose No Year if you don't know when she was born. When you've finished, tap outside the barrel roll to make it go away.

It's possible to add other dates, such as anniversaries, in the Contacts app, but they won't show up on the calendar unless you enter them directly in the Calendar app. To enter another date, tap Add Field and then tap Date. You can change the description of any date by tapping its label.

After you've added birthdays to your contacts, you can use the Calendar app to browse them by month, by week or in a list. The beauty of it is that when birthdays have been entered in Contacts, Calendar shows them every year for you automatically. Figure 5.3 shows the month layout for the Calendar app, including some friends' birthdays. You can tap the buttons at the top to select a different view, and you can use the year/month selector at the bottom of the screen to choose a different date.

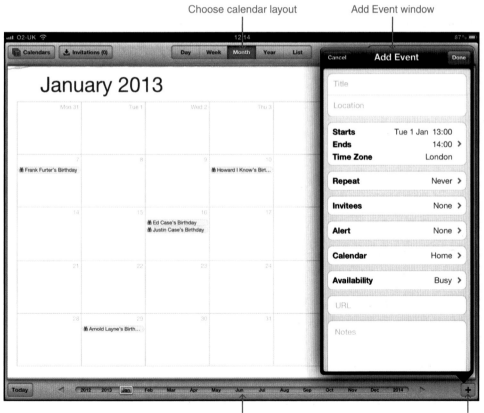

Figure 5.3

You can use Calendar for all kinds of other things, such as reminding you to pay your credit card bill each month, planning holidays or recording when the family will be descending for dinner. To add a new event, tap the plus button in the bottom-right corner to open the Add Event window. You can enter the date, description, how often the event should repeat (if at all) and an alert to make sure you don't forget about it. (See Chapter 8 for advice on managing alerts across all your applications.) You can also send invitations to your friends by email if you're planning a social event.

Searching your contacts

To search for somebody in Contacts, tap the search box and then start to type part of the name. It doesn't matter if you type the first name or surname. As you type, the iPad filters the list of contacts below the search box so that it shows only those that match what you've typed so far. The moment you see the person you're looking for, tap the name to see the person's contact details. To cancel the search and show the full list of results again, clear the search box by tapping the round X button inside it on the right.

One limitation of the search is that you can find somebody only by name. You can't search for everyone who lives in a particular town you're visiting, for example, or search by phone number to see who phoned you and didn't leave a message.

Spotlight search (see Chapter 4) will find your contacts, too. It will also find people by location, making it a much more powerful search option than simply typing a name into Contacts.

Summary

- The Contacts app is used to store information about your friends, family members and acquaintances.

- The information you enter in Contacts is available to the Mail, Messages, FaceTime and Maps apps.

- To select a contact, scroll through the list of contacts on the left.

- You can use the alphabetical index to speed up scrolling through the list or jump straight to people with a particular initial.

- You can also search by name from within Contacts or by using the iPad's Spotlight search, or the Maps and Mail apps.

- To add a contact, tap the Add Contact button.

- You can customise each contact page, adding your own boxes of information or changing the labels of the existing ones.

- The iPad's keyboard layout changes depending on which box you're filling in.

- You can ignore any boxes you don't want to complete.

- If you have a photo of your friend on your iPad, you can add it to that person's contact details.

Brain training

Is your address book under control? Try this short quiz to find out.

1. The plus sign below your contacts list is used to:

(a) Make new friends

(b) Add a contact

(c) Scroll the contacts list to show more

(d) Tell a friend you're cross with her

2. When you're entering an email address, you can find the @ sign:

(a) On the symbols keyboard (.?123)

(b) On the extra symbols keyboard (#+=)

(c) On the letters keyboard

(d) On the Home button

3. A round red sign with a white bar across it is used to:

(a) Warn you off entering anything in a box

(b) Delete a contact

(c) Delete some of a contact's information

(d) Tell you you're not allowed to call this friend

4. You can use the Calendar app to:

(a) See whose birthday is coming up this month

(b) Remind you whose anniversary it is next week

(c) Set an alert to remind you of your dental appointment

(d) Set a monthly reminder to pay the credit-card bill

5. You can use Spotlight search to see:

(a) Contacts, searched by name

(b) Photos added in the Contacts app

(c) Everyone you know who lives in France

(d) All your friends who are actors

Answers

Q1 – b

Q2 – c

Q3 – c

Q4 – a, c, and d (b is true only if you've added the anniversary separately in the Calendar app)

Q5 – a and c

Keeping in touch by email

6

Equipment needed: An iPad with a connection to the Internet (through Wi-Fi or mobile communications) and an email address, if you already have one.

Skills needed: Experience starting apps (see Chapter 3) and using the iPad keyboard (Chapter 4). Familiarity with the Contacts app (see Chapter 5) and experience using email on an iPhone or other smartphone may be helpful, but is not essential.

In this chapter, you find out how to send email messages to your friends and read their replies. If you've used email on your computer or an iPhone, you'll find it easy to adapt to using the iPad, especially now that you're an expert on the iPad keyboard. Before you can start emailing, though, you need to set up email on your iPad. We talk you through the steps to do so.

If you haven't used email before, you're in for a treat! The iPad makes it easy to keep in touch with friends and family by sending them messages they can read on their computers, their smartphones or their own iPads. With email, messages wait until somebody picks them up, so your friends don't have to be using their computers at the same time you're writing to them. It's a bit like sending a letter by post: Messages are delivered and sit in the email box in the same way that letters sit on the doormat until somebody comes home to read them. Email is easy to pick up, and once you've started using it to keep in touch with your friends, you'll wonder how you ever did without it.

It doesn't matter whether your friends have iPads. The emails you send can be read on a computer, mobile phone or any other email-enabled device. You can read the replies on your iPad irrespective of the device used to send you the message.

> Computer engineer Ray Tomlinson of U.S. technology company Bolt Beranek and Newman invented the use of the @ sign for email addresses in 1971. He is credited as being the first to send email across a network.

Creating an email account

To get started with email, you need to have an email account. Similar to the way that a bank account stores your money, an email account stores your email messages. Lots of companies can provide you an email account, some of them for free.

Having an email account also gives you an email address. This address is used to deliver your messages to you, in the same way your postal address is used to deliver letters to you (eventually). If you have an email address, you already have an email account, so you don't need to set up a new one. You can skip ahead to the later section, 'Using an existing account on your iPad'. If you don't have an email account, or if you want to use a different account on your iPad, the rest of this section shows you how to create an account.

Apple's iCloud service (**www.icloud.com**) comes with a free email address you can use. Your email address will be *something*@icloud.com, and you get to choose what the *something* is. With so many accounts already registered, you may find that your preferred email address is already taken, so you'll have to be creative to find one you like.

To create your iCloud email address, tap the Settings button; then tap Mail, Contacts, Calendars and finally tap iCloud. Tap the switch beside Mail to turn it on. If you don't already have an iCloud email address, tap Create when prompted. Enter your desired email address, and the iPad will tell you whether someone's already snaffled that one and, if so, ask you to try again. The iPad also suggests options for you. Click the Suggestions button to see variations based on your name or the pseudonym you were trying to use. Adding a memorable number (such as your year of birth) can help. It may take a few goes to find something you can use, so stick with it! Your iCloud email address can't be changed once you've chosen it, so check it carefully before confirming it (see Figure 6.1).

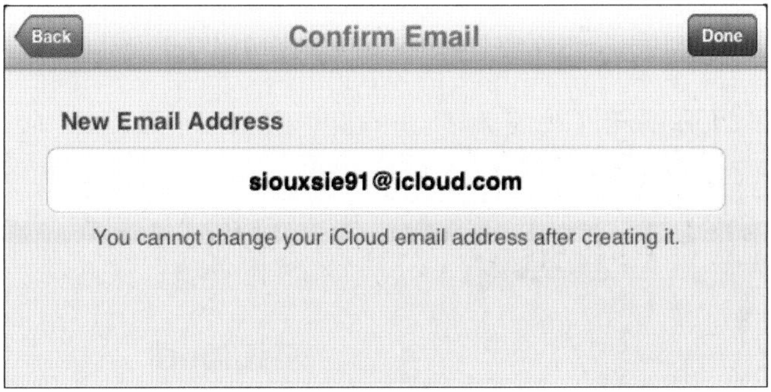

| Back | **Confirm Email** | Done |

New Email Address

You cannot change your iCloud email address after creating it.

Figure 6.1

Try adding numbers to your email address, using abbreviations for your surname, or picking place names or names related to your hobbies to come up with a memorable email address nobody else has taken.

After you've created your iCloud email address (or switched on Mail for iCloud, if you already have an iCloud address), your iPad is ready to use for email.

The default suggested name in an email account on the iPad is John Appleseed. This name is a reference to the legendary Johnny Appleseed (real name John Chapman), who distributed apple seedlings throughout the Midwestern United States. By the time he died in 1845, he owned 1,200 acres of orchards and had helped create many more.

When someone else is using your iPad, you can read your iCloud emails by logging in with your Apple ID on another device at the **www.icloud.com** website.

Using an existing email account on your iPad

If you already have an email account, you can use it on your iPad too. It's less hassle to use your existing email address than to switch to another email address and make sure everyone you know remembers to use it. To set up your email address, go into the Settings app; tap Mail, Contacts, Calendars and then tap Add Account. You see a set of logos showing the different email services you can set up (see Figure 6.2).

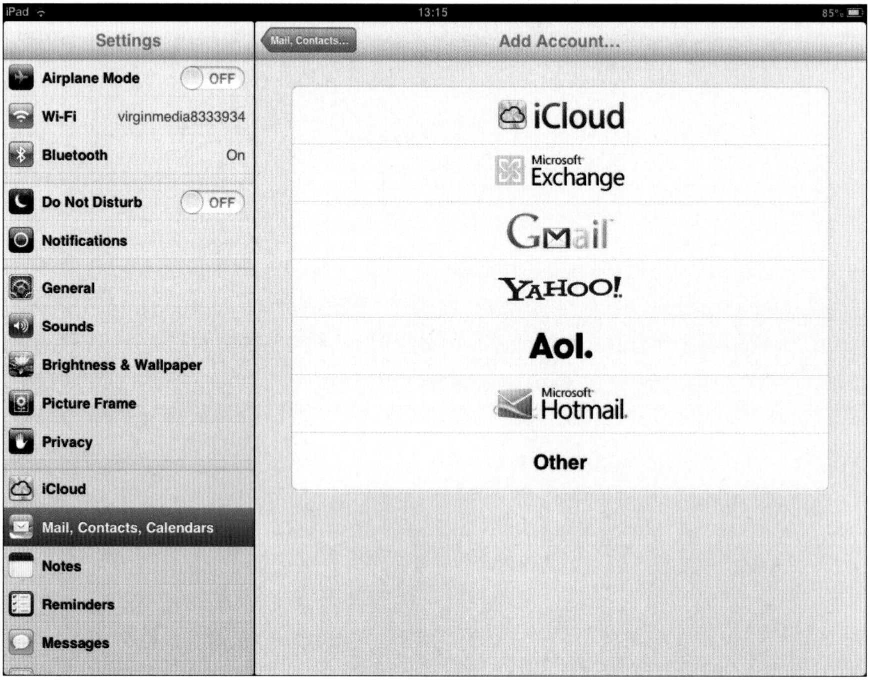

Figure 6.2

Although the logos are colourful, there's no explanation for them, so this screen can seem a bit unfriendly. The logos represent

● **iCloud:** If you already have an email address that ends in **icloud.com**, you can log in with your Apple ID (or create a new Apple ID) here.

● **Microsoft Exchange:** This service is used mainly for business email, and it's unlikely you're using it at home. Even if you use other Microsoft software on your computer, including Windows, this setting usually isn't the one you need.

- **Gmail, Yahoo!, AOL and Microsoft Hotmail:** These accounts are called *webmail accounts,* because people usually access them from a website. They're simple to set up, so if you need to create an additional email address, we recommend choosing one of these services. You can register for a free email address at their websites (**mail.google.com**, **http://mail.yahoo.com**, **www.aol.com** and **www.hotmail.com**, respectively).

- **Other:** This option covers all other email addresses, including email accounts provided with broadband subscriptions. If you usually store your email on your desktop computer, and you can read it there even when the Internet connection is switched off, this setting is most likely to be the option you need.

In the following sections, we show you how to set up the most common types of email accounts on your iPad: webmail and the mysterious 'other'.

Your iPad needs to be connected to the Internet so it can check that the account details you provide are correct, and so it can download your emails. You need to have an active Wi-Fi or 4G/3G connection (see Chapter 3).

Setting up Gmail, Yahoo!, AOL and Microsoft Hotmail email accounts

The iPad is programmed to recognise email accounts from Gmail, Yahoo! Mail, AOL and Microsoft Hotmail, so you don't have to type much information. Start by tapping the logo of the email account you want to use. Figure 6.3 shows the short form you need to complete:

- **Name:** Tap this box and enter your full name here. The iPad automatically uses a capital letter for the first character of each word. This name is the name your friends will see on any messages you send them, so they'll know to open them straight away. This option isn't shown for Windows Live Hotmail.

- **Address:** Tap this box and enter your full email address here. It will be something like *username*@gmail.com, *username*@yahoo.com or *username@* aol.com. When you're typing an email address, the @ sign is on the letters keyboard, towards the bottom-right corner.

- **Password:** Tap this box and enter the password you use to log in to your webmail. Remember that the characters of the password will appear briefly onscreen, so you should set up your email somewhere reasonably private. After you've set up your email, you won't have to enter your password again.

- **Description:** The iPad completes this box automatically, but you can change it to something else by tapping it and typing your description. It's useful only if you're planning to set up several email addresses on your iPad.

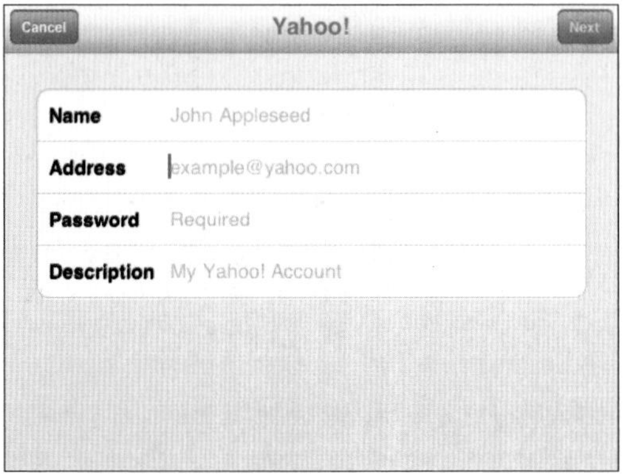

Figure 6.3

When you've finished, tap the Next button in the top-right corner of the form. The iPad checks that your information has been entered correctly, and, if it has, it gives you options to synchronise your calendars and notes, as well as email. They say that a man with a watch knows the time and a man with two watches is never sure. So if you use the calendar in Yahoo!, Windows Live Hotmail, or Gmail, it makes sense to synchronise it with your iPad so that they contain the same information. You can also synchronise contacts and reminders with Yahoo! and Microsoft Hotmail.

When you've finished, tap the Save button in the top-right corner of the form, and the iPad starts to download your emails (if you have any).

If you synchronise your notes, you can read them by signing in to your web-mail account. You can also synchronise more than one email account with your notes, in which case there will be new options for adding notes to your different email accounts in the Notes app. Access these options by tapping Accounts in the top-left corner of the Notes app. When you log in to your webmail in Yahoo! and AOL, your notes are located in a folder called Notes. In Gmail, they have the label Notes.

Setting up other email accounts

If you don't have an iCloud, Gmail, AOL, Microsoft Hotmail or Yahoo! email account, the option you're most likely to need is Other. This setting applies if you use an email address provided to you by your broadband supplier, satellite TV company, phone company or any other company.

Unfortunately, the Other option is much harder to set up than a webmail account, and you may need help from whoever originally set up your email account on your computer or from your email provider's technical support staff.

The first form is similar to the one for webmail accounts (refer to Figure 6.3), so follow the guidance for webmail accounts to complete it. Your email address will probably look like *yourname@yourprovider*.com or *yourname@yourprovider*.co.uk, although you may have full stops, underscores or numbers as part of your address.

The password is the first technical challenge because you may not even know that your email address has a password. It's usually stored in your email program so you don't have to type it every time you download email. To find out your password, check any correspondence you have from when you set up your email account originally, or seek technical support from your email provider. If you're calling them, don't dial yet, though. There's a whole lot more they'll probably need to tell you, so read on to see what else you need to know first. If you have a Mac, you can find the password in the Keychain Access utility.

After you complete the form, tap Next in the top-right corner. The New Account form (shown in Figure 6.4) carries forward some of the information you've already added but asks for additional information, which you need to get from your email provider.

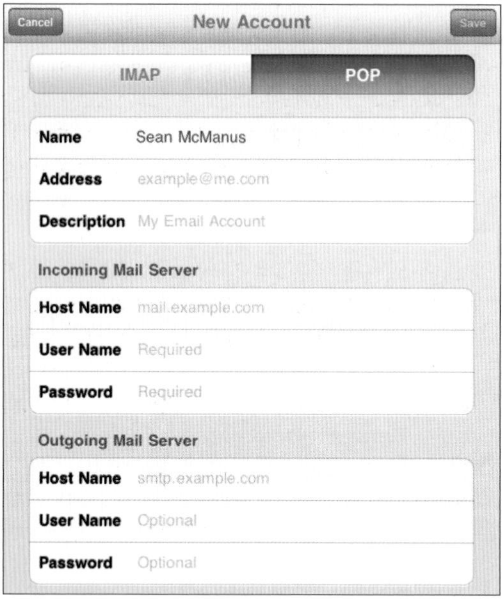

Figure 6.4

At the top of the form are two large buttons marked IMAP and POP; these button are the two different ways to access email. They work in slightly different ways, which really matters only if you're going to use multiple devices to access your email. If you read your email on POP, any other devices using the same email account won't know when you've read messages or made other changes to them. So you could read your emails on your iPad, but they would still show as new messages when you check your email on your computer. If you read your email messages on your iPad using IMAP, they will already be marked as having been read when you see them on your computer. As a rule of thumb, you can use POP if the iPad will be the only place you read your email. If you'll be using both your iPad and your computer to check your email, choose IMAP. Not all email services support both; if in doubt, check with your email provider to see which is available to you. Tap the POP or IMAP button to select it, and the button turns blue.

You also need to provide the host name for your incoming and outgoing mail servers. You need to get all these details from your email provider, but they're usually published on the provider's website. If you go to **www.google.com** and search for 'set up email' plus the name of your email provider, you should be able to find something helpful.

Your incoming mail server requires a username in addition to the password you've already provided. The outgoing mail server username and password are described as optional, but email providers require you to use them. If you frequently get email account login failures, double-check that you're using the right outgoing and incoming server settings.

To scroll the form so you can see the bottom part of it below the keyboard, touch the form and then drag your finger up the screen, similar to how you scroll notes (see Chapter 4). The scrolling won't work if you touch outside the form.

After completing the form, tap Save in the top-right corner, and your email will be set up.

You can add multiple email accounts to your iPad by repeating the instructions for setting up an email account. If you go into the Mail app before setting up an account, you'll be asked to set one up and will be given options like those in the Settings app, described in the preceding sections. If you want to add addresses or change your settings, though, you need to use the Settings app.

Sending an email

Now it's time to brighten up somebody's day by sending that person an email message. As long as you've got a friend's email address to hand, you're ready. If you don't know anybody else's email address, you could try sending yourself an email for practice, but don't expect any surprises in the reply.

To get started with email, open the Mail app. It usually sits on a shelf called the Dock, at the bottom of the Home screen. If you've moved it (see Chapter 14), you can find it by using Spotlight search (see Chapter 4).

To make sure you've noted a friend's email address correctly, check it against this simple guideline: An email address always has exactly one @ sign in it and at least one full stop after the @ sign. You can't use spaces in an email address.

To begin creating an email, tap the New Email icon in the top-right corner of the iPad's screen. It looks like a pen and a blank piece of paper (see Figure 6.5).

 — New email

Figure 6.5

Addressing your email

When you start to write a new email, a message window opens, and a keyboard slides into view, so your screen looks like Figure 6.6.

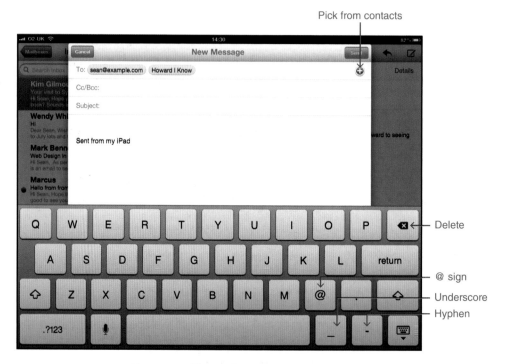

Figure 6.6

102

The cursor starts in the To box, which is where you enter your friend's email address. Because the iPad knows you're entering an email address, it gives you a keyboard that's designed to make that task easy. The letters keyboard is enhanced with the @ sign, hyphen and underscore characters (refer to Figure 6.6), so you can type them without having to switch to the symbols keyboard. If the email address has numbers in it, tap .?123 to open the numbers keyboard, as you do when typing notes (see Chapter 4). When you finish typing an address, tap the Return key, and a rounded box appears around the email address.

If the person you want to email is in your contacts list, and you've entered his or her email address there, you don't have to type it twice. If you want to browse your contacts list, tap the blue plus sign (refer to Figure 6.6). Alternatively, start typing your friend's name or email address, and the iPad will suggest matching contacts. The iPad also suggests the email addresses of people you've previously emailed. Tap a suggested email address to add it to the recipient list.

It's possible to send the same message to several people at the same time. After you've entered an email address, your cursor stays in the To box so that you can add more email addresses there, either by typing them or selecting them from your contacts list.

As well as adding multiple recipients in the To box, there are two ways you can address an email to somebody:

- **Cc:** This setting sends someone a courtesy copy of the email. This setting is often used when you want to keep someone informed about the conversation you're having but don't expect them to get involved in replying. Everyone who gets a copy of the email can see the email address of everyone who has been sent the message with To or Cc.

- **Bcc:** This setting works like Cc except that the *B* stands for *blind,* so nobody else can see that this recipient has received a copy of the email. Those who receive a Bcc copy can still see the To and the Cc recipients, though. If several people receive a Bcc copy, they can't see one another's email addresses. You can use this setting if you're emailing people who don't know one another and who might not want you to give out their email addresses.

If you want to use Cc or Bcc to address somebody, tap the Cc/Bcc box. Separate Cc and Bcc rows open. You can then tap these rows and enter the email addresses or contacts in them.

If you need to delete an email address from the email, tap that name or email address and then tap the Delete key on the keyboard (refer to Figure 6.6).

> When you finish typing in a box, you can tap Return to advance to the next box. If you want to Cc or Bcc someone, you have to tap the Cc/Bcc box, though, because tapping Return in the To box skips it and takes you straight to the email subject.

Writing your email message

After you address your email, you can compose your message. There are two parts to this message: the subject line and the message itself.

The subject line of the email is a short description of what it's about. It helps people tell different email conversations apart and find the messages they need more easily. In most email programs, the first things people see are your name and the email subject, and they have to open the email to see the rest. It's a good idea to have a clear, concise and meaningful description that uniquely identifies your message. Something like 'Planning August theatre outing' is much more useful than 'Chat', and emails with blank subject lines can be easily overlooked. On the iPad, the subject line is positioned between the addressees and the main message area, in common with other email programs you may have used.

Below the subject box is a large box in which you write your email message. You write your message in the same way you write notes (see Chapter 4), and the keyboard reverts to the same layout as in the Notes app. The Auto-text, selection, copy, cut, paste and editing features all work the same way as they do in Notes. You can include pictures as well as text in emails, if you find a picture on a website that you want to share. In iOS6 (the latest version of iPad software), tapping twice in the body of the email brings up the Insert Photo or Video menu so you can choose an image from your own Photo roll.

When you select text and tap the insertion point (see Chapter 4), you see some formatting options that you don't have in Notes. If you tap BIU from the options that appear, for example, you can choose among bold, italic and underlined formatting. There's also an option for Quote Level formatting. You don't need to use it, but you'll probably come across it in the menus at some stage. It's used to indent a piece of text to indicate that it's a quote from an earlier email.

When you've finished composing your message, tap the Send button in the top-right corner of the email form. If you have an Internet connection, your message is sent to the recipient immediately. Otherwise, you see an error message, but your email will be stored on your iPad and sent the next time you open the Mail app and do have an Internet connection.

If you decide to abandon the email, tap Cancel in the top-left corner. You'll have the option to save a draft of the email, which means that it won't be sent but will be kept in your Drafts folder so you can edit and send it later. If you delete the draft, the email is permanently deleted.

Cheekily, Apple puts a line at the end of each message that says "Sent from my iPad" to make sure all your friends think about buying one too. This line is the email *signature,* which concludes every message you send. You can change it to something else, if you prefer, such as your full name and favourite quotation. To edit the signature, go into the Settings app; tap Mail, Contacts, Calendars and then tap Signature. You can simply delete the 'Sent from my iPad' line if you prefer not to include a signature.

Email works a bit differently on the iPad to the way it works on a computer, so getting the hang of it may take a few minutes. When you do get it, though, you can send messages from anywhere you take your iPad and have an Internet connection. Give it a go!

Reading your emails

After you've sent out a few messages, we hope you'll get a few replies. If your iPad is set up with the same email account as the one on your desktop computer or your iPhone, if you have one, you may already have a stream of messages flowing in.

The Mail app probably looks a bit different to the email programs you've used before, so it may be hard to see at a glance how you do things like read an email, reply to one or delete one you don't need anymore.

When you go into the Mail app, it downloads your latest emails, and if you're using your iPad in landscape orientation, you see a screen like the one shown in Figure 6.7. If you rotate your iPad, you see just one email at a time, but you can swipe from the left of the screen to show the message list and can swipe it back the other way to hide it again. Portrait orientation is useful if you're reading long emails, but the landscape format stops you having to tap so often to open new messages, so we stick to that orientation here.

Figure 6.7

The column on the left shows a list of the messages in your Inbox, with the most recent at the top. You can scroll the message list up and down by putting your finger on it and dragging it up or down or by flicking it. To jump back to the top, tap the status bar above the list (refer to Figure 6.7).

> 💡 The number in brackets at the top of the list of messages tells you how many unread messages you have in your Inbox.

Each email has a summary box in the message list detailing who sent it, the time (today) or date (before today) the email was sent, the subject line and a short snippet from the start of the message. Unread emails have a blue bobble beside them so you can identify them quickly. When you tap the email's summary box, the email's entry in the message list is coloured blue, and the full email opens on the right, where you can scroll it up and down in the usual way. Figure 6.7 shows the welcome email from iCloud on the right.

If the email is part of an ongoing conversation, its entry in the message list includes a number in a grey box that indicates how many messages are in that conversation, or *thread*. (See the first email in Figure 6.7, which is part of a thread with two messages.) When you tap the email in the message list, the list changes to show only the previous emails you've received with the same subject line. To see all your messages again, just tap the Inbox button in the top-left corner.

> 💡 If the iPad spots an address, phone number, email address or link, it underlines that text in blue. Touch and hold the underlined text for options, including showing places on a map and adding details to contacts. Tap a location to see it on a map or a website link to visit it.

There are several things you can do with an email after you've selected it in the message list:

● **Save the sender as a contact.** Tap the sender's name, and you can create a new contact for her or add her email address to an existing contact. Because you can choose email recipients from your contacts list, this action can make it easier to send emails to that person in future.

● **Make the sender a VIP.** A new feature in the latest iPad software lets you designate a contact as a Very Important Person. Just click the Add to VIP button below the email address when you save that person's contact details. There's a special VIP filter below All Inboxes on the main Mail menu. Use this filter to see only messages from friends (and ignore marketing messages that may fill up your email Inbox).

● **Reply to or forward the email.** Tap the arrow in the top-right corner, and you can choose to reply to the email or forward it to somebody else. After that, the process is similar to writing a new email. If you reply to a message, a curved left arrow appears beside it in the message list. If you forward a message, a right arrow appears.

● **Print the email.** If you have a compatible printer, tap the arrow in the top-right corner to find the print option.

● **Delete or archive the email.** Tap the dustbin icon in the top-right corner, and the email you're reading is moved to the Trash folder. If you have a Gmail address, the dustbin icon is changed to an arrow pointing to an archive box. When you tap the archive-box icon, your email is archived, which means that it vanishes from your Inbox but is still available if you need it later (in the All Mail folder).

● **Mark the email as unread or flag it.** If you read a message but want to leave it marked as unread, tap Details in the top-right corner of the message; then tap Mark. From that point, you can mark it as unread or put a flag beside it in the message list as a reminder to yourself that you need to do something with it.

● **See all the recipients.** Tap Details at the top to see who else got a copy of the email.

● **View an attachment.** Scroll to the end of an email message to see any attachments it has. Tap the attachment, and, assuming there's a means of viewing it on your iPad, the file opens. Tap and hold the attachment if you have more than one app that can open it and you want to choose which app to use. When you've finished, tap Done in the top-left corner. (If necessary, tap the document first to make the Done button appear.) The iPad can also play audio or video attachments. Touch and hold a photo or video to save it in your Camera Roll album on your iPad (see Chapter 13).

You can also delete an email by swiping left or right over its entry in the message list and then tapping the Delete button that appears in the message list. If you don't want to delete, tap elsewhere in the message list.

Managing email folders

So far, everything you've seen has taken place in the Inbox, the folder where new emails are filed. There are other mailboxes you can use, which include the following:

- **Drafts:** If you abandon an email halfway through writing it but save it so you can finish and send later, this folder is where you'll find it.

- **Sent:** This folder stores the emails you've sent to others.

- **Trash:** This folder contains emails you've deleted. You can empty the Trash folder by going into it, tapping Edit and then tapping Delete All.

- **Archive**: This folder, where available, is there to store old emails.

- **Bulk Mail, Junk or Spam:** Where offered, this folder contains email that your email provider believes is junk email. It's worth checking this folder from time to time in case your email provider has moved a real message to this mailbox by mistake.

To access all your folders, tap Mailboxes in the top-left corner of the screen. Then you can choose a folder from the resulting list, which may look similar to Figure 6.8. If you have more than one email account, the Mailboxes button instead shows the name of your account. Tap this button to see all your folders and then tap Mailboxes to see a list of the email accounts set up on your iPad.

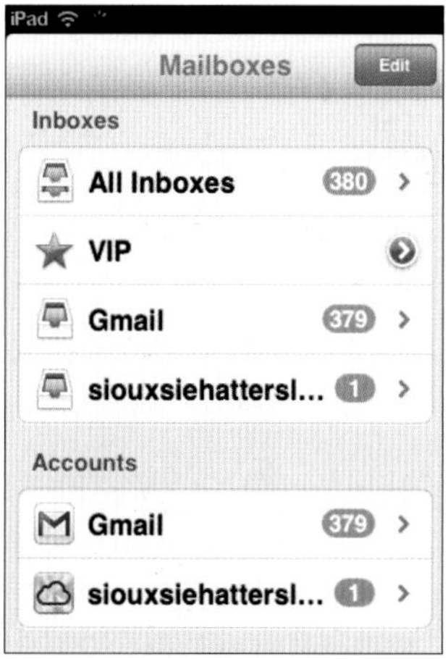

Figure 6.8

Choose All Inboxes to see all your incoming emails from different accounts in the same place. Choose VIP to see messages from your friends. We really like this feature, as it allows us to quickly view messages we actually want to read, rather than having to wade through marketing emails and unsolicited messages known as *spam*.

To create new folders on your iPad, view the mailboxes for an email and tap the Edit button. Then tap the New Mailbox button at the bottom to create a new folder so you can file away emails relating to particular people or activities. While you're organising your mailboxes, you can delete or rename some of them by tapping their names. The iPad won't let you meddle with Inbox, Drafts, Sent Mail and other essentials, though. When you've finished editing your mailboxes, tap Done at the top of the column.

When you're reading an email, you can move it into a different folder by tapping the Move button (refer to Figure 6.7) and choosing a folder. Be sure you choose carefully when archiving messages as after a certain period your email account provider will automatically delete them.

To move or delete lots of messages in one go, tap the Edit button at the top of the message list. Then tap the messages you'd like to select, and tap Delete or Move at the bottom of the column. If you're moving messages, tap the folder you'd like to move them to. Tap Cancel at the top of the message list if you change your mind.

Searching your emails

You can use Spotlight search to find emails, or you can use the search function built into Mail. Whichever you use, you can search only for people you received an email from or sent an email to or for a particular subject line. That's another reason why good subject lines are important.

The search feature built into Mail works in a similar way to the one in Notes (see Figure 6.9). You go into the appropriate mailbox, tap the search box in the top-left corner and then type the name or word you're looking for. Matching emails appear below the box, and you can tap any you want to read. Note that the iPad simply looks for corresponding characters you've typed. In Figure 6.9, a search for the name 'Ian' has also pulled up other emails containing that three-character sequence. To cancel the search, tap the Cancel button. To clear the search box and start looking for something else, tap the X inside the circle in the search box.

Figure 6.9

Downloading new emails

Your email messages are stored in a mailbox managed by your email provider. Your iPad downloads these emails to its internal storage over the Internet. It starts by downloading the most recent 50 emails. (You can change this number in the Settings app.) Then you can tap Load More Messages at the bottom of the message list to download another batch.

Whenever you go into the Mail app, your iPad checks for any new email messages in your mailbox. At any time you like, you can make it check for more new messages by tapping the Update info button at the bottom of the message list. Dragging downwards on the screen has the same effect.

Some types of email accounts (including iCloud) can automatically push new messages to your iPad shortly after they arrive in your mailbox as long as you have an Internet connection. *Push* means that you get messages almost as soon as they're available, but the drawback is that it runs down your battery more quickly.

For accounts that can't push messages to you, the iPad can automatically check at regular intervals (15, 30 or 60 minutes) to see whether you've had any new messages. Again, this feature is something that will run down your battery more quickly, and it isn't necessary if you won't be checking what's been downloaded for some time anyway.

By default, the iPad is set to allow emails to be pushed to your iPad where possible, but it doesn't have regular checking activated. You can change these settings by going into the Settings app and tapping Mail, Contacts, Calendars. If you want to conserve battery power, you can turn off automatic pushing of messages and regular checking.

If you tire of the pinging and whooshing noises, go into the General Settings to switch off the sounds you hear whenever you send or receive an email.

The Mail icon on the Home screen has a red circle in the corner of it showing how many unread messages you have in your main Inbox. You can customise how the iPad tells you about new messages, as you see in Chapter 8.

Summary

- You can use the iPad to read emails sent from any kind of device or computer. Emails from your iPad can be read on any email-compatible device, too.

- The Mail app is used for reading and writing emails.

- The easiest way to set up email is to use the free iCloud email account.

- You can set up the most common webmail accounts quickly by entering your email address and password.

- Use the Other option to set up most other types of email accounts, including those typically provided by broadband suppliers.

- You can pick people from your contacts list to send an email to.

- To send someone a copy of an email, use Cc. To send someone a copy of an email but hide that person's name from other recipients, use Bcc.

- Use a clear and specific subject line.

- To add the same text to the end of all your outgoing messages, such as your full name, edit the email signature in your Settings app.

- The message list shows a short preview of the messages in your mailbox. Tap a preview to read it in full.

- A *threaded email* is one that's part of a discussion. Tap it in the message list to see the previous emails with the same subject line.

- Tap the curved arrow in the top-right corner to reply to an email, forward it or print it.

- When you receive an email, you can add its sender to your contacts list so it's easier to email him in future. You can even make him a VIP and ensure that his messages are displayed in a separate VIP folder!

- You can move emails between folders.

- You can search for emails by sender name, recipient or subject line.

- Some types of email accounts can push email to your iPad when they arrive. Your iPad can also check for email regularly. To save battery power, turn off this automatic updating of email.

Brain training

At the end of that bumper project, relax with a short quiz to see how much you've remembered.

1. Which of these is a valid email address?

(a) fred@example@com

(b) www.example.com

(c) fred.bloggs@examplecom

(d) freddieboy@example.com

2. To set up a Gmail account on your iPad, you need to know:

(a) Your username

(b) Your incoming and outgoing server details

(c) Your password

(d) Whether it is IMAP or POP

3. A good subject line might be:

(a) Stuff

(b) Hello

(c) Thought you'd like this

(d) Booking tickets to see the Australian Pink Floyd

4. An email thread is:

(a) A group of sent messages

(b) An email message that's as long as a piece of string

(c) A group of emails with the same subject line

(d) A folder of messages

5. To find a party invitation email in your Inbox, search using:

(a) The name of someone else who got a copy of the invitation

(b) The name of the pub mentioned in the message

(c) The word *birthday,* which was in the subject line

(d) The name of the person who sent you the message

Answers

Q1 – d **Q2** – a and c **Q3** – d

Q4 – c **Q5** – a, c and d

Using FaceTime for video calls

7

Equipment needed: An iPad with built-in cameras and a Wi-Fi connection (a 3G or 4G connection can be used in some circumstances); a friend with a FaceTime-compatible device and the FaceTime app.

Skills needed: Familiarity with the Contacts app (see Chapter 5) is helpful.

If you have a first-generation iPad, which doesn't have built-in cameras, we're afraid that you can't use FaceTime. Skip ahead to the next chapter!

When Apple launched the second generation of the iPad (known as the iPad 2), it added a fantastic new video calling feature called FaceTime. For many years, technology like this – the ability to see who you're phoning as you speak to them – was the stuff of science fiction. In recent years, you might have used a webcam with your computer to have a video chat with people over the Internet, but that meant you only ever got to see people sitting in front of their computers. The iPad, with its two built-in cameras, makes this kind of technology much more portable, so you can chat to people from all over your house, as well as many other places.

You can chat anywhere there's a Wi-Fi connection. If you've got a third- or fourth-generation iPad running iOS6 (the latest version of the iPad software), you may also be able to make FaceTime calls using a 3G or 4G mobile connection. As well as needing to have the Wi-Fi + Cellular (3G or 4G) device and the latest iPad software, using FaceTime video calling this way depends on the mobile network you're using. Verizon in the United States allows such calls, and there are rumours that AT&T may soon follow suit. In the United Kingdom, you can use FaceTime over 3G, but Vodafone users may have to pay an extra fee to do so (£10 for a 2GB monthly allowance).

Sending video over a mobile connection will eat into your monthly data allowance, so this won't be something you'll want to do often. By contrast, Wi-Fi connections are often provided in cafés and holiday resorts, so it's usually easy to get connected for a chat. The upside of using Wi-Fi is that it's usually free – which, oddly, makes video calls cheaper than many phone calls.

The iPad comes with the FaceTime app already installed. The person you want to talk to must also have FaceTime, but she doesn't necessarily need to have an iPad; she may have FaceTime if she has an iPhone, an iPod touch or an Apple Mac computer, as FaceTime software is also available for these devices. Not all versions of these devices support FaceTime. iPhone and iPod touch owners must be running iOS5 or iOS6, while Mac users need to have OS X Lion or Mountain Lion.

FaceTime is a fantastic feature of the iPad. We've found that after a video chat, you really feel like you've met someone. It feels totally different to a phone call and is a much more satisfactory way of keeping in touch with far-flung relatives across the miles.

Tap the FaceTime app on your Home screen to get started.

If you don't have the FaceTime app on your Home screen, your iPad may not be compatible with it. Remember that you need an iPad with built-in cameras for FaceTime to work. If you do have a compatible iPad, check that you haven't disabled FaceTime in the Restrictions settings (see Chapter 3).

Logging in to FaceTime

To use FaceTime, you need to log in by using your Apple ID – the same email address and password combination you used when you set up your iPad. If you don't have an Apple ID, tap the Create New Account button.

If a friend wants to set up a FaceTime call with you, he needs to use your email address. The FaceTime app asks you which email address you want people to use to contact you. If you're happy using the same email address you use for your Apple ID, just tap Next in the top-right corner. Otherwise, tap the email address itself; then you can delete it and type a new address. Tap Next when you've finished.

> You can add more email addresses for yourself in the FaceTime section of the Settings app. This feature is useful if you have several email addresses through which friends may try to contact you.

When you enter an email address for FaceTime, you may need to verify that it's yours. If so, Apple will send you an email with a link in it. You need to check your email on your computer and click the link Apple sends you. This action proves to Apple that you own the email address and acts as a security measure for FaceTime because it stops people from using email addresses they don't own. You won't need to verify your email address if the email address you enter is already linked to your Apple ID or is one that you've already set up in the Mail app (see Chapter 6).

You can leave your iPad signed in to FaceTime so you don't have to enter your email address and password the next time you want to use it. If you want to log out for some reason (perhaps to enable someone else to use FaceTime with his own ID), you can do that by going into the Settings app, tapping FaceTime on the left and then tapping your Apple ID.

Starting a FaceTime call

The first shock you get when you start the FaceTime app is that you see your own face filling the screen (see Figure 7.1). (That's Sean, by the way.) Nice to meet you.

Down the right hand side of the screen is a list of people to call. If you tap the Recents icon at the bottom, you can see people you've recently called, tried to call or received calls from. The Favourites section shows you people you've labelled as favourites within FaceTime or the Contacts app. Tap Contacts to see people in your address book, which is shared with the Contacts and Mail apps. This is a great time-saver, because it means you don't have to enter a friend's email address again if you've already done so in Contacts or Mail. You can tap Groups at the top of your contacts list to access different groups of contacts.

If you haven't added the person you want to talk to as a contact in your iPad, you need to do that before you can call him or her. FaceTime makes it easy to add a contact by tapping the Add Contact button (the plus sign) in the top-right corner of the screen (refer to Figure 7.1). At a bare minimum, you should add his or her first name, last name and the email address or iPhone phone number he or she uses for FaceTime. You don't need to enter any further details to use FaceTime, but if you want to, you can flesh out your contact's profile with more details so it's there for you to refer to in the Contacts app. For advice on completing your contact's details and a refresher on how the Contacts app works on the iPad, see Chapter 5.

Figure 7.1

To find the contact you want to call, you can scroll the contacts list by touching it and dragging your finger up and down, or you can use the search box at the top of the screen. Tap somebody's name, and you see full contact details for that person. You also see three particularly useful options:

- **Add to Favourites:** Because not everyone in your Contacts will have FaceTime, you can save yourself a lot of time by adding those who *do* have it to your Favourites list. Then you can see a list of only these people by tapping Favourites at the bottom of the screen.

- **Edit:** To make a FaceTime call to your friend, you need to use the email address or phone number he asked Apple to associate with FaceTime. That email address may not be the same one your friend uses for correspondence; if necessary, tap the Edit button in the top-right corner and add his FaceTime email address or phone number to his contact details.

- **Start a FaceTime call:** There's no big button to tap! To start a FaceTime call, just tap the email address your friend uses for FaceTime or his iPhone phone number.

When you tap an email address or phone number, FaceTime attempts to call your friend, and you hear a simulated phone ringing sound. Your friend sees a message onscreen and hears an alert sound if alerts are enabled. When your friend answers, you see his face on the screen.

If the iPad tells you almost immediately that someone you're trying to call isn't available for FaceTime, it's probably because FaceTime doesn't know that email address. Check that you've got the right email address and that you've spelled it correctly.

Talking to a friend using FaceTime

During a call, the FaceTime screen looks like Figure 7.2. Most of the screen is filled with video of your friend, but overlaid on this video are a few controls.

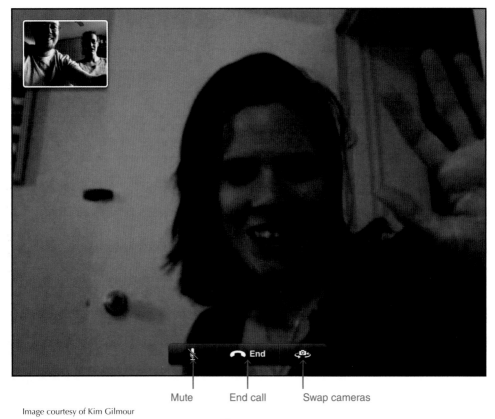

Mute   End call   Swap cameras

Image courtesy of Kim Gilmour

Figure 7.2

In the top-left corner is a small picture showing what your friend is seeing of you. If this picture is in the way of something you want to see in your friend's video, you can touch it and drag it to another corner of the screen, but you can't get rid of it. Most of the time, you can just leave it alone. (Check it from time to time, though, to make sure you're not covering the camera with your thumb or giving your friend an unflattering view up your nostrils.) The camera on the front of your iPad is opposite the Home button, so it's best to hold the iPad near its corners or to stand it up to avoid blocking the camera.

At the bottom of the screen are three buttons. On the left is a Mute button, which is probably more acceptable in business than in personal use. It seems a bit rude to stop someone you've called from hearing what you're saying, but if you need a moment of privacy, this button gives you it. The images continue, however, so don't rely on the Mute button if your friend can lip-read!

On the right is a button that lets you swap between the cameras on the front and back of your iPad. Most of the time, you want to use the front-facing camera so that you can see your friend onscreen and she can see you looking at her on the screen. Sometimes, however, you may want to share something that's going on, such as the view from your window or the action at a birthday party. Tap the Swap Cameras button, and FaceTime uses the camera on the back of your iPad instead of the front. That means your friend will be able to see whatever you point your iPad at, and you'll still be able to see what she's seeing – and her reaction to it – on your screen.

The back camera is in a corner near the Sleep/Wake button. Take care how you hold your iPad when you're using the rear camera, to make sure you don't cover the lens. To revert to using the front-facing camera, simply tap the Swap Cameras button again.

If you want to move around as you talk, try not to move too quickly. The image can become blocky and indistinct if you move too fast, so it's best to prop your iPad up on the desk if you're just chatting or move the iPad around slowly if you're giving your friend a tour.

You need a good Wi-Fi or mobile Internet connection to use FaceTime. If you move too far away from the Wi-Fi hotspot while you're chatting, your connection might break up, resulting in poor-quality sound and video.

If you rotate your iPad, the view on the other person's screen also rotates so that your friend always sees things the right way up.

You can break off the video chat to look something up on your iPad while you're still talking. You could look up someone else's address in the Contacts app, for example, if you're arranging to meet at his house later. Press the Home button to go to the Home screen, where you can start another app. The video your friend sees will be paused, and your own screen will be filled with the Home screen and whatever apps you use, so you won't see any video either. You and your friend can still hear and speak to each other, though. When you're ready to go back into FaceTime, tap the green bar at the top of the screen labelled 'Touch to resume FaceTime'.

When it's time to finish the call, tap the End Call button at the bottom-middle of the screen.

After you've had a successful call with someone, a video-camera icon appears beside that person's email address or phone number when you view her contact details in the FaceTime app, which is a helpful reminder of which one she uses for FaceTime when you want to talk to her again in future.

Receiving a FaceTime call

Your friends can request FaceTime chats with you, too. If your iPad has been muted (see Chapter 2), you won't hear anything; otherwise, your iPad makes an alert sound. If you've specified a ringtone for your friend in the Contacts app (see Chapter 5), your iPad uses that sound to let you know who's calling. You also see a message telling you who would like to have a FaceTime chat with you. You will see two buttons at the bottom of the screen: Decline, which blocks the call, and Accept, which starts the call straight away. If your iPad is locked when the Face-Time call is requested, a single control is available: a slider to start the call. If you've just stepped out of the shower and are in no state for video calling, you can ignore it or tap the Sleep/Wake button to put your iPad to sleep again.

If you don't want to be interrupted by FaceTime requests, you can turn FaceTime off in the Settings app.

Summary

- The FaceTime app enables you to have video calls with friends.

- The app is available for the iPad, iPhone and iPod touch and for Mac computers running OS X Lion or Mountain Lion (but not for the first generation of the iPad, which doesn't have built-in cameras).

- To use FaceTime, you need to have a Wi-Fi connection (though some iPads with 3G or 4G can also be used for FaceTime calls).

- You log in to FaceTime by using your Apple ID.

- People contact you by using any of the email addresses you've entered in FaceTime.

- You need to add a person to your contacts before you can call that person.

- To start a call, tap someone's email address or iPhone phone number in the FaceTime app.

- You can swap between the front and rear cameras when using FaceTime.

- If someone wants to have a FaceTime video chat with you, you see a message on your iPad's screen.

- In the Settings app, you can turn off FaceTime or add more email addresses that people can use to contact you.

Brain training

How did you get on with FaceTime? Find out with this quick quiz.

1. **You can use FaceTime to call some-one with:**

(a) A third-generation iPad

(b) A first-generation iPad

(c) A Windows PC

(d) An Apple Mac computer

2. **People contact you on FaceTime by using:**

(a) Your iPad's serial number

(b) Your phone number

(c) Any email address you have

(d) Any email address you've entered in FaceTime

3. **To use FaceTime on your iPad, you need to have:**

(a) An iPad with cameras

(b) A 3G or 4G Internet connection

(c) A Wi-Fi connection

(d) A Mac computer

4. **To turn off the video but keep the audio working in a FaceTime chat, you:**

(a) Tap the Mute button.

(b) Press the Home button.

(c) Tap the Swap Cameras button.

(d) Tap the End Call button.

5. **To make sure your FaceTime calls go well, you should:**

(a) Check that you're calling the right email address or iPhone number.

(b) Keep your fingers away from the camera lens.

(c) Make sure your iPad isn't muted so you hear the ringtone.

(d) Comb your hair.

Answers

Q1 – a and d   **Q2** – d

Q3 – a and c (b is also true if you have a 3G- or 4G-enabled iPad and are on a mobile tariff that allows FaceTime calls)

Q4 – b   **Q5** – a, b, c and d

Sending instant messages using iMessage

8

Equipment needed: An iPad and an Internet connection.

Skills needed: Experience using the iPad, including gesture controls, using the keyboard, and starting and using apps. Familiarity with the Contacts app (see Chapter 5) is helpful.

In Chapter 7, you find out how to have a video chat with friends using FaceTime. In this chapter, you discover a way you can chat with friends that's a bit more socially acceptable if you're still in your pyjamas.

The Messages app provides a convenient way to send text messages and photos to friends who also have an Apple device with the Messages app. This covers iPads, iPhones and iPod touches, as well as Mac computers running OS X Mountain Lion. If your iPad or iPhone isn't already running iOS5 or 6, iMessages is a good reason to update. This powerful communication tool works over Wi-Fi and lets you send messages complete with photos and web links without eating into your text message allowance. Even if you don't have Wi-Fi available, Apple doesn't charge you for sending or receiving messages, but you may have to use some of your mobile data subscription to exchange messages. This is different to standard mobile phone text messages (SMS), which typically are charged individually or included as part of a subscription package. The iPad's large keyboard makes it much easier to type messages than on a mobile phone, too.

The Messages app was introduced with Apple's iPad software update in October 2011 and was deemed so important that Apple made it the first app on the Home screen. If you don't have the Messages app on your iPad, see Chapter 3 for advice on updating your iPad software.

To send and receive messages, you need to have an Internet connection. To get started, tap the Messages icon on your Home screen.

The first time you use Messages, you need to sign in with your Apple ID. This ID is the same email address and password combination you use to log in to Face-Time, to buy content from the iTunes Store and the App Store, and to access other services on your iPad.

> The app is called Messages, but when you get into the app, you see that the service is called iMessage.

Sending messages

Figure 8.1 shows the Messages app with a conversation in progress. If you've used the Mail app on your iPad (see Chapter 6), the screen layout will feel familiar. Your conversations are listed on the left, and you can tap one to read it in the panel on the right or to pick up the conversation where you left off. You can scroll the conversation by touching the messages area on the right and dragging it up or down.

Here's how to send a message:

1. To start, tap the New Message button shown in Figure 8.1.

2. In the To box, enter the email address your friend uses for her Apple ID or the number of her iPhone. You can also just type someone's name to select her from your contacts list. If the person isn't registered with iMessage, her details are highlighted in red. Tap the details to remove them, and try another email address or phone number.

3. Tap the message box (with rounded corners) above your keyboard, and type your message. You can use the dictation feature, where available (see Chapter 4), if you prefer.

4. To add a photo or video, tap the camera button to the left of the message box. You can pick an existing one from your iPad or take a new one with the iPad's cameras.

5. Tap the Send button beside the message box when you've finished.

Message list   New message   Forward/delete

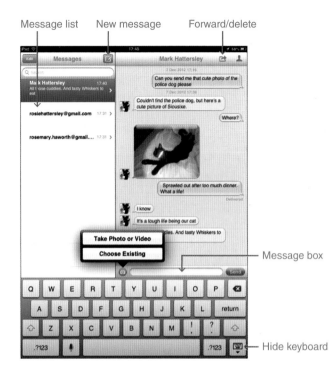

Message box

Hide keyboard

Figure 8.1

Your messages are shown on the right of the screen in blue speech bubbles, and your friends' messages to you are shown on the left in grey speech bubbles.

You may notice that your speech bubbles in iMessage are sometimes blue and other times green. If you message a friend who has an iOS device, the message is sent as a blue iMessage. A message to a non-Apple contact is sent as a standard SMS text message and appears as a green speech bubble in iMessage.

When your message has been read, the word *Delivered* appears below it if the recipient has enabled this feature. If delivery fails, and your friend has enabled read receipts, you'll see a warning to that effect, and you can tap the warning to try sending again. If you'd like your friends to see when you've read their messages, go into the Settings app and tap Messages, and then flick the switch to allow your iPad to send read receipts.

If you want to delete parts of a message or forward parts of it to someone, tap the Forward/Delete button in the top-right corner (refer to Figure 8.1). Tap which pieces of the conversation you want to forward or delete and then tap either the Delete or the Forward button at the bottom of the screen. If you choose to forward a message, enter the recipient's email address or phone number at the top and then tap Send next to your message.

You can send a message to several people at once. Just enter all their email addresses or iPhone numbers in the To box.

If you'd like to send someone a smile, you can use the Emoji keyboard, which has pictures representing a wide range of expressions (see Figure 8.2).

Return to letters keyboard

Recently used symbols   Switch between picture sets

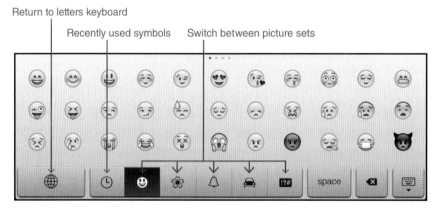

Figure 8.2

First, you need to enable this special keyboard. Go into the Settings app; tap General on the left and then tap Keyboard. Tap Keyboards and then tap Add New Keyboard. Among all the keyboards (including French and Spanish), you'll find the Emoji one. Tap its name, and when you go back into the Messages app, you see a globe key beside the spacebar. That key takes you to the Emoji keyboard and then back to the normal keyboard again when you've finished. You can swipe left and right across the faces on the Emoji keyboard to see more symbols. Tap the icons at the bottom to reveal new sets of symbols, including a jolly Santa, musical instruments and world flags. Tap a picture to add it to your message. This feature is a fun one, especially for surprising friends who haven't worked out how to do it yet!

Splitting the keyboard

You can make it easier to hold the iPad and type messages on it at the same time by splitting the keyboard into two smaller halves. Each half of the keyboard shrinks and moves to the outside edge so that you can rest the iPad in your fingers and reach all the keys on the screen with your thumbs. You can also move the keyboard from the bottom of the screen to the middle so it's easier to rest the iPad in your hands while typing.

To find these options, tap and hold the Hide Keyboard key and then tap Split or Undock (which moves the keyboard up). To return the keyboard to its normal form, tap and hold the Hide Keyboard key to find the options to Dock and Merge.

These options are perhaps most useful in the Messages app, but you can use them in any other app, too, including Mail, Contacts and Notes.

> You can also split the keyboard by putting two fingers on it and moving them apart horizontally. Reverse the gesture to merge the keyboard again.

Managing message alerts through the Notification Centre

If you're not using the Messages app when a message comes in for you, you can choose how the iPad alerts you. You can do that by changing your notification settings, which gives you control of how apps get your attention when they have new information or messages for you. That means you can decide how intrusive you will allow each app to be. In the case of Messages, you might let the app interrupt whatever you're doing with an alert because a friend is waiting for your reply.

To set up your notification settings, go into the Settings app, and tap Notifications on the left. On the right, you see a list of your applications. Tap an app's name, and you see its notification settings. Figure 8.3 shows our settings for the Messages app.

You have several options for notifications. First, you can choose whether you want them to appear in the Notification Centre – a panel that shows notifications from across different applications (see Figure 8.4). You can see this panel when you're using any app or Home screen. Just touch the status bar (or put your finger above the touchscreen area) and pull your finger down the screen to pull the panel into view.

If you tap an item in the Notification Centre, you can go straight into the appropriate app for more information or to take action. To stop an application from clogging up your Notification Centre, you can limit the number of recent items that appear there.

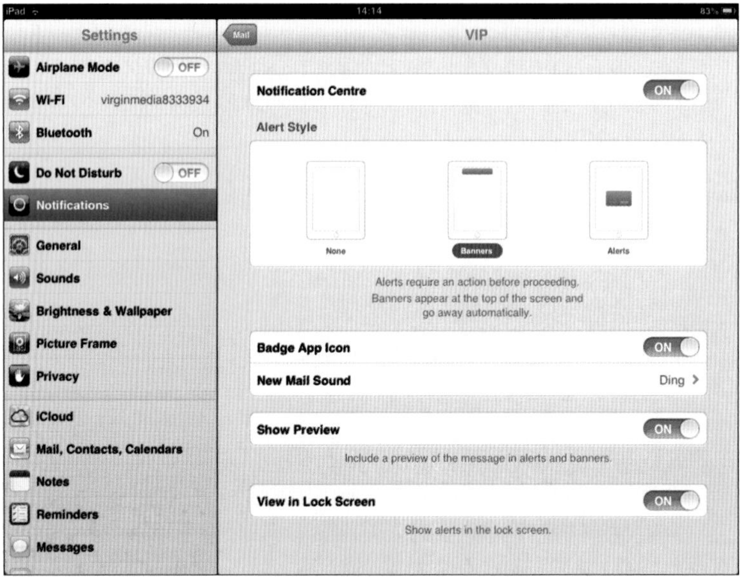

Figure 8.3

You can also choose to receive an alert or a banner when an app has new information for you. An alert pops up in the middle of the screen and won't disappear until you do something with it, such as tapping a button to make it go away. A banner appears at the top of the screen briefly and then disappears of its own accord. If you want neither of these options, you can choose None instead.

You can create your own ringtones and text message alert tones with the Garage-Band app, which is free for Mac users. Choose a snippet from a favourite song in your iTunes library and assign that snippet to a particular person. Then, without even looking at the screen, you know when he's sent you a message. In the Contacts app, select the name of the person and tap Edit to change the text tone that's used to tell you about a new message. A great selection of quirky noises is provided with the iPad, and you can buy additional tones in the iTunes Store (see Chapter 10), including classic lines from movies and snippets of hit songs.

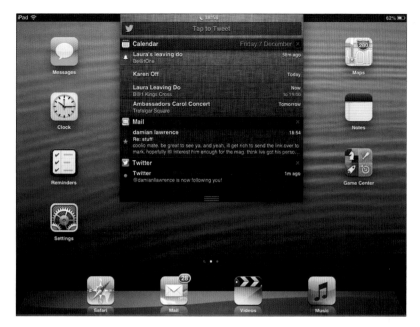

Figure 8.4

Some apps can also change the app's icon, perhaps by putting a number on it to show you how many unread messages you have (as the Mail icon in Figure 8.4 shows). Switch the Badge App Icon slider on (refer to Figure 8.3) to enable this feature where available

With iOS6, Apple allows you to install the social networking apps Facebook and Twitter without first having to download them. Scroll down your Settings list to reveal and install these apps. You can also set them to appear in your Notification Centre. Tap Notifications; then tap either Facebook or Twitter and tap to activate it. Now when you drag down to view your notifications on the iPad's Home screen, you see Facebook updates and have the option to tap to tweet or tap to post (to Facebook). To control which apps are set to notify you of things, tap the Notifications option in Settings to view a list of what's in use (see Figure 8.5).

For the Messages and Mail apps, you can also choose to show a preview of the message with the alert (which we recommend). The Messages app can also repeat the alert up to ten times if you miss it the first time, although this setting probably isn't the best idea if you often leave your iPad near other people. They could find it annoying to be stuck in a room with an unattended iPad that keeps chirruping.

Figure 8.5

A new feature introduced with iOS6 (the version of the iPad software that Apple introduced in September 2012) may be the most appropriate if you're in a meeting or don't want to advertise the presence of your rather desirable iPad. To activate the Do Not Disturb feature, go into the Settings app and tap Do Not Disturb. A crescent-moon icon next to the time on the status bar at the top of the iPad screen indicates that this feature is active. Go back to Settings and tap Do Not Disturb again to turn it off.

If you enable notifications to appear in the Lock screen, a box in the middle of the screen shows the update when you return to your iPad. You can unlock your iPad and go straight into the app associated with the update by touching the app's icon in the notification box (see Figure 8.6) and dragging it to the right.

Figure 8.6

To change or disable the sounds associated with different alerts, go into the Settings app, tap General on the left and then tap Sounds.

Summary

- The Messages app enables you to send instant messages, photos and videos to friends who also have the app.

- You can use a Wi-Fi or 4G/3G connection.

- Your conversations are listed on the left, and you tap one to enter it on the right.

- Your messages are shown in blue speech bubbles on the right, and your friends' are shown in grey bubbles on the left.

- You can address a message to someone by using his email address or iPhone number. You can pick someone from your contacts by typing her name.

- You can choose a photo or video from your iPad or use your iPad's cameras to create one.

- To make it easier to hold the iPad and type, you can split the keyboard and move it towards the middle of the screen.

- The Notification Centre gives you updates from across your apps in one place.

- You can also choose to see an alert or a banner when there's a new message for you.

- A new feature, Do Not Disturb, prevents you being interrupted by messages or alerts when you're busy or trying to sleep!

Brain training

Let's finish, as usual, with a short quiz.

1. When you've finished writing your message, you should:

(a) Tap Return on the keyboard.

(b) Tap the Send button.

(c) Tap the New Message button.

(d) Tap the Hide Keyboard button.

2. If you swipe from the status bar down the screen:

(a) You return to the Home screen.

(b) You reveal the Notification Centre.

(c) You go to another open app.

(d) You can crop a photo.

3. If you put your fingers on the keyboard and move them apart horizontally:

(a) You zoom in on the message.

(b) You move the keyboard to the centre of the screen.

(c) You split the keyboard.

(d) You type some strange meaningless characters.

4. If you want to see how many messages you have waiting for you on the Home screen:

(a) Turn on alerts for the Messages app.

(b) Turn on banners for the Messages app.

(c) Turn on the Notification Centre for the Messages app.

(d) Turn on the Badge App Icon setting for the Messages app.

5. To customise the sound played when a friend sends a message:

(a) Change the ringtone associated with that person.

(b) Change the sounds in the Settings app.

(c) Change the text tone associated with that person.

(d) Go into the iTunes Store, and choose a tone to denote him or her.

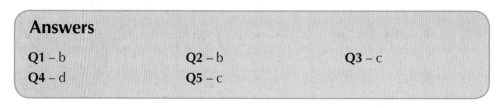

Answers

Q1 – b	Q2 – b	Q3 – c
Q4 – d	Q5 – c	

Browsing the web

9

Equipment needed: An iPad with an Internet connection (Wi-Fi or 3G/4G).

Skills needed: Experience using the iPad keyboard (see Chapter 4) and connecting to the Internet.

One of the best features of the iPad is the ease with which you can browse the Internet. From the comfort of your sofa or a café, or even in bed, you can look at family photos on Facebook, book your holiday, do your banking or search for the answer to pretty much any question. Almost anything you can do online with a conventional computer, you can do with the iPad.

We say *almost* anything because one thing the iPad doesn't support is Adobe Flash animation. So the iPad won't play things that use Flash technology: some animations, online games and video clips embedded in websites. It's not a big problem, though, as Flash technology is being phased out. And when it comes to games and video on the iPad, as Apple would say, "There's an app for that" (as you see in Chapter 14). What's more, the iPad offers a much more reassuring web experience in terms of security than the Windows computer you may have used.

Although you still need to ensure that you don't give out too much personal information while surfing the web, the Internet is a far friendlier place when experienced through the iPad.

To get started, you just need a web connection. (See Chapter 3 for details on how to get online.) The app you use for viewing web pages on the iPad (known as a *web browser*) is called Safari. You can find it on the Dock at the bottom of your Home screen, on the left.

If you're using a 3G/4G connection, don't worry about how long you're connected. Surfing the web isn't like a phone call, in which you're charged by the minute. You pay only for the content you download, so it's the amount of content you need to be aware of, not the amount of time you spend on the web. It doesn't matter how long you spend reading a web page before going to another one.

In this chapter, we show you how to get the most from Safari. You build on the skills you acquired in using the keyboard and editing text in Chapter 4, and on your experience using the Internet on other computers. Don't worry too much if you don't already know how to use the Internet; we show you how to explore it as we go.

Start the Safari app, and you're ready to go!

There's a small risk that somebody could intercept the information you send over the Internet when you're using public Wi-Fi, so it's best to avoid online shopping, banking and other sensitive activities when you're using Wi-Fi in public places like cafés and hotels. See Chapter 3 to read more about connecting to secure Wi-Fi networks.

Entering a website address

The Safari browser looks much like a browser on a desktop computer, so if you've ever used the Internet, there will be few surprises when the Safari app starts. At the top, you see two boxes: one for the website address and the other for searching the web (see Figure 9.1).

Bookmarks bar   Address field   Clear address field   Search field

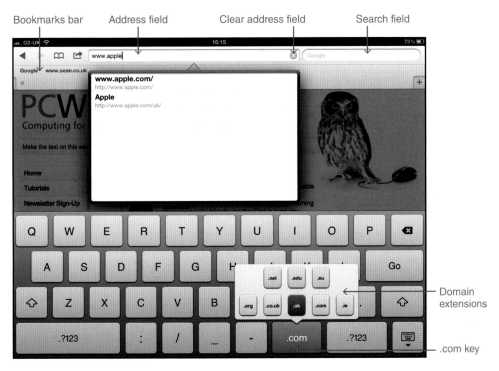

Domain extensions

.com key

Figure 9.1

To go straight to a particular website, you need to tell the browser its website address. This address usually starts with www, followed by a word or phrase, followed by a domain extension such as .com, .co.uk or .org. Website addresses you've probably used before include **www.bbc.co.uk** and **www.google.com**. A short address like either of these takes you to the website's home page, which is designed to welcome new visitors.

Every page of content on the website has its own, longer website address, too. You could type the longer address to jump straight to a particular article on a website, but it's usually easier to go to the website's home page and then click some links to find what you want or to use a search engine (Google is the best known, but Yahoo! and Microsoft Bing are also available) to go there.

To enter a website address on the iPad, start by tapping in the address field at the top of the screen (refer to Figure 9.1). The keyboard appears so you can type the website address.

It's generally fine if you leave out the 'www' at the start, as this is often inserted automatically. So you can save time by typing just **bbc.co.uk**, for example.

If you mistype anything in the address field, you can edit what you've typed. Tap and hold in the address field, and the magnifying glass appears so that you can easily position your insertion point. Then you can type missing letters or use the keyboard's Delete key to remove characters. You can also paste a website address if you've copied it from an email or the Notes app, for example. Before you paste a new website address into the address field, clear the old one by tapping the Clear Address Field button (the X) at the right end of the address field.

When you've finished typing your website address, tap the Go key, which is where the Return key normally is on the right side of the keyboard.

While a page is loading, you see a cross icon inside the address field on the right. Tap this icon to stop a page loading. When the page has loaded, the X sign changes to a circular arrow. Clicking this arrow *refreshes* the page (reloads the information on it).

A couple of iPad features are designed to make it easier to enter website addresses. First, when you're typing a website address, the keyboard includes the symbols you're most likely to need and incorporates a .com key, saving you from having to type the most common website address suffix. To add .com to the end of your address, tap the .com key. To insert .co.uk, .net, .eu, .org or .ie instead of .com, tap and hold the .com key. A bubble appears (refer to Figure 9.1), showing the other domain extensions. When it does, slide your finger over to the domain extension you want and then release your finger. If you're a speedy typist, you'll probably find it just as quick to type the website suffix manually.

The web address extensions in the bubble include both .co.uk and .uk. Most of the time, you probably need .co.uk, but .uk is the one that's highlighted initially. Make sure you pick the right one!

The other way Safari helps you enter websites is by suggesting websites based on what you type. These suggestions are drawn from sites you've previously visited, popular website addresses such as **www.bbc.co.uk** and those you've bookmarked (see 'Adding bookmarks', later in this chapter). The suggestions appear below the address field.

Each suggestion has the title of the page in bold, with its full website address below in grey. If you're returning to a website, keep an eye on these suggestions. The moment the iPad offers the correct suggestion, you can tap it to go there straight away.

Using the search box

You can also find websites by using the search field on the right. While you type, Google suggests phrases that match what you're typing. If one of them is what you want, you can stop typing and just tap it. If not, when you've finished typing, tap the Search key on the keyboard. You'll find it in place of the Return key.

The search feature also enables you to find words or phrases within a web page you're viewing. Above the keyboard is a Find on Page box (see Figure 9.2). Tap this box and then type the word you want to search for. As you type, Safari looks for your search term on the page and jumps to the first occurrence, highlighting it in yellow. You can move to the next time the word or phrase appears by tapping the Next button, and you can go back to the one before by tapping the Previous button. When you've finished searching in the page, tap the Done button above the keyboard on the right. If you want to see more of the web page while you search it, you can tap the Hide Keyboard button. The Find on Page controls will still be there at the bottom of the screen.

Previous

Next

Find on
Page

New Web
Page

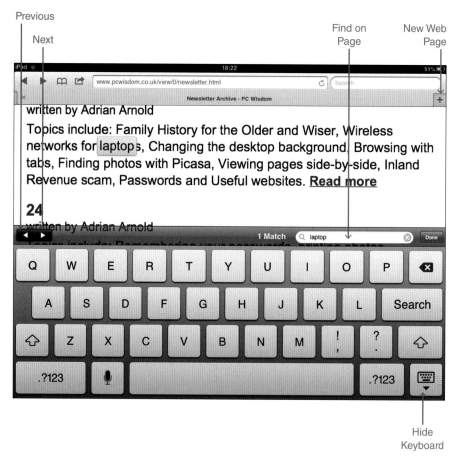

Hide
Keyboard

Figure 9.2

Zooming the page

Many websites were designed to be viewed on screens much larger than the iPad's. And some pages use text that's too small to read comfortably on an iPad. As we discuss in Chapter 2, going into the Settings app and then tapping Accessibility lets you turn on the option to zoom the whole screen. This feature is ideal for people with impaired vision because it enables them to enlarge the iPad's onscreen buttons as well as the content. The drawback is that it sometimes moves the controls off the screen, so you may have to do more scrolling around to find them again.

If you just want to see part of a web page more clearly, it's easier to simply enlarge the content of the web page. Double-tap an area of the screen, and it's enlarged to fill the width of the screen. Double-tap again, and the screen zooms back in so you can pick another area to zoom in on. The same double-tap action can be used elsewhere to zoom in on photos and other items.

There's also a gesture used for zooming, called the *pinch*. It works like this: You put two fingers on the screen, near the content you want to enlarge (see Figure 9.3). Slowly move those fingers apart, and the screen zooms in on the space between your fingers (see Figure 9.4). You can use the index finger and thumb of the same hand or two fingers of different hands.

PC Wisdom is © 2000-2011 by John Wiley & Sons, Inc.

Figure 9.3

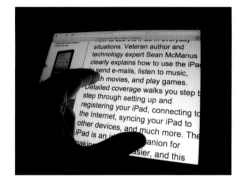

PC Wisdom is © 2000-2011 by John Wiley & Sons, Inc.

Figure 9.4

The pinch motion is also used for zooming in on photos (see Chapter 13). Practice the movement, and you'll find that it gives you a lot of control over what you see on your iPad screen.

Pictures can become indistinct when they're zoomed in too far, but the text of a web page sharpens when you use the pinch motion to zoom in.

To go back to the web page's original size, perform the pinch in reverse. Start with your fingers apart on the screen and then bring them close together. If you shrink the page too far, it snaps back to fit the screen when you release your fingers.

Scrolling the page

A web page often spills off the available screen area, especially when you zoom in. To scroll the page so you can see a different part of it, put your finger anywhere on it and then drag it across the iPad's screen. As you move your finger up or down the screen, the web page scrolls in that direction. If the web page is wide or has been zoomed in, you can also scroll sideways.

While you are scrolling, a thin scrollbar appears at the right and/or bottom of the screen to give you a visual clue of which part of the page you're looking at. The longer the line, the more of the page's total height or width you're looking at. The position of the line also tells you where you are on the page.

Figure 9.5 shows a zoomed-in page. Because now you can't see everything that's on the page within the viewable area, scrollbars have appeared at the bottom and on the right. The scrollbar at the bottom indicates that you're looking at about 80 percent of the page's width and at the right side of it. The scrollbar along the right side of the screen shows you that you're looking at only about 10 percent of the page's height and that you're roughly halfway down the page.

On a Windows computer, you might be used to seeing a scrollbar at the side of the screen all the time to tell you if there's more to see. You don't get that feature on the iPad, so it's a good idea to try scrolling the page to see what you might be missing.

You can use the flick gesture (refer to Chapter 4) to move quickly in any direction on the web page, but it's particularly useful for zipping through pages that are several screens deep.

The navigation options for a website are usually at the top of the screen. When you finish reading a page, you can jump to the top of it by tapping the status bar, indicated in Figure 9.5, so that you can find its links.

Back Forward   Status bar

Figure 9.5

💡 You can often see more of a web page by rotating the iPad. Try both landscape and portrait orientations to see which you find more comfortable for reading.

Using links on websites

As you may know from your experience with desktop computers, web pages are connected by links. Web links can be indicated in the text, in which case they're usually underlined, or they can look like buttons or other graphical elements.

To follow a link on a website, whether it's text or an image, just tap it. The iPad decides that you've tapped a link only when you remove your finger again. If you move your finger before lifting it, the iPad guesses that you intended to scroll. If you put two or more fingers on the screen at the same time, you don't select a link for either of them because you can't choose more than one link at the same time.

Web pages on the iPad look the same as they do on a desktop computer, but there's one significant difference. On a PC, your mouse cursor can be over a link without you clicking it. Doing so reveals a menu or other previously hidden information. This trick cannot be used on the iPad. Your finger is either touching the screen or it isn't. (You can, however, press and hold your finger on a link to show the URL it will go to.) On a well-designed website, it should still be obvious where the links are, but you may have to tap first to open menus that normally pop up automatically when you're using a desktop computer.

Like a desktop computer's web browser, the Safari browser on your iPad can take you back to the last page you looked at or forward again after you've gone back. The Back and Forward buttons are in the top-left corner of the browser (refer to Figure 9.5).

Entering information on websites

The way you enter information on a website is similar to the way you add information in the Settings app or address emails, but there are a couple of things to look out for.

As you might expect, tapping a text box brings up a keyboard so you can type something in that box. The keyboard layout can change, however, depending on what you're typing. Some websites tell the iPad you're entering an email address, so you get a keyboard with an @ sign within easy reach, for example, but not all websites do that.

Note that the Return key on the keyboard is replaced by a Go key. You may have tapped the Return key to move to the next box that you need to complete, but tapping the Go key submits your form as though you'd tapped the Submit button for the form.

If you tap the Go key before you finish filling in all the boxes, you may have to go back to the beginning and complete the form all over again.

To enter information in other boxes on the web page, tap the next box rather than the Go key. While the keyboard is in view, you can still scroll the underlying web page to make sure you can complete all the information you need to.

To select an option, such as an answer in a questionnaire, regardless of whether it's a round radio button, a box you need to tick or a dropdown menu choice, just tap it. In the case of a pulldown menu, the menu opens so that you can tap your option.

Launching multiple websites with tabbed browsing

If it's been a few minutes since you visited a page, it may take a couple of seconds for the information to load up again. If you're likely to want to go back to a page, it's worth tapping the Open New Tab button – the + icon in the top-right corner – and navigating to the next web page while leaving the current web page open (see Figure 9.6). This technique is called *tabbed browsing* because Safari opens additional pages that look like the tabs in a file. Tap the website name on a tab to make that web page the active view.

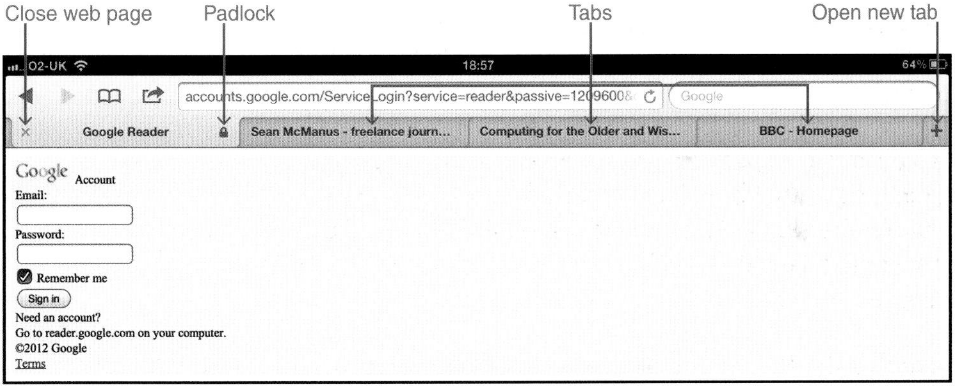

Close web page   Padlock   Tabs   Open new tab

.ıl O2-UK 🛜	18:57	64% 🔋

accounts.google.com/ServiceLogin?service=reader&passive=1209600&   ↻   Google

| ✕ | Google Reader | 🔒 | Sean McManus - freelance journ... | Computing for the Older and Wis... | BBC - Homepage | + |

Google **Account**
Email:
[   ]
Password:
[   ]
☑ Remember me
(Sign in)
Need an account?
Go to reader.google.com on your computer.
©2012 Google
Terms

Google screenshot courtesy of Google

Figure 9.6

Safari lets you have up to nine web pages open at the same time. This is useful when you're shopping online and comparing offers from different websites, when you're coordinating flight bookings in one window with hotel reservations in another, or even when you just want to take a short deviation and read something such as an encyclopaedia article before continuing to read a news report.

Sometimes when you tap a link, it opens in a new tab of its own accord, but you can choose to open a new tab and then use the address field or search box to open a new web page in that tab. The tabs resize depending on how many you have open, so they always fill the width of the screen.

To close a web page, tap the X on the left side of its tab. If you're not already viewing that web page, you need to tap its tab first to make it the active page.

Tabbed browsing means you can switch quickly between all the web pages you have open at the same time. Tabbed browsing was introduced in the iPad iOS5 software update in October 2011. If you don't see tabs at the top of your Safari browser window, you may need to update your iPad software to be able to use this feature. See Chapter 3 for details on how to update to iOS6.

If you're entering sensitive information on the website, such as credit-card details, make sure you're using a secure web page. To check, look at the web page title in its tab. A secure web page has a tiny padlock icon to the right of the page title (refer to Figure 9.6). Don't be tricked by any padlocks in the web page content. If the padlock icon isn't inside the tab, it doesn't count.

When you tap a link, it usually opens in the same tab, but you can choose to open it in a different tab. To do that, tap and hold the link until a menu appears (see Figure 9.7).

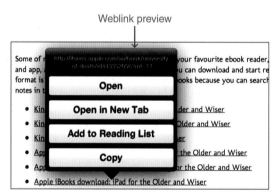

Figure 9.7

At the top of this menu, you see the website address the link goes to. You can open this menu if you're not sure where a link will take you and want to check its destination before you follow it.

Here are the options from this menu:

- **Open:** Tap this option to open the link in the current tab (that is, to replace the page that is open with the new one). The same thing happens if you just tap the link, but this option gives you a chance to check first where the link goes.

- **Open in New Tab:** Tap this option to open the link in a new tab.

- **Add to Reading List:** Tap this option to add the linked page to the Reading List. The Reading List keeps a record of web pages you plan to read but don't have time to read right now. There's more about the Reading List later in this chapter.

- **Copy:** Tap this option to copy the link's website address. If you want to send somebody the link, you could use this option to make a copy of its address and then paste it into an email in the Mail app.

- **Do nothing:** There isn't actually a Do Nothing option on the menu, but if you tap outside the menu, it closes again. That's good to know if you open the menu by accident.

The tabbed browsing feature in Safari can be extremely useful, but you need to take care with it. If you use all nine tabs and then tap a link that opens in a new tab, you lose the contents of one of your previous tabs. That doesn't matter so much if you're just reading a website, but if you'd started to write something in Facebook or were midway through ordering a new fridge freezer, it might be annoying. This won't be a problem if you are using iCloud Tabs (see 'Deleting bookmarks' later in this chapter), as pages you visit and any tabs you create are automatically saved.

If a page is taking a long time to download, you can try reading another page in a different tab while you wait.

Managing bookmarks, history and web clips

If you find a website you want to remember, you can bookmark it. Bookmarking stores a link to the website in your browser so you can easily find it again.

The idea of bookmarking websites isn't limited to the iPad. You may well have come across it on your computer. If so, you can synchronise your computer's bookmarks with your iPad (see Chapter 3). As long as you have iCloud active on your iPad and your Windows or Mac computer, your bookmarks automatically appear on all your devices. Windows computer users will need to download the iCloud applet from **www.apple.com/icloud/setup/pc.html**. At present, only Mac computers additionally support iCloud Tab synching. You need to have the latest iPad software (iOS6), though, and be using the same Apple ID across your devices. See Chapter 3 for details on how to update to the newest software version.

Visiting websites by using bookmarks

Your iPad comes with a few bookmarks on it already, including one that takes you to the iPad User Guide.

There are two ways you can visit a website that's in your bookmarks list. The first way is to use the address field. As you type in it, your browser checks your bookmarks to see if any of them match what you're typing. If any bookmarks do match, the iPad suggests those websites so that you can just tap a website's name to visit it. These suggestions appear automatically whenever you're using the address field. Start typing **bbc.co.uk**, for example, and you'll see any pages on the BBC site that you've bookmarked, which could be the news section or sites dedicated to your favourite shows.

You don't have to type an address in the address field to find a bookmark; you can also type words that are in your bookmark title. Try typing **user** in the address field, and the iPad User Guide link appears, even though its actual address doesn't include the word *user*.

The other way you can visit websites you've bookmarked is to browse your book-marks. If you don't have a particular website in mind and just fancy meandering through some of your favourite websites, this approach is the better one.

To open your bookmarks, tap the Bookmarks button, which has an icon like a book (see Figure 9.8). A menu opens, showing your bookmarks, including any that you've synchronised from your desktop computer. Each bookmark has a book icon beside it. Tap the name or the icon to visit the website.

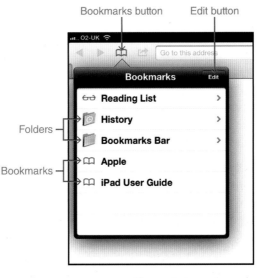

Figure 9.8

If you have lots of bookmarks, you can scroll the menu by dragging it.

As you can see in Figure 9.8, Safari already has two folders and another special bookmark set up on it:

● **Reading List:** This folder is used to keep note of web pages you want to read later. If you just want to see the pages you haven't read yet, tap the folder name and then tap Unread at the top of the folder's contents. Note that when you tap a page from your Reading List, the iPad assumes that you've read it and removes it from the Unread list. To find it again, tap the Reading List glasses icon and then tap the All option to view everything you've saved to this menu.

- **History:** This folder stores links to the websites you've visited recently. You can't add your own bookmarks to this folder, but you can tap the History folder and then tap Clear History to delete this record. Your web browsing history is used to suggest websites when you're typing in the address field, which makes it easier to visit sites you've been to before.

- **Bookmarks Bar:** The bookmarks bar appears below the address field when you're using it. This bar is a good place to keep your favourite websites. To visit one of them, tap the address field to make the bookmarks bar appear and then tap the name of the bookmark. Your bookmarks bar will be empty at first, but we're about to show you how to add websites to it.

Adding bookmarks

Navigate in the usual way to the site you want to bookmark. To create a bookmark for the web page you're viewing, tap the Bookmark/Share button (denoted by an arrow coming out of a box). The menu that appears offers these options:

- **Add Bookmark:** Tap this option to add a bookmark. The name of a bookmark is taken from the title of the web page, so some bookmarks make more sense than others. You can change a bookmark's name to anything you like. You can use the editing controls you've seen in the Mail and Notes apps. Tap and hold to make the magnifying glass appear so you can reposition the insertion point for editing; then tap the X button in the title box to clear it. Below the bookmark name, you can see the folder it will appear in, which is usually Bookmarks. That means it will go into your bookmarks collection without being filed in a folder. If you want to put the bookmark in a folder you've created, tap the folder box and then choose which folder you want to put your new bookmark in. Note that you need to create a folder before you can add a bookmark to it. You can also add the bookmark to the bookmarks bar. When you've finished, tap Save.

- **Add to Reading List:** Reading List pages aren't suggested when you type in the address field and the iPad separates out unread content in the folder. So the Reading List is best used for keeping a temporary note about a particular article you want to read. As with bookmarks, your Reading List can be synchronised with other devices (see Chapter 3 for more on synchronising), so you can add something to your Reading List on your computer and read it on your iPad later (or vice versa). As we note earlier in this chapter, if you have iCloud enabled and also have the latest iPad software, iCloud tabs appear automatically.

- **Add to Home Screen:** If you tap this option, the web page you're viewing gets an icon on your Home screen, like the icon of an app. This icon is called a *web clip*. You'll be prompted to enter a short name to go below the icon. You have only about 10 to 15 characters, depending on how wide they are; otherwise, your iPad abbreviates the name to the first few and last few letters. Some websites provide icons designed especially for web clips, but the iPad uses a tiny picture of the web page if no icon is provided. When you tap the icon on the Home screen, Safari opens and takes you straight to that web page. We recommend that you add your favourite web pages to the Home screen. In Chapter 14, we show you how to organise and delete icons on your Home screen, including web clips.

Whatever you type in the bookmark's title, you can use to find it later by typing that text in the address bar. So feel free to add any words to the end of your bookmark titles that may make the bookmarks easier to find later.

Organising your bookmarks in folders

Are you one of those people who spends more on stationery than on bread, or are you happy to throw your paperwork into a big box and hope you never need to find a gas bill at the bottom of it? Organised types will be pleased to know that you can arrange your browser bookmarks in folders. If getting organised isn't at the top of your to-do list, feel free to skip this bit. You can always jump straight to a bookmark by typing part of its name or address in Safari's address field. Organised bookmarks are much easier to browse, though.

If you synchronise your iPad's bookmarks with those on your computer, they'll arrive on your iPad in the folders they are in on your computer.

You need to create a folder before you can add a bookmark to it. To create an additional folder, tap the Bookmark/Share button and then tap the Edit button. A new menu appears, with a New Folder button in the top-left corner (see

Figure 9.9). When you tap New Folder, you're asked to enter a title for the new folder. You have room for only a few words here, so keep the title short, and put the important words at the start.

Figure 9.9

It's possible to have folders inside folders, so below the folder title, the iPad shows you which folder your new folder will appear in. Usually, this folder is titled Bookmarks, which means that you'll see your folder as soon as you open your bookmarks. You can leave this setting alone, but if you tap it, you can pick one of your other folders to put this new folder inside.

When you've finished setting up your new folder, tap the Bookmarks button in the top-left corner of the menu, or tap Done on the keyboard. When you're in edit mode, you can change the order of your folders. Put your finger on the Arrange icon (three short lines) to the right of the folder name, and without removing your finger, move it up or down the list to change where that folder appears. The folder stays where your finger is when you lift it from the iPad. You can use the same technique to rearrange the order of your bookmarks, but you can't change the order of Apple's default bookmarks and folders.

Deleting bookmarks

You can delete all except Apple's default bookmarks or folders. When you edit a folder of bookmarks, red buttons appear beside the items you can remove (refer to Figure 9.9). Tap one of these buttons, and a red button marked Delete appears to the right of the item. Tap the Delete button to confirm, and your folder or bookmark disappears.

You can also swipe your finger left or right across a bookmark to make a Delete button appear when you're browsing your bookmarks. You don't have to tap the Edit button first if you do that, so it's a bit quicker.

> When you're creating or deleting folders or bookmarks, don't tap the Edit button until you're looking at the folder or bookmarks you want to change. If you want to delete a bookmark that's in another folder, for example, tap that folder name first to show the bookmark and then tap Edit so you can delete it.

Another helpful feature is support for iCloud Tabs. Introduced with the iPad mini and the latest version of the iPad, iOS6 software allows you to synchronise bookmarks and tabs across your Mac computer, iPhone web browser and iPad. This means that if you're looking something up on your iPad that you later want to refer to on your Mac computer, all the web pages you visited and any bookmarks you saved are automatically shown on the computer (and vice versa). You can use iCloud Tabs with your Mac only if it is running OS X Mountain Lion, though. To synchronise your tabs and bookmarks, enable iCloud in the Settings menu and check that the Safari option is active within your iCloud Settings list. When you turn on this setting, you get a message asking you to confirm whether you'd like your Safari data to be merged with iCloud (see Figure 9.10). Once iCloud tabs have been set up, Safari shows a cloud icon on its toolbar next to the Reading List icon.

Sharing website content

The web is all about sharing information, and you often come across information or pictures online that you want your friends to enjoy too. Safari has several features that make it easy to share website content.

iCloud

Account	siouxsiehattersley@gmail.com	>

Mail — ON

Contacts — OFF

Merge Safari

Your Safari data will be merged with iCloud.

Cancel　　Merge

Calend — ON

Remin — ON

Safari — ON

Notes — OFF

Find My iPad — OFF

Find My iPad allows you to locate this iPad on a map and remotely lock or erase it.

Only your main account can use Photo Stream, Documents & Data, and Backup.

Figure 9.10

Firstly, you can copy text or a mixture of text and images from a web page by using one of the techniques you use in Notes or Mail. Tap and hold your finger on text near the content you want to copy, and the magnifying glass appears. When you lift your finger, you can select the area you want to copy by moving the grab points (refer to Chapter 4). When you tap Copy, the text and images and their layout are kept in the iPad's memory. Then you can go into your Mail app or other compatible apps and use Paste to put the content in a new message or other document. For this technique to work, it's important that you tap and hold ordinary text, not a link or image; otherwise, a menu appears instead of the magnifying glass.

Sometimes you can select a whole section of a web page by tapping and holding that section.

If you want only to copy a picture, tap and hold it. You'll be given the option to copy the picture so that you can paste it into an email or other document or save it. If you save the picture, it's stored with all your other photos on your iPad. In Chapter 13, you see how to use the Photos app to view the pictures on your iPad.

Now that you know how to save photos from websites on your iPad, why not find a great image online and use the Settings app to make it your iPad wallpaper? Choose Brightness & Wallpaper, and select the photo you saved from the web from your Camera Roll.

In addition to the Bookmarks, Copy and Reading List options we've already mentioned, you see six options when you tap the Bookmark/Share icon in Safari:

- **Mail:** Tap this option, and an email box opens, with a new email already started. In the body of the email is a link to the current web page, and the subject line is the web page's title. When you send a link, the person to whom you send it can tap the link to go straight to the website you want him to see. The link may not mean much to him without some context, however, so it's worth writing a few words to explain what's on the website and why you're sending it to him. You can send an email in this way without leaving the Safari app, so you can carry on browsing where you left off after sending your message.

- **Message:** Tap this option to send a friend an iMessage containing a link to the page or image. This option is faster than writing an email, as it's only text-message length.

- **Facebook:** Facebook is a social network on which you can post messages and web links, share whole albums of photos, play online games and let friends know what music you're currently listening to. The Facebook app is preinstalled on the latest iPad models (or can be downloaded for free). When you pull down on the Notifications bar, you'll see a 'Tap to post' option in which you can compose a new status update to share on Facebook.

- **Tweet:** Twitter is a social networking site that enables you to share short messages with friends and strangers online. If you're a Twitter user, you can enter your Twitter account in the Settings app and then use it to post messages and photos from within the Camera, Photos, Maps, Safari and YouTube apps. Each message on Twitter is called a *tweet*. When you tap the Bookmark/Share button and then tap Tweet, a box opens, where you enter a message to go with your web page link. When you tap the Send button, your message is posted on Twitter.

- **Add to Home Screen:** Ideal for frequently visited websites, this option adds a permanent link to the site so you don't need to enter its web address whenever you want to visit it. In Figure 9.11, we've added the BBC Good Food website so we can easily access its recipe library.

- **Print**: If you have an iPad-compatible printer, you can tap this option to print the page. This option feels like the odd one out in this menu to us, because the others are all about keeping and sharing links to the web page. But if you imagine that you're printing for a friend, it's easy to remember where to find the Print button.

Figure 9.11

💡 You can look up words and phrases in websites by using the built-in dictionary. This feature works the same as in Notes. See Chapter 4 for a refresher.

Using Reader to make it easier to read pages

Some websites are packed with adverts and have designs that clash so horribly, it's hard to concentrate on the content. The Reader feature in Safari attempts to streamline a web page so that you see only the article you want to read, without any of the adverts or other clutter. If you're reading an article that's split across multiple web pages, Reader can also collect the whole article for you so you don't have to keep following links to the next page. It does sometimes filter out useful content such as videos and comments, though, and it's not available for every web page.

To use this feature, when available, tap the Reader button in the address field (see Figure 9.12). A plain box opens, displaying the stripped-down page content. You can drag the content up and down and tap links in the usual way. Tap outside the box to close the Reader view.

Reader button

Figure 9.12

Using Private Browsing mode

Don't spoil the surprise! If you've used the iPad to book a romantic getaway or order flowers, you may be rumbled if your partner sees the websites you've visited. This could easily happen because the history of websites you've visited is used to suggest websites when someone types in the address field.

To remove the trail of websites you've visited, go into your Settings app, and tap Safari. Then you can clear history (a list of visited websites), cookies (small files websites use to recognise you when you return) and data (files from websites stored on your iPad to speed return visits). You can also clear the history by tapping the Bookmarks icon in Safari and then tapping the History folder.

To stop your iPad keeping any records of your visits, go into the Settings app, tap Safari and then switch on Private Browsing. When you're in Private Browsing mode, the top of the browser changes from a silvery-grey to a charcoal colour. You can turn off Private Browsing in the Settings app when you've finished shopping.

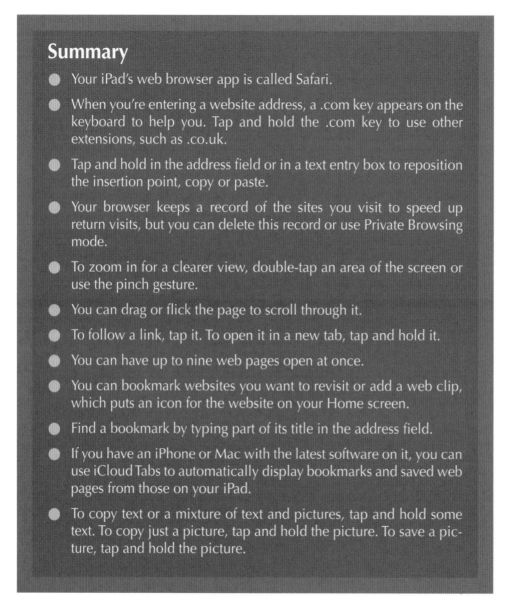

Summary

- Your iPad's web browser app is called Safari.

- When you're entering a website address, a .com key appears on the keyboard to help you. Tap and hold the .com key to use other extensions, such as .co.uk.

- Tap and hold in the address field or in a text entry box to reposition the insertion point, copy or paste.

- Your browser keeps a record of the sites you visit to speed up return visits, but you can delete this record or use Private Browsing mode.

- To zoom in for a clearer view, double-tap an area of the screen or use the pinch gesture.

- You can drag or flick the page to scroll through it.

- To follow a link, tap it. To open it in a new tab, tap and hold it.

- You can have up to nine web pages open at once.

- You can bookmark websites you want to revisit or add a web clip, which puts an icon for the website on your Home screen.

- Find a bookmark by typing part of its title in the address field.

- If you have an iPhone or Mac with the latest software on it, you can use iCloud Tabs to automatically display bookmarks and saved web pages from those on your iPad.

- To copy text or a mixture of text and pictures, tap and hold some text. To copy just a picture, tap and hold the picture. To save a picture, tap and hold the picture.

- You can use the Reading List to keep track of articles you'd like to read later.

- The Reader feature strips a web page down to its basics, but it can leave out important content and isn't always available.

Brain training

How will you fare in the traditional end-of-chapter quiz?

1. To put a link to your favourite website on your Home screen, you:

(a) Add a bookmark to the Bookmarks Bar folder.

(b) Create a web clip.

(c) Add a bookmark to the website.

(d) Tap and hold the address bar.

2. If you want to strip the advertising from a web page so you can read it more easily:

(a) Add the page to your Reading List.

(b) Tap and hold a link.

(c) Tap the Reader button in the address bar.

(d) Tap the X on the page's tab.

3. When you finish typing information in one box on a form and want to go to the next, you should:

(a) Tap the Go key on the keyboard.

(b) Tap the Return key on the keyboard.

(c) Tap the next form box on the web page.

(d) Drag the web page.

4. To view a web page in a new tab, you can:

(a) Tap the address field.

(b) Tap the small tab with a plus sign on it.

(c) Tap and hold a link.

(d) Double-tap a link.

5. To enlarge the website content, you can:

(a) Put two fingers on the iPad and move them closer together.

(b) Put two fingers on the iPad and move them farther apart.

(c) Double-tap an area of text.

(d) Put your finger on the page and move it up the screen.

Answers

Q1 – b

Q4 – b and c

Q2 – c

Q5 – b and c

Q3 – c

PART III
Music, Videos and Photos

I've downloaded our entire music collection from iTunes. Now nobody will be able to see what appalling taste we have.

Adding music and video

10

Equipment needed: An iPad with an Internet connection. Your credit card or an iTunes gift card, if you plan to download from the iTunes Store. Payments can also be made using a PayPal account. A computer with a CD drive, if you want to copy CDs.

Skills needed: Experience using apps and gestures. Skills using the web browser (see Chapter 9) are particularly valuable.

One of Apple's shrewdest moves was creating the iTunes Store, which sells audio and video content, and makes certain programmes available for free download. The iTunes Store was launched in 2003 for iPod music players and has made Apple one of the most powerful companies in the entertainment business. What it means for you is that you can find Hollywood blockbusters, TV shows, recent or classic albums and educational content from the comfort of your sofa.

The programmes, films and music you select are copied straight to your iPad from the Internet, through a process called *downloading*. When your music or programmes have been downloaded, they're kept on the iPad so you can play them whenever you like. The process of downloading is fast and convenient. You can discover a new album, hear snippets of the tracks, buy your favourite songs, download them and start listening to them, all within a few minutes.

A fantastic catalogue is on offer, including many classic films, TV series and songs that you might have thought you'd never experience again. You'll even find vintage episodes of *Doctor Who* and rare tracks by some of your favourite bands.

There's a wealth of music in the iTunes Store, from top acts of the 1950s and 1960s to today's chart-toppers. If you've got a favourite record you've lost or a golden oldie you'd like to hear again, the iTunes Store might help. iTunes has an equivalent version for use on your Windows or Mac computer, so you could simply use it as your main music manager.

There's some potential for confusion: Apple uses the name *iTunes* to refer both to the software you run on your computer to manage your iPad and the store where you buy content for it.

In this chapter, we show you how you can use the iTunes Store to download audio and video content for your iPad. Even if you don't want to buy music or films, it's worth investigating the iTunes Store, as there's plenty of free content there too.

What about your CD collection? The good news is that you can use the iTunes software on your computer to copy your music CDs to your iPad. We show you how to do that later in this chapter in the section 'Adding CDs to your iPad using your computer'.

More than 10 billion songs have been downloaded from the iTunes Store since it launched. The 10 billionth was "Guess Things Happen That Way," by Johnny Cash, downloaded on 24 February 2010.

Browsing the iTunes Store

To get started, tap the iTunes icon on your iPad's Home screen. This icon's name is short for *iTunes Store,* so when it opens, you see something that looks a bit like a shopping website. Figure 10.1 shows you what the iTunes Store's home page looks like.

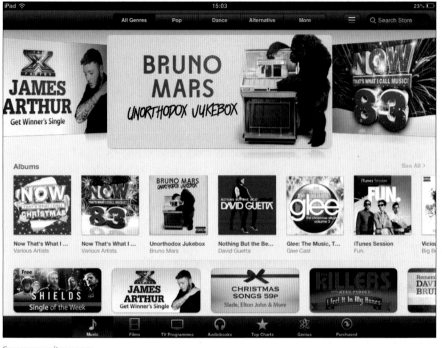

Source: www.itunes.com

Figure 10.1

You navigate the store similar to the way you navigate a website (see Chapter 9). You can drag the page up to see content that doesn't fit on the screen and then tap the status bar to jump back to the top of the page. When you see a product or promotion you want to find out more about, tap it to open it the way you do with a link on a web page. At the bottom of the scrolling page are buttons that let you manage your account, redeem gift vouchers or seek support. Across the top of the screen are buttons that let you select different genres (such as Rock, Pop or Comedy) and see the best-selling content (tap Top Charts).

Where you see a group of offers, such as those in the bottom half of Figure 10.1, you can often swipe them horizontally to see more. This tip also applies to the App Store (see Chapter 14) and the iBookstore (see Chapter 16).

165

Along the bottom of the screen, at all times, is a series of buttons that you use to navigate the different types of content in the iTunes Store:

● **Music:** Music includes music videos and ringtones. Free downloads are made available from time to time, including a free single of the week, but you have to pay for nearly all the content in this section. You can find ringtones (called Tones) by tapping Genres in the top-left corner.

● **Films:** You can buy a film or rent it, which costs less. Buying a film means you can watch it as often as you like, for as long as you like. Rented films expire 48 hours after you start watching them (24 hours in the United States) and then are automatically deleted from your iPad. If you don't get around to watching a film you've rented, it's deleted after 30 days anyway.

● **TV Programmes:** The programmes on offer include U.S. and UK dramas, comedies and children's shows. As with music, free downloads are available occasionally, but nearly all the content is for sale.

● **Audiobooks:** Audiobooks are professionally recorded readings of books and radio programmes. You have to pay for them.

● **Top Charts:** Tapping this item brings up lists of the most popular songs, albums, TV programmes, music videos and films. Each category is presented as a top 100, with a search option always available in the top-right corner and a genre-based view option in the top-left corner.

● **Genius:** The Genius feature comes into its own after you've made a few purchases. Genius tries to work out what you enjoy listening to or watching and presents suggestions to help you discover new artists and programmes.

● **Purchased:** This option enables you to download to your iPad music and TV shows that you've already bought or downloaded for free from the iTunes Store.

● **Downloads:** This option shows you the progress of content you're currently downloading to your iPad.

To search the iTunes Store, tap the search box in the top-right corner of the screen. It doesn't matter what part of the store you're in when you do this, because the search returns results from across the store.

Buying music and video from iTunes

We've all bought an album in a shop and felt cheated when we got it home because it had only two good songs on it. In the iTunes Store, you run much less risk of this happening because the store allows you to preview the music tracks first to make sure you like them. You usually can buy individual songs without having to buy the whole album, too. Buying one song is cheaper, but a whole album is often better value than cherry-picking several songs.

When you've found an album you'd like to buy (by browsing the featured products or using the search), tap its artwork to see the tracks on it. A new window opens in the middle of the screen, as you can see in Figure 10.2. You can drag this window up and down to see more information, including reviews by other customers where available.

Buy album

Stop preview   Buy track

Source: www.itunes.com

Figure 10.2

To hear a sample of a track, tap its name. You can stop the song playing again by tapping the Stop button that appears in place of its track number. If you don't hear anything, check that the iPad's volume is switched on. To close the album's window and carry on browsing the iTunes Store, tap outside the album window.

When you've found a track you want to buy, tap the price beside the track name. To buy the whole album, tap the price below the album's name (both indicated in Figure 10.2). The Price button changes to a Buy Song or Buy Album button. Tap that button, and you're prompted to log in to your iTunes account. This account is the same one you created when you set up your iPad (see Chapter 2). Usually, your credit card, PayPal account or gift certificate balance is charged, and your content is downloaded. Note that you need to enter the details of your iTunes gift card before you choose what to buy. Otherwise, Apple will simply debit the account associated with your iPad and Apple ID.

The first time you buy something, you're required to confirm your payment information. You'll be shown your account information, and you need to tap beside the words *Security Code* and enter the three-digit security number on the back of your credit card or the four-digit number on the front of an American Express card.

When you've finished confirming your details, tap Done in the top-right corner of the window. You get a last chance to back out, but when you tap Buy, your account is charged and your music starts to download.

Tap Artist Page, in the top-right corner of an album's window, to find other albums by the same artist. This option isn't shown for compilation albums.

The process of downloading TV shows and films is similar to the process of downloading music. You can search for a particular programme or browse the featured titles. When you find something you like, tap its artwork to open its window. The main difference is that for TV episodes, you tap the picture from the episode to see the preview, and for films, you tap the Preview button on the right.

For video content, you may be offered two formats: high definition (HD) and standard definition (SD). HD is the higher-quality video format and looks much sharper on the iPad's screen, but SD is acceptable and is the only format available for older TV shows. HD films take longer to download than SD files do and are usually more expensive than SD films.

To download free content, tap the Free button that appears in place of a price. Note that unlike older versions of iTunes, podcasts are no longer played through the Music app. Instead you have to use the separate Podcasts app that was introduced with iOS6. You need to download and install this app before you can access any podcasts. See Chapter 11 for more information on this subject.

Content is queued up and downloaded one item at a time. It can take several minutes for a film to download, but you can use other apps on your iPad while the downloading continues in the background. To check the progress of your downloads, tap the Downloads button at the bottom of the screen in the iTunes app.

The process of buying is quick and convenient – so much so that you can forget you're spending money. It feels very different to handing over £10 notes in a record shop, so keep an eye on how much you're spending in the iTunes Store.

For advice on playing music, audiobooks, and video on your iPad, see Chapters 11 and 12.

Using the iTunes Store on your computer

If you prefer, you can download content from the iTunes Store on your computer. Open the iTunes software on your computer, and click iTunes Store on the right. Across the top of the screen are buttons that take you to the different types of content (such as music, films and TV).

The iTunes Store on your computer has a few additional features. For one, you can now add content to a wishlist by clicking the arrow button beside its price. You can view all the items on your wishlist by clicking the arrow beside your email address in the top-right corner.

Sometimes you buy a single track and then want to hear the whole album by an artist. You can download the remainder of an album by choosing the Complete My Album option next to its iTunes Store listing. Since you've already paid for part of it, Apple discounts the purchase accordingly. Similarly, if you already bought individual episodes of a TV series, you can buy the complete series for a discounted price.

Another useful addition is that you can subscribe to podcasts so that your computer automatically downloads the latest episodes when you open iTunes. However, as noted above, you first need to install the Podcasts app. When you view a podcast's details in the iTunes Store on your computer, you can click the Free button beside an episode to download just that episode, or you can click the Subscribe button below the podcast's artwork to subscribe for free.

When you synchronise your iPad with your computer (see Chapter 3), any content you downloaded on your computer can be copied to your iPad. You can also enable content to download on your iPad automatically over Wi-Fi when you buy it on your computer (see Chapter 3).

Removing content and downloading it again

Over time, you might find that you've bought more music and video than you can fit on your iPad at the same time, especially if you're a film fan. You can change what's stored on your iPad, though. If you remove some albums or shows to make room on the iPad, you can download them again from the iTunes Store later for free. Apple recently changed the terms of its film purchases so you can download again films you bought from the iTunes Store and subsequently deleted. You can also keep a copy of purchased films on your computer and synchronise them to your iPad from there.

In the case of audio content, you remove it by using the Music app. We give you a detailed tour of this app in Chapter 11 when we show you how to use it to play your music. For now, here's how you use the Music app to delete content:

- To delete a song, tap Songs at the bottom of the screen. Find the song you want to remove and then swipe across it. Tap the Delete button that appears.

- To delete an album, tap Albums at the bottom of the screen. Tap and hold on the album you want to remove and then tap the X button that appears in the top-left corner of its artwork.

- To delete all of an artist's albums, tap Artists at the bottom of the screen. Tap and hold on the artists you want to delete and then tap the X button in the top-left corner of their artwork.

Films and TV shows take up a lot of space on your iPad, so it's a good idea to delete them from your iPad after watching them. Take care when you delete films, though: If you delete a film you've rented, it's permanently deleted, and you have to pay again to get it back.

To remove films and TV shows from your iPad, you use the Videos app. Again, we show you in Chapter 11 how to use this app for playing content. To delete a programme or series from your iPad, tap and hold its artwork and then tap the X button that appears in its top-left corner. To delete multiple programmes or series, tap the Edit button in the top-right corner when viewing their artwork and then tap the X button of those you want to remove. When you've finished, tap Done in the top-right corner. To delete an individual episode of a TV series, tap the artwork to view the list of episodes and then swipe your finger from left to right (or right to left) across the episode summary to reveal the Delete button.

To download music or videos from the store again, go into the iTunes Store app and then tap Purchased at the bottom of the screen. This option gives you access to iTunes in the Cloud, Apple's service that looks after your music and TV-show collection so you can access it on any compatible devices. The screen looks like Figure 10.3. Drag the list of artists on the left and tap one to see the content by that artist that you've already downloaded from the iTunes Store.

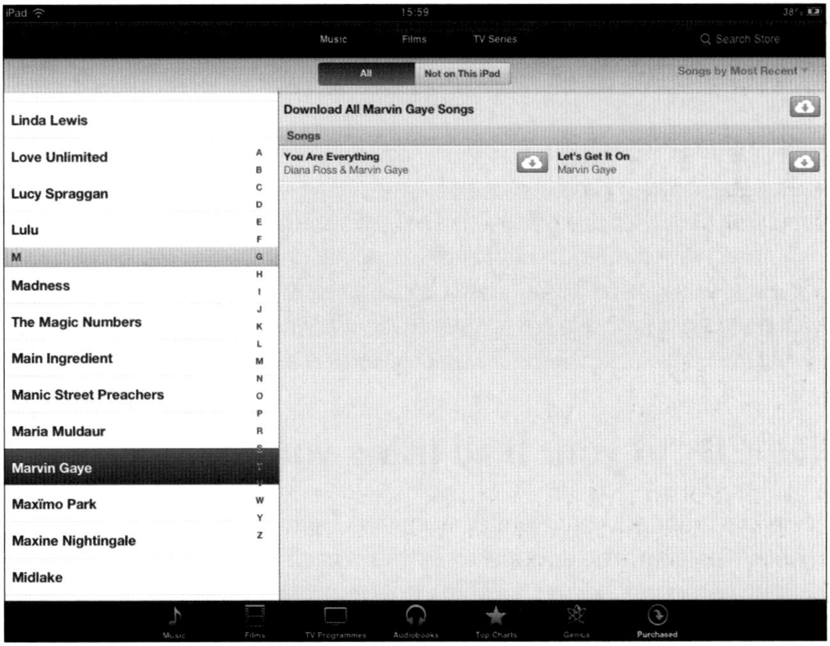

Figure 10.3

Along the right-hand edge of the artist list is an A-Z index (indicated in Figure 10.3). Tap a letter to jump to it, or run your finger down the index to scroll rapidly through the artists.

If you've bought tracks from more than one album, you can tap the Songs or Albums buttons at the top to view the music organised in albums or as a full song list. You can download a track again by tapping the button with a picture of a cloud on it. A button in the top-right corner allows you to download all the tracks by a particular artist.

By default, you see the music that you've bought or downloaded, but the tabs at the top of the screen let you view TV Series or Films instead. Tap a programme name and then tap the series to see individual episodes. Then you can download your favourite episodes or the whole series.

Note that iTunes displays all instances of content by an artist (including collaborations with others), but you may not have all of it currently stored on your iPad. The Not on This iPad button at the top of the screen lets you view items that aren't currently on your iPad. Assuming that you've an active Internet connection, you can tap an item and have it download so you can listen to it. A search box above the artist or programme list lets you quickly find what you're looking for.

Apple warns that previous purchases of music, video, apps and books may not be available to download if they've been removed from the iTunes Store since you bought them. Don't forget that you can keep a copy of everything on your computer and synchronise any content you want from there (see Chapter 3).

Adding CDs to your iPad using your computer

Most of us have already paid good money to own the music we love, so we'd rather not buy it again. The good news is that you can transfer CDs to your iPad as long as your computer has a CD/DVD drive. In December 2012, UK copyright law changed to allow you to make a single back-up copy of any CD you bought and still possess. (Most people considered it ethical to do that in any case.) Copying CDs to your computer this way is called *ripping* them.

Often it's cheaper to buy a CD and rip it by using your computer than it is to buy the same album as a download.

To add a CD to your iPad, follow these steps:

1. Start the iTunes software on your computer, and insert your music CD into the CD/DVD drive. iTunes downloads the names of songs and artists from the Internet, if possible.

2. If the download fails, or if you need to correct a piece of information, right-click a song; choose Get Info from the contextual menu; click the Info tab of the Get Info dialog; and then add or edit the song title, band name, genre and year. To change information that applies to all the tracks at the same time, press Ctrl+A (PC) or Command+A (Mac) to select them all; then right-click a track and choose Get Info from the contextual menu.

3. Untick any songs you don't want to copy.

4. Click Import CD from the list of options that appears in the top-right corner. The CD/DVD drive starts to whirr, and your CD is copied to your computer.

If your computer asks whether you want to add the CD to your iTunes library when you insert it, you can just click Yes if the album and song information is correct and you want to copy all the songs.

You can play any CDs you've copied to your computer, and any content you've downloaded from the iTunes Store by using the iTunes software on your computer as well as your iPad. Find the content you want to play by clicking the content type on the upper left (for example, music) and then using the search box if necessary in the top-right corner. You can double-click a song name to start it playing. CD-player-like controls in the top-left corner let you pause and jump forward or back a track.

⚠️ You can't copy DVDs to your iPad by using iTunes, unfortunately, because DVDs have encryption to stop them being copied. You can use third-party software, available online, to copy DVDs into iTunes, but rapidly expanding video rental and download libraries mean that it's far easier to go the rental route (and you don't have to worry about piracy laws).

When you synchronise your iPad with your computer, any CDs you've added to your computer are copied from your computer to your iPad in accordance with your synchronisation settings (see Chapter 3). If your CD doesn't get copied to your iPad, check that you've set your computer to synchronise either all music or that particular artist, album or genre. If you were using Windows Media Player or another music manager, any albums associated with them can easily be imported into iTunes.

Using iTunes Match to copy music to your iPad

iTunes Match is a subscription service provided by Apple that lets you access your iTunes music collection from the cloud. If you have a large CD collection, this service enables you to access it easily on your iPad, which means you can play the songs anywhere. It works like this: Apple analyses your music collection, including the CDs you've ripped and any music you've downloaded from rival stores to see whether Apple has the same music in its iTunes catalogue. If it does, Apple makes a note that you've bought this music and lets you download it on your iPad. If the music is not in its iTunes catalogue, Apple copies your music to a storage area on the Internet. The result is that Apple will let you download any of your music on your iPad at any time, whether or not you originally bought that music from Apple.

To download the music, you need to have an Internet connection, but music that you download stays on your iPad as long as there's space, so you can play it later without having an Internet connection. An advantage of iTunes Match over some digital songs you may have downloaded or ripped to your music library is that every track is offered at a very high quality audio setting of 256Kbps (kilobits per second). So if you had a rather poor recording of a favourite track in the past, listening to the iTunes Match version could be a revelation.

> ⚠ iTunes Match is available only if you have fewer than 25,000 songs that weren't bought from iTunes, so it's not for the most ardent music fans with large CD collections!

To use iTunes Match, go to the iTunes software on your computer, and click iTunes Match at the top. Click the Subscribe button (the current price is £21.99 per year) and log in with your Apple ID to make the purchase. The process of analysing your collection and uploading unknown tracks may take a while; for a collection of about 3,000 songs, the whole process can take about six hours. You can continue to use your computer and iTunes while this is going on, though.

You need to turn on iTunes Match on your iPad, so go into the Settings app, tap Music on the left and then turn on iTunes Match. You can't use iTunes Match together with music synchronised from your computer (nor do you need to), so any existing music will be removed.

When you go into the Music app, you see your entire collection, available to play. When you play a song, it's downloaded to your iPad. You can also download songs without playing them by tapping the buttons with clouds on them. If a download button doesn't appear next to a particular song, it's already stored on your iPad.

When you run out of room on your iPad, iTunes Match automatically removes some songs that you haven't played for a while to make room. Those songs remain stored in iTunes Match, however, so you can always download them again later.

Now that you know how to add music and video to your iPad, turn to Chapter 11, where we show you how you can play it.

One popular way of storing music on a computer is in a file called an MP3. Your iPad can play any song in that format. You can buy MP3 music downloads from Amazon and other music download services using your computer. When you search in Amazon for a particular album or artist, you're often given the choice to download an MP3 album instead of buying a CD. Amazon provides some free software that copies the MP3s you buy to your iTunes software for you automatically. You can't buy music downloads from Amazon on your iPad. Instead, shop on your computer, and you can copy your purchases to your iPad by synchronising with your computer or by using iTunes Match. Amazon often has a different product range and pricing structure to the iTunes Store, so it's worth shopping around.

Summary

- You can download music and video content from the iTunes Store, either on your iPad or by using your computer. The iTunes Store also offers free lectures and podcasts, as we learn in the next chapter.

- You have to pay for most content; the single of the week is free.

- You navigate the iTunes Store similarly to the way you navigate a website.

- You can buy individual songs or TV episodes, or a whole album or TV series.

- For a brief sample before you buy on your iPad, tap the name of the music track, the picture of the TV show or the Preview button for a film.

- High-definition (HD) films and TV programmes are better quality than their standard-definition (SD) counterparts, but older films and programmes are available only in SD.

- HD content takes up much more space on your iPad than SD content does, and because the file itself is much larger, it takes longer to download.

- You can delete music and TV shows you've bought from iTunes from your iPad to free up space and then download them again later when you want to listen to them.

- In the latest version of the iPad software (iOS6), podcasts are separated out from iTunes, so you need to install and launch the new Podcasts app to find them.

- You can copy your music CDs to your computer by using the iTunes software on it. Then you can copy the music to your iPad from your computer when you synchronise your iPad with your computer.

- The iTunes Match service analyses your music collection on your computer and enables you to download any music you own on your iPad any time you have an Internet connection.

Brain training

We hope that your iPad is now packed full of great videos and music you can enjoy. Use this quick quiz to check whether you've mastered the art of adding music and video to your iPad.

1. You can buy content for your iPad by using:

(a) The Music app on your iPad

(b) The iTunes app on your iPad

(c) The iTunes software on your computer

(d) The App Store app on your iPad

2. To be able to watch a Hollywood film on your iPad whenever you like and as often as you like, you can:

(a) Rip a DVD using iTunes.

(b) Buy a film in the iTunes Store.

(c) Rent a film in the iTunes Store.

(d) Download in high definition.

3. To play the CDs you've ripped to your computer on your iPad, you can:

(a) Synchronise your iPad with your computer.

(b) Go into the iTunes Store app and tap Purchased.

(c) Subscribe to iTunes Match.

(d) Tap and hold an album's artwork.

4. If you tap the price beside a song in the iTunes app, the app:

(a) Starts a preview of that song

(b) Starts the buying process for that album

(c) Starts the buying process for that song

(d) Downloads that album to your computer

5. If you tap the picture beside a TV episode in the iTunes app, the app:

(a) Enlarges the picture

(b) Shows you the chapters in that episode

(c) Starts the buying process for that episode

(d) Plays a preview of the episode

Answers

Q1 – b and c   **Q2** – b   **Q3** – a and c

Q4 – c   **Q5** – d

Playing music and audiobooks

11

Equipment needed: An iPad with audio and/or video content loaded onto it (see Chapter 10) or an Internet connection for listening to online radio. Earphones or speakers, if you'd like to use them.

Skills needed: Good command of gestures, including tapping and dragging.

The iPad enables you to take your favourite music and videos with you wherever you go, and gives you a number of interesting new ways to enjoy your music collection. If there is one track in the middle of your favourite album that really niggles you, or if you've always wanted a jukebox that plays your favourite songs in a random order, the playlists feature can help.

The iPad's high-quality screen is ideal for watching films, whether these are full-length movies you've bought or rented or short films published on the Internet. The iPad mini's screen doesn't offer quite the exceptional image quality that the standard-size iPad does, and of course it's a little smaller. Nonetheless, you should find it comfortable for watching video, too.

In this chapter, we show you how to play music and listen to podcasts on your iPad. In the next chapter, we look at video viewing options. We assume that you've successfully added music or video to your iPad by downloading it from the iTunes Store or by ripping music from your CDs. Both of these options are covered in

Chapter 10, so head there for a refresher, if necessary. We pay another visit to the iTunes Store when we go in search of audiobooks. We also look at ways of enjoying video and podcasts on your iPad that don't involve an iTunes Store purchase.

Playing audio content on your iPad

The app used to play music is called simply Music, and you can find it on the Dock at the bottom of your Home screen. Tap it to start.

You can choose whether you want to listen to your music by using earphones (which you need to buy separately). There are also speakers designed specifically for amplifying your iPad. Bluetooth speakers are ideal as they connect wirelessly to your iPad. Speaker docks are less flexible. See the appendix for other caveats to consider. If you have earphones, plug them into the round hole on the back of your iPad. It's in the top-left corner when the Home button is at the bottom. The iPad's built-in speaker is quite loud, so you may want to have your fingers at the ready to adjust the volume. Buttons that adjust the volume are on the right side of the iPad, towards the top. Keeping the Home button on your right, swivel the iPad around to landscape view whenever you can watch a video, and the volume buttons will be on the top left. There are also onscreen volume controls, as you see shortly.

Browsing and playing your music

The Music app gives you several ways to browse through your music collection. By default, you see your content sorted by Songs, but you can tap the buttons at the bottom of the screen (see Figure 11.1) to see your music organised by Artists, Albums or Playlists. The numbers in the right column of each track (such as 4:31 and 2:30 in Figure 11.1) are the length of the track in minutes and seconds.

If you tap the More button, a menu opens so you can choose to view your music by genres or composers. You can also specify whether the music is sorted by its title or by the artist name. Composers view is particularly useful if you're a classical music fan, but most rock and pop-music fans will rarely stray from Songs, Artists and Albums views. To see your list of songs again, tap the Songs button at the bottom of the screen.

Figure 11.1

You can drag the song list up and down, or use the search box in the bottom-right corner to find a particular track, album or artist. When you've found something you want to play, just tap the song name, and it starts to play. A speaker appears next to that track in the song list, and its artist, track name and album name are shown at the top centre of the screen. Your music will continue to play even if you put the iPad into sleep mode, or if you press the Home button and go into another app. If you want to stop it playing again, go back into the Music app, and tap the Pause/Play button.

At the top of the screen are various playback controls, as indicated in Figure 11.1. In the top-right corner is a volume slider. Drag the circle to the left to turn the volume down or to the right to turn it up. You can also press the Home button twice quickly and then swipe from left to right at the bottom of the screen to reveal the volume controls when you're not using the Music app.

If you can't hear anything, check the volume control. It's easy to accidentally hit Mute or turn down the volume when you thought the switch did something else entirely. We've all spent time shaking and tuning radios that just needed their volume nudged up.

In the top-left corner are playback controls that are similar to those you may have seen marked on a CD player. The central button is used to start or pause playing. Tap the button to the left of it (indicated as the Back button in Figure 11.1) once to restart playing the current track from the beginning or twice to go to the previous track. The button to the right of the Pause/Play button (the Forward button in Figure 11.1) skips to the next track.

You can also tap and hold these two buttons to fast-forward or rewind through a track, but it's easier to use the playback controller to the right. Drag this controller left or right to go to any position in the song. The bar shows the relative progress through the song rather than denoting a specific amount of time that has elapsed.

Have a go at playing a few tracks to familiarise yourself with how the Music app works and how to skip backward and forward through portions of a song.

Tap the Artists button at the bottom to see your music alphabetically sorted by artist, with details of how many songs and albums you have by each artist. Because the iPad can't tell the difference between the name of a person and the name of a band, it doesn't sort artists by surname, as you might expect. Instead, it sorts everything from the first letter of the first word, which means that Paul McCartney comes after Frank Zappa. This can throw you a bit at first, but it makes a lot more sense than hunting for Pink Floyd under F or having the Rolling Stones under S. An exception to this sorting method is that iTunes ignores the word *The,* so you will still find The Beatles under B. If you tap the name of an artist, you can see which of that artist's tracks and albums you have on your iPad. Tap any one of these to play it.

Albums view is the most attractive (see Figure 11.2), showing the artwork for all your albums arranged in rows. As with Songs and Artists views, you can drag up and down to see more. When you tap an album, a large central panel opens to show you the tracks on it, and you can tap a track name to start that song playing. Note that if you ripped the CD on your computer, the album artwork may not have been included; iTunes doesn't recognise every compilation album and may not display the album art for many such imports. If you go into the iTunes app and choose Get Album Artwork in the Advanced menu, however, iTunes tries to find the missing image.

Figure 11.2

Mac users will find the same tool in File, Library, Get Album Artwork. Be warned: ask iTunes to find one album cover and it will search for missing images for your whole music collection – a potentially lengthy process.

The different views aren't purely cosmetic; when one song finishes, they also decide what song will play next. If you choose Songs view, the next song will be the next song alphabetically according to the song title, no matter who the artist is, even if you've sorted the songs by artist. In Albums and Artists views, it's the next song on the same album. If you've used the search box in the bottom-right corner, the next song to play will be the next one in the list of search results.

Looping and shuffling your music

When a song is playing, the iPad will behave in either of two ways: It will have the song's artwork filling its screen or show a small version of the artwork beside the Forward button so you can continue browsing your music on screen. If you tap the small Artwork icon (see Figure 11.3), you can make it fill the screen.

Album artwork © Tom Hingley

Figure 11.3

When the artwork is filling the screen (Artwork view), you can tap it to reveal the standard playback controls. There are some new controls at the bottom (indicated in Figure 11.3):

● **Show Songs on This Album:** Tap the list view button in the bottom-right corner to see all the songs on the same album as the song that's playing. In this view, you can also rate your music, giving it one to five stars by tapping one of the five dots below the playhead control.

● **Close Artwork View:** Tap this button to go back to Songs, Artists, Albums, Genres or Composers view.

In previous incarnations of Apple's iTunes software, podcasts were part of the mix; they are now handled by a separate app. In iOS6 (the iPad software that Apple introduced in September 2012, which comes preinstalled on the iPad mini and the latest iPad), Apple also changed how iTunes U content is played. iTunes U is an excellent source of lectures and other learning materials. We thoroughly recommend exploring what it has to offer.

Previously shown and played through the Music app, podcasts and iTunes U (categorised as podcasts, too) now have dedicated apps through which you can play them. You can search for iTunes U lectures and courses in the iTunes Store, but the iPad will prompt you to install the dedicated app before you can download anything. Both apps are made by Apple and are free. Tap the link to download and install the set of five apps Apple recommends (see Figure 11.6). To use the Podcasts or iTunes U app to play audio content, tap Open. Each app has its own library for you to browse. Tap the Catalogue button in the top-left corner of the iTunes U library to see what's available to download. You can choose a single lecture or subscribe to a series.

Figure 11.6

If you downloaded podcasts or iTunes U lectures in the past, when you update your iPad to iOS6 you need to install the respective free app (Podcasts or iTunes U) to access those titles again. You won't need to pay for your podcasts again, though. (iTunes U lectures are free, anyway.)

Summary

- The Music app is used to play audio content on your iPad.

- You can browse and play your music by Songs, Artists, Albums, Genres or Composers.

- Shuffle plays an album, playlist or other music selection in random order.

- You can loop a list of songs or an individual song so that it plays over and over again.

- You can create playlists on your iPad or on your computer.

- Audiobooks are ideal if you don't have perfect eyesight or if you want something to listen to in the car. Books are often read aloud by the author or a well-known celebrity.

- The Podcasts app is used to play audio recordings. These recordings are usually free and can be downloaded from the iTunes Store.

- iTunes U is an area of the iTunes Store containing free lectures and learning materials. You can listen to a single lecture or follow a course. iTunes U has its own app through which lectures are played.

Brain training

The iPad is a fantastic entertainment device, as well as a great way to enjoy music, films and educational content. Refresh your knowledge of the key points in this chapter with a quick quiz.

1. The playhead control is used to:

(a) Move to a different point in a song

(b) Skip to the next track

(c) Show how much of an audiobook has downloaded

(d) Create a playlist

2. To listen to lectures downloaded from the iTunes Store, you use:

(a) The YouTube app

(b) The Podcasts app

(c) The iTunes app

(d) The iTunes U app

3. You tap and hold the Forward button to:

(a) Skip to the next song

(b) Skip to the next film chapter

(c) Fast-forward through a song to the guitar solo

(d) Fast-forward through a boring bit in a film

4. If you tap the 1x button when listening to an audiobook:

(a) That section repeats once.

(b) The speed of playback changes.

(c) The last 30 seconds play again.

(d) The volume resets.

5. iTunes U lectures typically cost:

(a) A fortune

(b) Nothing as long as you're a student at that university

(c) Single episodes are free, but a subscription is not.

(d) Everything on iTunes U is free.

Answers

Q1 – a and c

Q2 – d (iTunes U content now plays through a dedicated iTunes U app)

Q3 – c and d

Q4 – b

Q5 – d

Playing video

12

Equipment needed: An iPad with some video content on it (see Chapter 10) or an Internet connection for watching YouTube videos. Earphones or speakers, if you'd like to use them.

Skills needed: Good command of gestures, including tapping and dragging.

In Chapter 10, you see how to add video content to your iPad, such as vintage TV shows and Hollywood blockbusters. The chapter particularly looks at buying or renting films and TV shows via the iTunes Store. In this chapter, we cover how to play this video content and also explore options for accessing video from other sources. The most obvious option here is video footage you've taken yourself. As long as you have an iPad with cameras (any iPad except the very first model), you'll be able to shoot videos on it. We look at how to do this in Chapter 13.

Watching videos on your iPad

If you have the latest iPad or the iPad mini (or have updated to iOS6), you should find two apps for playing video:

- **Videos:** This app is used to watch videos you've bought or downloaded from iTunes (see Chapter 10). If you try to play a music video in the Music app, you hear the music but don't see the video.

- **Photos:** This app is used to watch videos you've filmed using your iPad. We cover this app in Chapter 13.

If your iPad is using a software version earlier than iOS6, you should have a third option for viewing videos: the YouTube app. (For iOS6, Apple decided not to pre-install YouTube.) YouTube enables you to watch short films from the video-sharing website **www.youtube.com**. Anyone can publish a video on YouTube, so the site features lots of homemade movies as well as content from major broadcasters. Whether or not you've downloaded any videos from the iTunes Store, you can always watch free online films from YouTube. Even if YouTube isn't pre-installed on your iPad, you can still use YouTube to watch videos; you simply need to download and install the app for free from the App Store.

Using the Videos app

You find the Videos app on your Home screen. Unless you've already down-loaded a video, when you launch the Videos app you see a message stating that the iPad has no videos and that you can download them from the iTunes Store. A tiny arrow appears to the right of this message. If you can, tap this arrow to follow the link to the video section of the iTunes Store. It's much easier, though, to press the Home button to exit the Videos app, open the iTunes Store app on your iPad and select Film or TV Programmes when you're there.

Assuming that you already have some video available to view when you start the Videos app, you can choose what type of content you want to watch (a film, TV programme, video podcast, music video or iTunes U course) by tapping the appropriate button at the top. As with audio content, it's easier to use the iTunes U courses from within the dedicated app, but you can find them here, too, for convenience.

Each show is represented by its artwork or a still image taken from it (see Figure 12.1). Drag the page up if you have more than one screenful of programmes.

To start viewing a programme, tap its artwork or still image. If you choose a TV show, you're shown all the episodes of that show on your iPad. If you've down-loaded individual episodes, you see an option to complete the series (at cost, of course; see Figure 12.2). Tap the image of a particular show to start playing it. If you tap the round Play button at the top, the iPad begins playing the entire series (or as many episodes as you have) from the start.

When you tap a movie's artwork, you see information about the film, which might include its summary and cast list. Tap the round Play button to start the film from the beginning. If you like, you can often skip ahead to a particular 'chapter' (sec-tion) of the film. Tap the Chapters button, drag the chapters list to find the one you want and then tap it to start the film from that point.

While a video is playing, you can tap the screen to show the controls. At the bottom are Back and Forward buttons, which you tap and hold to rewind or fast-forward. If the video has chapters, you can tap these buttons to skip through them as well: Tap the Back button once to start from the beginning of the current chapter, and tap it again to jump to the previous chapter. Tap the Forward button to advance to the next chapter.

Between the two Back and Forward buttons is a Play/Pause button, and below them is a slider that controls the volume. You can also use the physical volume control on the side of your iPad.

At the top is a playhead slider you can use to see how far through the programme you are and to move through the programme.

If you're watching a widescreen programme, you can double-tap the screen to change between widescreen mode (which leaves black spaces at the top and bottom of the screen) and standard mode (which chops off the sides of the image so it can fill the screen).

Figure 12.1

Figure 12.2

In the top-left corner is a Done button, which takes you back to the Videos app so you can choose what video you'd like to play next. Your iPad remembers how much of a TV programme or film you've watched. When you come back to a programme next time, it starts playing from where you left off. To play a film from the start, tap the first chapter. For a video without chapters, start it playing and then tap the Back button to go back to the start.

Watching online films from YouTube

As we've already noted, Apple no longer ships the iPad with the YouTube app already installed, but it's free to download and provides a gateway to a world of free online video content. Unlike the Videos app, the YouTube app needs an Internet connection. That's because YouTube films are stored on the Internet, and you watch them over the web (something known as *streaming*). Because the programmes aren't stored on your iPad permanently, you can happily watch YouTube until your eyes go square – unlike content you buy from the iTunes Store, a limited amount of which will fit on your iPad. It's better to watch YouTube videos over a Wi-Fi connection, though, as watching video over a 3G or 4G connection will use up your monthly data allowance very quickly indeed.

YouTube is free to watch, and it offers a wealth of comedy, tutorial and dramatic content. Full-length films and programmes are available, but most YouTube videos are just a few minutes long, making them perfect for snacking on between other programmes.

Anyone can put videos on YouTube, including members of the public. YouTube says that more video is uploaded to YouTube in one month than the three major U.S. TV networks created in 60 years. A total of 60 hours of video are uploaded to YouTube every minute, and more than 4 billion videos are viewed every day.

Start the YouTube app, and you see a selection of featured videos, which you can drag up to see more. You can tap the buttons at the bottom of the screen to explore the top-rated and most-viewed films. There's also a button you can use to quickly find any films you've marked as your favourites.

Most of the time, though, you'll want to use the search box in the top-right corner to find something to watch. Try entering some words related to your hobbies or interests, or, if you know the username of a friend who posts content on YouTube, try entering that. The screen fills with film suggestions. For each one, you see a still picture, the length (03:44, for example, means 3 minutes and 44 seconds) and how many times the video has been viewed. Tap a film, and it starts to play.

As with the Videos app, the controls fade away so you can concentrate on the film, but you can bring them back by tapping the screen. Because the film has to download from the Internet, it can take a moment or two to begin to play. The runner for the playhead control along the top of the screen fills with grey to show how much of the video has downloaded to the iPad.

Figure 12.3 shows the YouTube player in action. This short film is a trailer created to promote the first edition of this book. Most of the controls indicated in Figure 12.3 may be familiar to you from the Videos and Music apps. There are a few additional controls, however: You can add videos to your favourites so you can find them quickly later, and you can tap the Show Film Full Screen button to make the film fill the screen.

Figure 12.3

When the film finishes playing, the app takes you to the information page for the film you've been viewing (see Figure 12.4). Below the film, you can read a summary of it, provided by the person who published the film on YouTube. Across the top of the film are buttons you can use to add the video to your favourites, share the video (by email or using Twitter), or give the video a thumbs up or thumbs down.

Although anyone can share films on YouTube, other people's copyrights must be respected. Sometimes, you tap a link to a video and find a message stating that the video is no longer available because its owners have made a copyright claim. Similarly, you shouldn't find any inappropriate footage on YouTube. Should you do so, you can report it by tapping Flag to flag inappropriate content to the service's owners. To block younger family members from using YouTube, use restrictions in the Settings app (see Chapter 3) to disable YouTube.

You can watch films on YouTube as much as you want without having an account, but certain features are restricted to registered users. You need to register before you're able to tap the Like and Dislike buttons, add comments to videos and publish your own films. You can also subscribe to a channel so you automatically get to see new episodes from your favourite YouTube auteurs. To get your free account, visit **www.youtube.com** in the Safari app (see Chapter 9) or on your main computer. YouTube is owned by Google, so if you've already registered for other Google services (such as a Gmail email address), you can use that account for YouTube also.

Add to Favourites   Share   Flag inappropriate content   Show film full screen

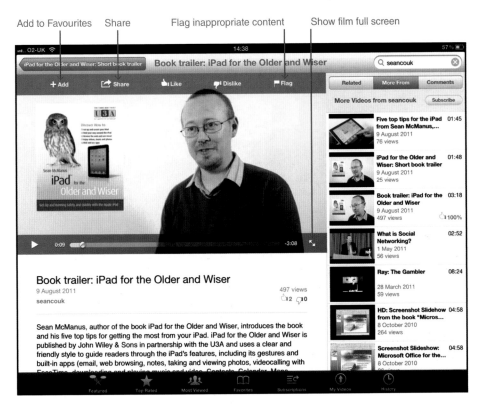

Figure 12.4

The column on the right of the information page helps you find other films to watch. If you want to see what else the same film-maker has made, tap More From at the top. If you prefer to see what others have filmed on a similar theme, tap Related.

Also on the right, the Comments button shows you comments by other viewers and gives you a chance to add your own. Any comments you enter can be read by anyone on the Internet, so take care about what information you share here.

Using catch-up TV services

A particularly popular development in the past couple of years has been the launch of catch-up TV. For UK users, the best-known example is BBC iPlayer (see Figure 12.5). This app offers a combination of the streaming Internet video offered by YouTube and the Download and View Locally option of the iTunes Store's video library. To ensure that you don't get any nasty bills, the BBC iPlayer app downloads programmes only over Wi-Fi.

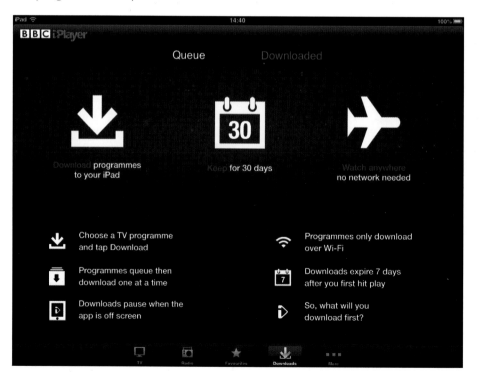

Figure 12.5

If you want to email your creations to someone, tap one of the thumbnails and then tap the Use Photo button that appears in the bottom-right corner in place of the Swap Cameras button. Tap any of the thumbnails to select them (tap again to deselect), and tap Email to send them in a new email message. Who can you surprise with a weirdly warped family portrait?

Viewing photos

Whether you take photos with your iPad or copy them from your camera or computer, the iPad is ideal for showing them off. The Photos app is designed to do exactly that, so fire it up to get started.

You can use the iPad Camera Connection Kit (sold separately) to copy photos from your digital camera to your iPad. Ensure that you choose the right connection kit. For the iPad mini and the latest (fourth-generation) iPad, you need the Lightning to SD Card Camera Connector. Older iPads take the wide, flat 30-pin connector, so choose the right connector type.

As you can see in Figure 13.3, your photos are organised in several ways. You can tap the Places button at the top to see your photos arranged on a map. This feature uses positioning data stored in photos taken on the iPad if you enable Location Services. More impressively, it picks up place names in any descriptive tags you've added to your photos in Windows or a program like iPhoto or Adobe Photoshop Elements. Tap a pin on the map to see one of the photos taken there and then tap that picture to see them all.

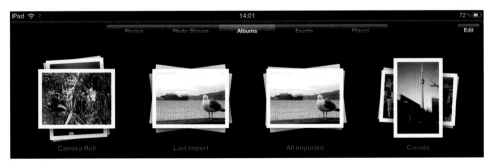

Figure 13.3

The Photo Stream feature of iCloud enables you to share your photos with other devices. Users of the latest iPad software (iOS6) can also use this option to share photos privately or publicly through shared PhotoStreams. In the PhotoStream library, tap on a photo and choose the PhotoStream option. You can then select who to share the album or photo with, as well as specifying whether the album may be viewed publicly at **www.icloud.com**.

The Events button at the top of the screen lets you see photos you've imported from your camera organised by date. This button doesn't appear for photos you've synchronised from your computer or photos you've taken with your iPad.

You can also tap Photos to see all the pictures on your iPad or Albums to see your photos organised in folders. What folders you see on your iPad depends on what pictures you have on there and how they got there, but they might include the following:

- **Camera Roll:** This folder stores images created on your iPad, including photos you've taken with it.

- **All Imported:** This folder includes all the photos you've imported from your digital camera or SD Card if you have the iPad Camera Connection Kit.

- **Last Import:** This album makes it easy to find the last batch of photos you imported from your camera by using the iPad Camera Connection Kit.

- **Folders from your computer:** If you synchronise your iPad with your computer using iTunes and include photo-syncing, there's an option to have your photos organised in the same folders they were in on your PC. In Figure 13.3, the Canada folder has been synchronised from a PC with the iTunes software on it. Your iPad might also show the albums used to organise your photos on your computer in software such as iPhoto on the Mac and Photoshop Elements in Windows.

> The Photos button at the top of the screen provides easy access to all your photos, including all those from your computer, irrespective of which folder they're in.

Tap an album, and thumbnails of all the photos in it appear. Tap a photo or use the pinch gesture to enlarge it, and it expands to fill the screen. You can use the pinch gesture to zoom (see Chapter 9) and can drag the enlarged picture around to see different parts of it. When you rotate your iPad, the picture rotates too. If you use the iPad in the same orientation as the photo (such as viewing a landscape-shaped picture with the iPad in landscape orientation), the picture enlarges to fill the screen.

Figure 13.4 shows the controls that are available to you when you're looking at a photo.

Figure 13.4

The following list describes the photo viewing controls:

● **Album browser:** See another photo in this album by touching its tiny thumbnail at the bottom of the screen. You can just roll your finger along this strip of thumbnails. You can also flick the main photo that fills the screen to the left to see the next photo or flick right to see the previous one in the album.

● **Delete photo:** This icon deletes a photo from your iPad. If you delete a photo from the Photo Stream folder, it is also deleted from other devices that use your Photo Stream, such as your computer. You can't delete photos that have been synchronised from your computer via the iTunes software. To remove them from your iPad, you have to remove them from the folder or album on your computer that's synchronised with your iPad. Then, when you next synchronise your iPad with your computer, the photos will be removed from your iPad.

● **Use photo:** Tap this icon to email the photo, send it in a message (see Chapter 8), set it as your iPad wallpaper, assign it to one of your contacts (see Chapter 5), print it or copy it so you can paste it into another app. If you use the Twitter or Facebook social networks, you can also post to those from here.

● **Back:** The button in the top-left corner takes you back to the album so you can see thumbnails for all the pictures in it. In Figure 13.4, the button reads *Camera Roll* because that's the name of the album this photo is in. You can also use a pinch (zoom out) gesture to close a photo and go back to the album. When you're looking at the album, a button in the top-left corner takes you back to see all your albums so you can choose another one.

If you admire your photo for a moment or two, the controls disappear so you can see it clearly. To bring the controls back, tap the photo. You can double-tap a point on the photo to zoom in on it and double-tap the screen again to zoom out.

Watching a slide show

A slide show is a great way to enjoy your photos. You can start it running and then hand the iPad to a friend to watch, or use the iPad's Smart Cover or Smart Case to stand up your iPad so it works like a digital photo frame.

To start a slide show featuring photos from the album you're browsing, tap the Slideshow button in the top-right corner and a menu opens.

Several special effects (called *transitions)* are used between the photos, and you can tap to choose among several effects. These effects range from the simple Dissolve, in which one photo fades into another, to the elaborate Origami, in which your photos are combined into collages that fold like pieces of paper.

If you have music on your iPad, you can choose a song to accompany your slide show by switching the Play Music switch on and then tapping Music below the switch to pick a song.

Tap Start Slideshow, and the slide show begins. You can tap the screen to stop it again.

You can change how long each slide is shown and whether photos repeat or appear in random order (shuffle). Go into the Settings app, and tap Photos on the left.

The iPad also has a Picture Frame option, which you can use without unlocking your iPad. This option works independently of slide shows in the Photos app. To change the transition, timings and photos shown, go into the Settings app, and tap Picture Frame on the left. To start the Picture Frame when your iPad is locked, instead of sliding to unlock it, tap the Picture Frame button in the bottom-right corner (which looks like a picture of a flower).

The Picture Frame feature is set to show all photos by default. Because you can use Picture Frame when the iPad is locked, anyone can use the Picture Frame feature, even if your iPad is protected with a passcode. For privacy reasons, you may prefer not to allow the use of this feature. In the Settings app, you can choose to restrict the Picture Frame so that it shows only folders of photos that you don't mind anyone seeing. You can also turn off the Picture Frame by going into the Settings app, tapping General and then tapping Passcode Lock.

Setting up and sharing Photo Streams

Photo Stream works with iOS5 and iOS6, so you may need to update your iPad in order to use this feature. (See Chapter 3 for instructions on updating your iPad software.)

To enable Photo Stream on your iPad, go into the Settings app and choose Photos & Camera. Tap My Photo Stream to send new photos you take to your other devices (such as your computer) when a Wi-Fi network is available. These photos appear on the other devices as soon as a minute or two after you take the photos.

You can also allow photos to be copied to your iPad automatically from your iPhone, iPod touch or computer. A new Photo Stream section appears in your Photos app. Tap this section to see all the photos in Photo Stream, both those taken on the iPad and those sent from other devices. (See Chapter 3 for details on setting up iCloud to back up your Photo Stream.)

Shared Photo Streams is a newly introduced option in Photos & Camera Settings. When it's active, a new option appears in the top-right corner of your iPad's photo browser when you tap the Share icon (see Figure 13.5). Tap Photo Stream, and you'll be able to send that photo or album to a friend by typing his or her name. To display the album publicly at **www.icloud.com**, tap to turn on the Public Website option, and name your album.

Figure 13.5

Organising your photos in albums

To make it easier to organise your photos for viewing, you can create albums and add photos to them. Because you can show slide shows of an album, and because you can set the Picture Frame feature (in the Settings app) to show only a particular album, creating an album is a good way to sort photos before displaying them. Any folders you create on your iPad aren't synchronised back to your computer, though. Here's how to create an album:

1. Go into the Photos app.

2. If you only have a few photos so far, the Photos app may show a full-screen one at this stage. If this happens, tap in the top-left corner to go to that photo's album; then tap in the top-left corner again to see all albums. If you instead see thumbnail images of your photos, ignore the preceding instructions.

3. Tap Albums at the top of the screen and then tap Edit in the top-right corner.

4. Tap New Album in the top-left corner.

5. Enter a name for your new album in the box that appears and then tap Save.

6. Choose the photos that will go into the album. The iPad shows you all your photos. You can tap a photo to choose it and tap again to deselect it. Your chosen photos have a blue tick on them. You can drag the page up and down as necessary to see all your photos and can tap the buttons at the top to browse photos by which album they're already in or by events.

7. Tap Done in the top-right corner.

To add photos to an album in future, go into the album, tap the Use Photo button in the top-right corner and then tap Add Photos.

There's also a Select All button at the top of the screen. To choose all but a few photos, tap the Select All button and then tap to remove the tick marks from the ones you don't want to include.

Note that when you add a photo to an album, it doesn't remove it from the album it was previously in. If you add a photo to a new album, any edits you make to it will be made to the copies of the photo in *both* albums. That's because there's really just one copy of the photo, but the albums provide different ways of finding and viewing it.

Editing your photos

When you're viewing a photo, either in the Camera Roll or in the Photos app, an Edit button appears at the top of the screen. When you tap it, four new editing options appear at the bottom of the screen:

- **Rotate:** Tap this button to rotate the image to the left by 90 degrees. If you need to rotate an image 90 degrees right, you have to tap the button three times. Tap Save in the top-right corner to keep your rotated picture.

- **Enhance:** When you tap this button, the iPad adjusts the picture's contrast, colour saturation and other qualities to improve it. You can't control these settings, but if you don't like the iPad's changes, you don't have to keep them. Tap Save in the top-right corner to keep the enhanced version, or tap Cancel in the top-left corner to discard the changes.

- **Red-Eye:** The iPad doesn't have a flash built in, so you're unlikely to have red-eye in photos you take with it. You can fix red-eye in a photo you've copied to the iPad, however, so you could take a photo with your best digital camera or your iPhone and then fix any red-eye on your iPad's larger screen. Tap the Red-Eye button and then use the pinch gesture to zoom in and tap each eye. The iPad shows you a white ring around the eye once it's applied the red-eye reduction. If the iPad can't find red eye to correct, an error message appears in the bottom-left corner. If you correct an eye and then tap it again, the red-eye is put back. When you've finished, tap the Apply button in the top-right corner, or tap Cancel in the top-left corner to abandon your changes.

- **Crop:** Cropping is used to cut edges off the photo to get rid of distracting detail or improve the composition. To use it, tap the Crop button, and a grid appears (see Figure 13.6). Touch a corner of the grid and drag it, and the size and shape of the grid change as you move its corner. When you lift your finger, the screen display adjusts to focus on the area inside the grid, which will be staying in your picture. Anything outside the grid is shaded out and will be cut off the picture when you've finished. When you've got the crop roughly right, you can adjust it to fit a particular shape, such as a perfect square or 4x6 inches. To adjust the dimensions, tap Constrain at the bottom of the screen and then tap one of the options. You can also pinch to zoom while cropping. When you've finished, tap Crop in the top-right corner to keep your changes, or tap Cancel in the top-left corner to discard them.

You can tap Undo in the top-left corner repeatedly to reverse the edits you've made, in order. Tap Revert to Original to discard all your edits.

Take care, because any edits you make will overwrite the original picture. The exceptions are photos synchronised from your computer via the iTunes software, which can't be overwritten or deleted on the iPad. If you edit one of these photos, a new version of the picture is saved in the Camera Roll.

Figure 13.6

Photos added to the Camera Roll can be copied to other devices with the Photo app, but be warned: Any edits you make on the iPad may not show up on other devices or in other software programs. At present, iPad edits aren't shown in Windows at all when photos are copied to your PC with the iCloud Photo Stream. Before spending too much time editing photos you intend to use on other devices, we recommend that you do a quick test to make sure the edits work on your other devices or programs.

Viewing and editing videos

If you've shot your own videos with the iPad, you can find those videos in your Camera Roll album in the Photos app. The videos appear as thumbnails mixed in among your still photos. When you tap one, the first frame fills the screen; to play it, just tap the Play button in the middle of the screen or in the top-left corner. Across the top of the screen is a control showing different frames from the film. Touch this control to jump to different parts of the film; play or pause by tapping the button in the top-left corner.

When you tap the Use Video button in the top-right corner (it looks the same as the Use Photo button indicated in Figure 13.4, earlier in this chapter), you can email the video or upload it to the video-sharing site YouTube so anyone can see it on the Internet.

Before sharing your videos this way, you may want to edit them. In the Photos app, tap on Camera Roll and select a video you want to edit. Start playing the video; then tap on the visual timeline at the top of the screen. Use the sliders to select start and end points, trimming off portions before the action started. Note that the editing option is only available if the video is played from the Camera Roll view. The iMovie app (£2.99 from the App Store) is recommended if you'd like to do more than make basic trims to your video footage.

Summary

- The Camera app is used to take photos on iPads with built-in cameras.

- If you allow the camera to use your location, you can view the photos you take with your iPad on a map.

- When taking photos with the iPad, tap the most important part of the picture to focus.

- You use the pinch gesture to zoom the camera.

- To take a picture, put your finger on the Take Picture button on screen, steady the camera and then lift your finger.

- You can also press the physical Volume Up button to take a photo.

- Images and videos created with the iPad go into your Camera Roll album.

- The Photo Booth app that comes with iPads that have built-in cameras enables you to take pictures with special effects applied.

- Even if you don't have an iPad with cameras, you can use your iPad to view your photos.

- The Photos app is used to view photos.

- The Photos app is also used to view videos you've created on the iPad.

- You can start a slide show of photos from the Photos app, including your choice of musical accompaniment.

- The Picture Frame feature enables your iPad to work like a digital photo frame.

- You can make basic photo edits on the iPad: rotating photos, fixing colours and red-eye, and cropping.

- If you save edits to a photo on your iPad, you overwrite the original unless the photo was synchronised from your computer via the iTunes software.

- You can organise your photos in albums to create slide shows or to make them easier to find.

- You can trim video clips you take with your iPad, but only from the Camera Roll view in the Photos app.

Brain training

Now that you're an expert on browsing photos and videos with your iPad, and on taking them yourself if you have an iPad with cameras, try a short quiz.

1. When taking a photo with the iPad, you can zoom in by:

(a) Using the pinch gesture

(b) Pressing the Volume Up button

(c) Using the front camera

(d) Tapping and holding the Take Picture button

2. The Camera Roll is:

(a) What happens when you rotate your iPad

(b) The album containing photos you've copied from your camera

(c) The album containing the photos you've taken or images you've made on your iPad

(d) A somewhat dry and crunchy sandwich

3. To see the videos you've shot on your iPad, you use:

(a) The Camera app

(b) The Videos app

(c) The Photo Booth app

(d) The Photos app

4. To zoom the view of a photo you've taken, you can:

(a) Tap the photo, and use the zoom control.

(b) Rotate the screen so the photo fills it.

(c) Use the pinch gesture to zoom in.

(d) Double-tap the photo.

5. To start the Picture Frame feature, you need to:

(a) Tap its icon on the Home screen.

(b) Tap the flower icon on the lock screen.

(c) Tap Picture Frame in the Photos app.

(d) Go into the Camera app.

Answers

Q1 – a   **Q2** – c   **Q3** – d

Q4 – b, c and d   **Q5** – b

PART IV
Using apps on your iPad

Don't the photos of you and Mark
look fantastic on this iPad? You can
see every little wrinkle!

Adding and managing apps

14

Equipment needed: An iPad with an Internet connection.

Skills needed: Experience using the iTunes Store (see Chapter 10) is helpful but not essential. Familiarity with gesture controls is helpful (see previous chapters).

So far in this book, you've discovered the many things your iPad can do, using the apps that Apple installs on your iPad for you. That's only the start of the story, though. Thousands of programmers out there are constantly coming up with new apps that allow you to use your iPad in all kinds of imaginative ways. However obscure you think your hobby is, there's bound to be an app for it among the 300,000 apps designed for the iPad.

In this chapter, we show you how to download new apps to your iPad, how to remove them and how to organise them. We also suggest some apps you may want to try out.

Lots of free apps are available, and many people spend more time using apps they've downloaded than the built-in apps. In some ways, this chapter is the most important one in this book.

Downloading apps to your iPad

All the apps you add to your iPad, including the free ones, come through the App Store, which is part of the iTunes Store. When you tap the App Store icon on your Home screen, you see a screen that looks similar to the iTunes Store for music and video (see Chapter 10).

You navigate the App Store like a web page (see Chapter 9). To see more offers, drag the screen upwards. To jump back to the top, tap the status bar. To find out more about a particular app or offer, tap its artwork. As in the music and video store, you buy and/or download an app by tapping its Price button.

At the bottom of the screen (see Figure 14.1) are buttons that take you into different parts of the App Store. It's worth checking what's new in the Featured section from time to time, because this section shows Apple's hand-picked recommendations of the best apps. The Top Charts section shows you the most popular paid and free apps, which is another nice way to uncover some gems. You can also tap the All Categories button to see apps organised by categories such as books, business, education, health and fitness, music, lifestyle, news, travel and weather.

If you go into the Genius section by tapping the button at the foot of the page, the App Store recommends new apps for you based on others you've downloaded. You first need to turn on Genius for apps and accept the terms and conditions. This feature is a great way to find new apps you'll like.

You can search for apps by using the search box in the top-right corner of the screen. The search results screen has several filters across the top, so you can refine your results to focus on a category such as games (and subcategories of games), new releases, apps with top ratings and free apps.

There are three types of apps:

● **iPhone apps:** These apps are designed for the iPhone and iPod touch, which are pocket-size devices. Their apps work fine on the iPad, too, but they use only a tiny portion of the screen. When you're using an iPhone app, you can tap the 2x button in the bottom-right corner to enlarge it to fill the screen, but that can make the content appear 'blocky'.

- **iPad apps:** These apps are designed for your iPad and make full use of the available screen space. These apps are sometimes called HD (short for *high definition*) apps, although that doesn't necessarily mean they make full use of the higher-quality screen on the third-generation iPad. The term was originally used to differentiate iPad apps from those designed for the iPhone's smaller screen.

- **Hybrid apps:** These apps are designed to work well on both the iPad and the iPhone, so you can use them with confidence on your iPad. If you have an iPhone or iPod touch, you can also use the app on those devices, and it will often have a different screen layout to accommodate the smaller screen. Hybrid apps are indicated by a tiny plus icon in the top-left corner of the Buy/Download button.

Figure 14.1

You can filter your search results to show only apps that are designed for the iPad. On the search-results page, tap Device at the top and choose iPad. The search on the iPad also prioritises apps designed for the iPad and shows them higher up the screen.

When you find an app you like the sound of, tap its icon to see its information page, which is organised like Figure 14.1. You can drag the page up to see more information, including ratings and reviews by previous customers at the bottom of the screen. You can drag the screenshot left to see more pictures, too. The description is provided by the developer, and some pages also show information about what's new in the latest version of the app. Tap More at the bottom to show the description and information about what's new in full.

Most apps work on all the iPad models, but it's worth checking the requirements before downloading, especially if you have a first-generation iPad. iOS is the name of the iPad's software, and you can check which version your iPad has by going into the Settings app, tapping General and then tapping Software Update. Chapter 3 explains how to update your iPad software if necessary. If you have the Messages and Reminders apps, your iPad has at least iOS 5.0 on it, so it should be able to use any app requiring a lower version number than that.

Some apps are free to download but enable you to buy additional content from inside the app. These 'in-app purchases' are sometimes used to buy the latest content for a newspaper app or additional characters for a game app. Where an app enables in-app purchases, you can see a chart of the best sellers on the left. It's worth looking out for this feature, because you can sometimes download a free app only to find that it's empty and you have to buy the content to fill it! The app's reviews normally warn you if this is likely to happen.

App creators sometimes release versions of their apps for free so you can try them out. Tap the Developer Page link in the top-right corner of the page to see other apps by the same developer, which might include a free version of the app you're looking at. Note that the free versions sometimes include adverts that aren't in the paid version. Others try and get you to unlock features by paying a small amount to use them. To do so, you'll need to have 'In-App Purchases' enabled. This is in the Settings app under General, Restrictions. A lot of work goes into making apps, and the developers have got to make money somehow!

To download and install an app, tap the Buy/Download button (the button below the app's logo that shows its price). The button goes green, and you just need to tap it again to confirm that you want to install the app. If the app is a paid app, your credit card will be charged. If you're not already logged in, you'll be prompted to log in by using your Apple ID, which is the same one you use for Find My iPad, music downloads and other services that Apple provides.

If you haven't previously downloaded any music, video or apps to your iPad, you need to verify your payment information before you can proceed, even if the app is free. You're shown your account information; you need to tap beside Security Code and enter the three-digit security number on the back of your credit card (or the four digits on the front of an American Express card). You can also use a PayPal account, if you have one. When you've finished confirming your details, tap Done in the top-right corner of the window.

When you've confirmed the purchase or free download, the App Store closes, and your app begins to download to your Home screen. You can watch the download-ing progress in a bar that goes across the app's icon, or you can use other apps while you wait. When the download is finished, tap your new app's icon to start using it.

You can also download apps by using the iTunes software on your computer (click on the left to go into the iTunes Store and then click App Store at the top of the screen). Any apps you download to your computer can be synchro-nised to your iPad via iTunes (see Chapter 3).

When you run an app for the first time, you may be asked whether you want to allow push notifications. These notifications enable the app to give you new infor-mation when you aren't using it, perhaps by displaying a 'new message' alert on screen or showing you how many messages you have waiting on the app's icon. You can change which apps may use notifications by going into the Settings app and tapping Notifications on the left. (See Chapter 8 for a guide to managing noti-fications on your iPad.) Since some app developers insist on using zany ringtones and alerts, you may find it expedient to adjust the notifications settings.

You may also be asked whether you want to allow the app to use your location. Some apps, such as travel apps that find restaurants near you, need this information to work properly. Other apps can be enhanced by Location Services, such as photography apps that store the location with each photo you take so you don't have to remember it. There are privacy implications, though, because an app could in theory publish your location on the Internet or use it to target advertising to you (although few apps do). We recommend that you give an app permission to use your location only if it's necessary for the app to do what you want it to. You can change which apps can use your location by going into the Settings app and tapping Location Services on the left.

Many apps have their own settings available in the Settings app. If you can't get the app to do something you want, check there.

From time to time, the makers of apps update them. The App Store icon on the Home screen shows you how many updates are available for the apps you have installed on your iPad. The number is in a red circle in the top-right corner of the App Store icon. To get your updates, go into the App Store and then tap Updates at the bottom. You can either Update All your apps, or view which apps have updates and a summary of what's changed. Click the Update button beside each app to implement it. Selectively updating makes sense as not all updates are welcome. Updates are usually free and bring new features to the app. Occasionally, app creators remove features from their apps, too, so read the version information and reviews to make sure that the update won't cut off a feature you like.

Rearranging your apps and web clips

In this section, we show you how to organise the apps on your Home screens, but the same ideas apply to web clips (web-page bookmarks that you've added to your Home screen; see Chapter 9).

You can have up to 11 screens of apps. The screen indicator at the bottom of the screen (see Figure 14.2) shows you how many screens there are (each screen is represented by a dot) and which one you're viewing (the dot coloured white). To move between screens, flick left and right. This is the same way you bring up Spotlight search (see Chapter 4).

As you've probably noticed by now, when you rotate your iPad, the apps change their position on the screen. In portrait mode, you have five rows of four apps, and in landscape mode, you have four rows of five apps. The apps are arranged in the same sequence in both modes, filling the rows from the top left, but the different lengths of the rows mean that many of your apps move to a different position onscreen when you rotate the iPad.

Figure 14.2

Using your iPad to rearrange your apps

To rearrange the icons on your iPad, go to a Home screen, and tap and hold one of the icons. All the icons start to jiggle around, which means you're in the mode for arranging icons. Touch an icon and keep your finger on it, and the icon enlarges. Without lifting your finger, move it across the screen; the app icon goes with it. Move your app to a space near another app and keep it there, and that app jumps out of the way to make room. When you release your finger, your app drops into that space.

 Be careful when moving apps around. It can be easy to press and hold an app and accidentally delete it. You should get a warning before the iPad carries out the delete action. If you're not sure what you're doing, just press the Home button to cancel the current action and stop all the apps jiggling about.

Apps aren't like folders on your desktop computer, which you can put anywhere on the screen, because you can't have empty spaces between apps. Apps are always arranged in rows starting at the top of the screen. You can't add an app to the second row until the first row is filled. If you want to drop an app into the last available space, move the icon across the screen and hold it in the empty space for a moment before lifting your finger. The app bounces into the next space, just after the last app on the screen.

The shelf at the bottom of the screen is called the *Dock*. The Dock has the same icons on every Home screen. It has room for six apps or folders, and you can move the default apps (Safari, Mail, Photos, Music) into the normal Home screen area to make room for your own apps on the Dock. When the Dock is full, if you want to add a new app to the Dock, you need to move one of the apps from there to the Home screen above to make room.

If you put an app directly on top of another app and then release your finger, a new folder containing both apps appears, as shown in Figure 14.3. All the other app icons fade into the background, so just the apps inside the folder are clearly visible. You can enter a name for the folder, rearrange the apps inside it and leave the folder again by tapping outside it. To add new apps to the folder, move them onto the folder's icon, hold for a moment and then release your finger. To remove apps from the folder or change the folder's name, tap it when you're in arrangement mode (when the apps are jiggling about and their positions can be freely swapped). Then you can edit the name box or drag the icons from the folder into the greyed-out parts of the Home screen to lift them out of the folder. To delete a folder, simply remove all the items from it. When you've finished viewing a folder, just tap outside it to go back to the Home screen. Each folder can hold up to 20 apps.

Moving apps to a different screen is a tricky manoeuvre. You need to move an icon to the right or left edge of the screen and then hold it there a moment until the next screen rolls into view. If you go too far and move off the screen, the app bounces back into place, and you have to start again.

To stop arranging icons, press the Home button. The apps stop jiggling, and you can start apps by tapping their icons in the usual way. To start an app that's inside a folder, first tap the folder to open it and then tap the app's icon.

Figure 14.3

Using iTunes to rearrange your apps

You can also use the iTunes software on your computer to organise the apps on your iPad, which makes it much easier to move apps between different screens. Connect your iPad to your computer and then click Apps at the top of the screen to view the Apps pane. A list of the apps you have on your iPad appears on the left. Tick the box beside any apps you'd like on your iPad, and untick the box beside any apps you don't want on your iPad now. You can install them again later, if you want to.

On the right, you can arrange where each app appears on each of your screens. You use the large picture of a screen to arrange icons and the smaller pictures below it to choose between screens. Click a small screen picture to choose that screen, and you see its apps in the large screen picture. If you want to change an app's position on the screen, click it, hold down the mouse button, drag the app to the space where you want it and then release the mouse button. The other icons rearrange themselves to make room. To move an app to a different screen, click its icon and drag it in a similar way to the small Home screen box below. To start a new screen, drag your icon onto the greyed-out box to the right of your choice of screens. To make a folder containing apps, use your mouse to drag one app directly on top of another app. Using iTunes is an easier way to organise your apps, but it does mean that you have to use your computer to do it.

Deleting apps and web clips

When you're in arrangement mode, all the apps and web clips you've added to your iPad have an X in the top-left corner. To delete a web clip, tap this X and then confirm that you want to delete the clip. (You can't delete web clips by using the iTunes software on your computer.)

Tap the X in the top-left corner of an app's icon, and the iPad asks you to confirm that you want to delete the app and all its data from the iPad. Don't worry if you change your mind later. You can download any removed apps again by going into the App Store and then tapping Purchased at the bottom of the screen.

Multitasking with apps on your iPad

When you quit an app by pressing the Home button, the iPad keeps a record of the state the app was in when you did that. This means you should see the same documents and information onscreen when you return to the app.

There's a quick way to switch between apps you've recently used. If you press the Home button twice quickly, the Home screen fades out, and the Multitasking bar pops up from the bottom of the screen below the Dock, showing the icons for the apps you used most recently, as you can see in Figure 14.4. Tap one of these icons to go back into it, or flick the bar to the left to see more apps. If you don't want to use one of these apps, tap in the faded-out area or press the Home button to return to the Home screen.

Figure 14.4

Not all apps will run in the background while you do something else. You can play music or have an app download while you surf the web or compose an email, for example, but you can't watch a film or play a game at the same time as anything else. Removing apps you aren't currently using from the Multitasking bar closes the app and can extend the life of your battery. Press the Home button twice to show the list; then tap and hold one of the icons. All the icons start to jiggle. Tap the minus sign in the top-left corner of an icon. The app closes and is removed from the list. To finish, tap outside the Multitasking bar or press the Home button.

Flick the Multitasking bar to the right, and you can call up brightness, volume and Music-app playback controls. There's also a button in the bottom-left corner of this panel to lock the screen orientation. Normally, the screen contents adapt to which way up you hold your iPad, but locking the screen orientation stops this behaviour.

Using multitasking gestures

You can use three gestures to switch between apps and the Home screen:

- Put four or five fingers on the screen and pinch them together to return to the Home screen from any app.

- Put four or five fingers on the screen and drag them up the screen to show the Multitasking bar so you can switch between apps quickly.

- Put four or five fingers on the screen and swipe left or right across the screen to move between apps. This enables you to hop between apps without going through the Home screen or the Multitasking bar.

Try the gesture to move between apps. It really does make multitasking on the iPad much easier.

Checking out some more apps

Part of the fun of the iPad is exploring the App Store to find the apps that are perfect for you. The apps on someone's iPad are as much an indicator of his personality as the books he owns. We mention several apps in the preceding chapters. You can download Apple's own apps Find My Friends, Podcasts, iTunes U, iBooks and Find My iPhone just by tapping a podcast listing in the iTunes Store and following the prompt that appears. We also recommend BBC iPlayer and YouTube for free video and TV viewing. The apps for social networks Twitter and Facebook are already on your iPad; just go into the Settings menu and scroll down to find and install them. If you're a keen gamer, tap the Game Center icon on your Home screen to find games that you can play against your friends over the Internet.

Here are some other apps you may want to take a look at. Many of these apps are free at the time of writing, but prices and specifications change from time to time, so check the App Store for the latest information.

- **Alltop:** This app offers a quick means of viewing the latest headlines and features across a wide range of topics. You can customise the topics and the sources that you're shown. You can easily hop between articles on different websites.

- **Cut the Rope:** This addictive puzzle game for the iPad has cute graphics. First, try the free 'lite' version, which includes a tutorial.

- **Draw Something:** Challenge friends or strangers in this game, in which you take turns drawing something or guessing what your co-player has drawn.

- **Evernote:** Write notes, save web clips and photos, share research with friends, and never forget an appointment or omit to email yourself something you need when you're out and about. Evernote securely stores everything.

- **Flipboard:** This interactive newspaper shows stories of interest to you, as well as headlines from your favourite magazines and websites. Tap a story to read the full article.

- **Fotopedia Heritage:** This app features 25,000 photographs of the UNESCO World Heritage Sites.

- **GarageBand:** Apple's simple music studio enables you to play an onscreen keyboard, drum kit, guitar and sampler.

- **Guardian Eyewitness:** Every day, a new, high-quality reportage photo is downloaded to your iPad, together with a photography tip.

- **iWork:** The iPad might not be a computer, as such, but apps allow you to view, edit and even create documents, spreadsheets and presentations on it. Apple iWork is a collection of productivity apps consisting of Pages, Numbers and Keynote.

- **Paint Sparkles:** Children we've played this with loved this app, which gives them animal pictures to colour in. You can try a free version with a limited number of pictures to colour in before deciding whether to buy the full version.

- **Waze:** You contribute to this free satellite navigation app by using it. It shows traffic jams you encounter and you can report road work and traffic accidents while you're stationery. As a bonus, it helps you track down the cheapest place to refuel.

Summary

- You can enhance your iPad with free and paid apps.

- All apps are downloaded from the App Store. Use the App Store app on your iPad or the iTunes software on your computer.

- Your iPad can run iPhone apps too, but they use only a small portion of the screen.

- To download an app on your iPad, tap its price in the App Store.

- Free updates for your apps are available in the App Store too.

- Push notifications enable apps to give you an alert even when the app isn't running.

- Tap and hold an icon on the screen to go into arrangement mode (the icons will jiggle about, indicating they can be freely moved about).

- In arrangement mode, you can rearrange your app icons or create folders for your apps.

- You can have up to 11 screens of apps.

- Apps on the Dock are always visible onscreen, whichever screen you're viewing.

- To see recently used apps, press the Home button twice quickly.

- The best app on the iPad is whatever turns out to be your favourite. Everyone's different, so explore the App Store!

Brain training

Are you app happy or appsolutely confused? Try this quick quiz to refresh the key points in this chapter.

1. The 2x button is used to:

(a) Download an app again

(b) See the apps you recently used

(c) Enlarge an iPhone app to fill the screen

(d) Cheat by making two moves in the Noughts and Crosses app

2. Pressing the Home button twice quickly:

(a) Takes you into arrangement mode

(b) Takes you to Spotlight search

(c) Shows you recently used apps

(d) Provides a quick way to lock the screen orientation

3. If you drag one app on top of another app in arrangement mode:

(a) Your iPad creates a new folder containing both apps.

(b) Other apps jump out of the way to make room for the app you're dragging.

(c) The apps swap places.

(d) The app you're dragging jumps to the next free space.

4. If you put four fingers on the screen and pinch them together:

(a) You return to the Home screen.

(b) You show the Multitasking bar.

(c) You close the Multitasking bar.

(d) You enter arrangement mode.

5. To download an app from the App Store on your iPad:

(a) Tap its artwork.

(b) Tap its name.

(c) Tap its price.

(d) Tap More.

Answers

Q1 – c	**Q2** – c and d	**Q3** – a
Q4 – a	**Q5** – c	

Finding your way with Maps

15

Equipment needed: An iPad with an Internet connection (Wi-Fi or 4G/3G).

Skills needed: Experience starting apps (see Chapter 3), using the keyboard (see Chapter 4), managing bookmarks (see Chapter 9) and using the Contacts app (see Chapter 5).

If you get lost, your trusty iPad can show you the way. It uses information about the Wi-Fi network or cellular network you're using, plus satellite positioning technology if you have a 4G/3G iPad, to work out where you are. Wi-Fi–only versions of the iPad lack the GPS functionality, so you can't use them for real-time turn-by-turn navigation. Nonetheless, the iPad is ideal for route planning and getting directions.

With iOS6, Apple replaced the established and proven Google Maps with its own Apple Maps. As a result, we've provided two separate sets of information regarding maps in this chapter. If you don't like the less detailed Apple Maps, it's perfectly possible to make use of Google Maps in any case. You can either install the iPhone version of the Google Maps app or use the web version of Google Maps (see Figure 15.1).

As we explain in Chapter 9, you can navigate to a web page – in this case, **https://maps.google.com** – and then click the Share button to the left of the address bar and choose Add to Home Screen to make that page a permanent fixture. To install the Google Maps iPhone app, tap the App Store icon on your Home screen, tap the iPhone Apps option at the top and enter **Google Maps** in the search box.

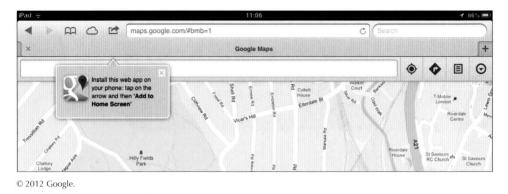

© 2012 Google.

Figure 15.1

To use the Maps app, you need to have an Internet connection.

Which iPad Maps app have I got?

To establish which version of Maps you have, look carefully at the app's icon. Both Apple Maps and Google Maps are represented on the iPad with a U.S. Highway 280 sign. The Google Maps icon has a red 'drop pin' on one of the streets, while Apple Maps has a blue arrow and a blue vertical line. There's another clue when you tap the Maps icon and launch it. If a Google logo is displayed faintly in the bottom-left corner of the screen (see Figure 15.2), you'll know that's the mapping software you've got. Conversely, tap the turn-page indicator in the bottom-right corner of Apple Maps (see Figure 15.3), and you see a tiny TomTom logo above the three rows of options.

Finding where you are with Google Maps

Google Maps enables you to view street maps, satellite photos, photos of buildings and traffic jams. Google Maps uses many ideas you've come across in previous chapters, including bookmarks, the pinch gesture (see Chapter 9) and contacts (see Chapter 5).

Tap the Maps icon on your Home screen or use Spotlight search to start the app. If you're using the web version, tap the monochrome Google Maps icon that has been added to your Home screen.

TomTom logo

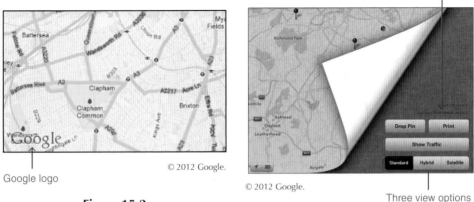

© 2012 Google.

Google logo

Figure 15.2

© 2012 Google.

Three view options

Figure 15.3

When Maps opens, it shows you where it thinks you are, using a blue pin. Around it is a blue ring that tells you how confident the iPad is in its guess: The larger the ring, the less precise the position is. Usually, it's accurate enough for you to find your way around easily. If there's no blue ring, the location should be spot-on.

If you've disabled Location Services in the Settings app to preserve battery life, you need to enable them again to enable the Maps app to find your location. To get an idea of the surrounding area, you can use a couple of gestures you've seen in other apps. You can drag the map around by putting your finger on it and moving it. New bits of the map are downloaded from the Internet as they're needed, so it may take a moment for the new map information to appear. At any time, you can jump back to your current location on the map by tapping the arrow icon, indicated in Figure 15.4. In the web version of Google Maps, your location is indicated by a blue diamond icon with a pale blue turn arrow inside.

Assuming that you have a Wi-Fi connection, Google Maps tries to work out where you are. For accuracy, enable Location Services in the Settings menu. You can use the pinch gesture to zoom in and out. You can even zoom all the way out to see where you are on a global map.

Arrow   Search box

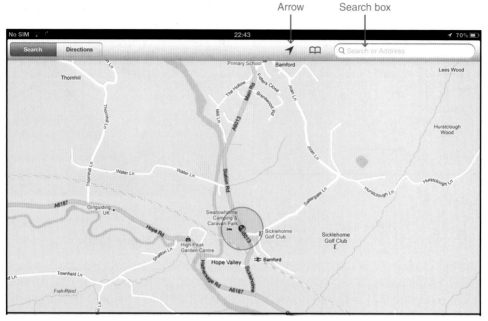

Figure 15.4

 A double tap zooms in, and you can double-tap repeatedly to keep enlarging the map until you can't zoom any further. A single tap with two fingers zooms out.

This app offers four different map types:

- **Standard:** Shows a street map
- **Satellite:** Shows satellite photographs
- **Hybrid:** Shows satellite photos with roads overlaid on top
- **Terrain:** Uses colour to indicate the height of the land

To change between views, tap the bottom-right corner of the screen to 'peel back' the map and reveal the options (see Figure 15.5). You can also switch on the Traffic option, which colour-codes some roads to show you whether the traffic is currently flowing (green), slow (yellow) or jammed (red). The traffic information works best with iPads that support cellular communications. If you have a printer that supports AirPrint, you can print maps and directions in these options too.

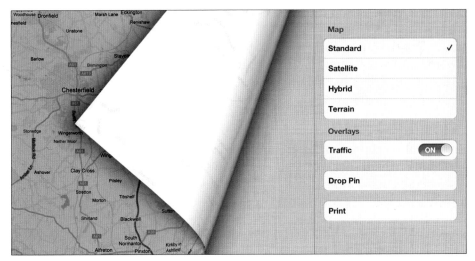

©2012 Google.

Figure 15.5

The iPad enables you to drop a pin on the map as a place marker. Just tap and hold the map, and a purple pin drops from the sky at that point. If you tap the Drop Pin button, which appears when you tap the bottom-right corner of the map, a pin is placed in the middle of the map. You can have only one dropped pin at a time, so it's best to create a bookmark for places you want to remember.

The iPad has a compass built into it, too. Tap the Arrow icon so that it shows your current location and is coloured purple, and then tap it again. To calibrate the compass, you may need to wave the iPad around in the air in a figure-of-eight pattern. (Seriously, we're not making this up!) You see instructions onscreen if you need to do this. When the compass is active, you see a North indicator in the top-right corner of the map, and you can rotate the iPad to orientate it towards North. You can use the pinch gesture to zoom, but if you tap or drag the map, the compass turns off. The Arrow icon changes its appearance when the compass is active, and you can tap it again to turn the compass off.

See if you can find a satellite photo of your house or wherever you are at the moment. Start by finding your current location, switch the view to satellite and then zoom in.

Finding where you are with Apple Maps

If you've got the latest iPad model or the iPad mini, or if you updated your iPad software to iOS6 sometime after September 2012, your default mapping app will be Apple Maps rather than Google Maps. Apple Maps has some differences from Google Maps, but the way you use it is almost exactly the same.

Start by tapping the Maps icon on your Home screen. To have Apple Maps show your current location, tap the arrow in the bottom-left corner of your screen. To find a monument or specific location, type the address or the institution's name in the search box in the top-right corner (see Figure 15.6). If it finds several matching addresses or locations, Maps presents a list with pins indicating the approximate locales. Tap one of these pins to be taken to the location. An option in the top-left corner offers directions from your current location to the place you've just identified on the map.

With the pinch-to-zoom gesture you've been using throughout this book, you should be able to zoom in closer and have a look at what's near by. Bus routes and street names are shown, as well as parks and rough indications of building shapes and sizes. The 3D mapping is much more limited than in Google Maps, so you often get more of a feel for how a place looks by using Satellite view. Tap the page curl in the bottom-right corner to reveal viewing options. Choose Satellite or Hybrid. When you've zoomed in enough, you may also notice either a 3D or a skyscraper icon in the bottom-left corner of the page. Known as Flyover view, you'll only encounter this option when viewing well-known landmarks and large cities. The skyscraper icon indicates that landmarks are visible in relief view; zoom in some more to view them. Using two fingers, you can turn the map to change the viewing angle or to see more or less a fully realised 3D landmark. Depending on the amount of detail, it may take a few seconds for the image to render properly (as we found when exploring Olympic Park in East London in this way).

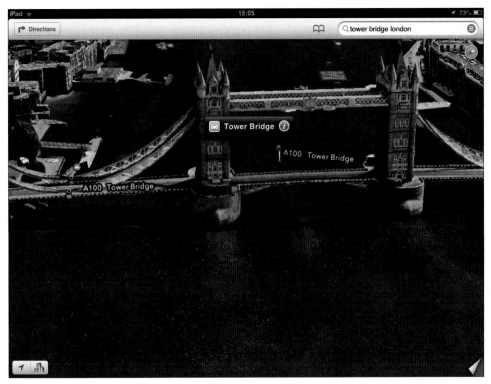

Copyright © Apple, Inc.

Figure 15.6

Getting directions to a friend's house

You can find any place in the world by typing a place or business name in the search box in the top-right corner of the screen of either Google Maps or Apple Maps. Try typing **Eiffel Tower** or **Buckingham Palace**, for example. If you enter a street name with more than one match, Maps asks you which one you want before displaying it.

You can also use the addresses in the Contacts app. To get directions to a friend's house, follow these steps:

1. Tap the Bookmarks icon.
   This icon looks the same as it does in Safari. When you tap it, a menu opens.

2. If your contacts aren't showing, tap Contacts in the bottom-right corner of the menu (see Figure 15.7).

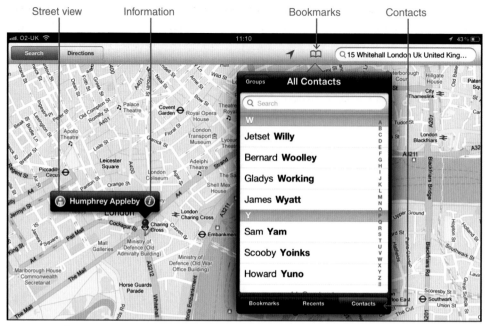

©2012 Google.

Figure 15.7

3. Use the search box at the top of the menu or scroll the alphabetically sorted list to find your friend and then tap his or her name. The map moves to your friend's house, and a red pin is dropped with his name above it, as you can see for Humphrey Appleby in Figure 15.7.

The instructions we give here are essentially the same for Google Maps and Apple Maps (or for any third-party mapping software you install and use instead). At present, Apple Maps shows a much more limited level of detail, so don't be surprised if the screenshots we've used for illustration are more informative than what you see on your iPad screen. Mapping information is stored online, so you won't need to update your Apple Maps software to see more detail as it's added. You'll simply see improvements over time.

When you've found your friend's house, you can zoom in. If there's an icon of a person next to the name above the pin, you can tap it to see a Street View of your friend's road, which we'd like to assume will look similar to the one in Figure 15.8.

This view shows you panoramic photos that have been taken of the street by one of Google's roving cars, tricycles or (more rarely) snowmobiles. Street names appear down the middle of the roads, and you can tap the arrows on them to move along the street. You can pinch to zoom or touch the screen and move your finger around to spin the view through 360 degrees or look up and down. This is a great way to check for landmarks on the route before you leave . If your friend says you need to take the lane after the post office, for example, you can do a recce on the iPad first and recognise it more easily while you're driving along at 30mph. When you've finished, tap the circle with the map in it in the bottom-right corner to go back to the map.

Apple Maps doesn't have a Street View mode, but it does offer a Satellite view of wherever you're visiting.

©2009 Google.

Figure 15.8

If you tap the information icon on the label on someone's pin, Apple Maps shows you the address and allows you to choose whether you want directions to her house or from her house. If you tap for directions to the person's house, a blue line is drawn on the map for each suggested driving route. You tap a route to select it, and the blue bar at the bottom of the screen shows the estimated distance and journey time for your chosen route. The selected route is shown with a thick blue line, but the semitransparent line used for the other routes can be hard to differentiate from motorways and rivers. One tip is that most routes merge at the start and end of the journey, so this part of the route is always be shown with a highly visible thick blue line. You can tap this shared part of the journey to switch between selecting the alternative routes.

The same method is used to locate and get directions to business premises. Type 'Hamley's' into Maps, then tap on its pin and you'll see contact and address information. In Apple Maps you'll also see how highly it's rated by customers. To view these reviews, you'll need to install the Yelp app from the App Store. Beneath the address you'll see options to get 'Directions to Here' or 'Directions from Here'. Tap on this, then select a mode of transport and confirm you're travelling from your 'current location' (indicated in blue in the Start box). Tap Route to begin travelling.

The blue bar at the bottom of the screen also has three icons for mode of travel: by car, by public transport and on foot. Tap your preferred mode of transport, and you see the estimated travel time. Tap the Start button in the blue bar to begin your directions.

Note that Apple Maps does not yet include detailed public transport information. Install another mapping service, such as Google Maps or Waze, however, and when you tap on the public transport (train icon), you will be offered a choice of them to use for this purpose.

If you're using public transport, Google Maps users can tap the clock icon in the blue bar (where available) to see the timetable. It's a good idea to double-check with the transport operator directly, because schedules are subject to change, and these changes may not be reflected in the iPad app.

You can advance through the directions in the blue bar one at a time by tapping the Next and Previous buttons, shown in Figure 15.9. If you tap the List button, the directions are shown in a list (see Figure 15.10). You can scroll this list and tap the steps to see them illustrated on the map. To hide the list, tap the List button again.

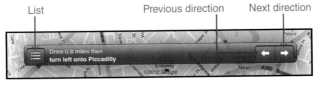

© 2012 Google.

Figure 15.9

Maps can give you directions between any two places. Tap Directions in the top-left corner first (see Figure 15.10); then enter the start and end places in the boxes in the top-right corner. Either will give you the option to choose from places you've recently searched for or dropped pins on. The button between the two boxes is used to reverse the start and end locations so you can see directions for your return trip. After you've used Maps a few times, you'll notice that previous trips you've undertaken will show up in the suggested list of destinations.

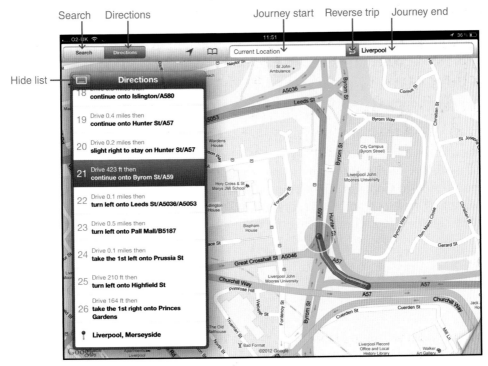

©2012 Google.

Figure 15.10

If there's a place you want to remember, tap and hold the map, and a pin drops there. Like the pins your contacts have, this pin has an Information button that you can use for plotting routes, as well as a Street View button. You can have only one dropped pin at a time, so if you want to keep a record of an address, you need to create a bookmark for it. Tap the pin's Information button and then tap Add to Bookmarks. Enter a name for the bookmark and then tap Save. You can see your bookmarks by tapping the Bookmarks button and then tapping Bookmarks in the bottom-left corner of the menu that opens.

When you've finished with your directions, you can bring back the search box again by tapping Search in the top-left corner (refer to Figure 15.10). If your journey has worked up a thirst, try searching for a café (or pub!) to see all the refreshment stops on the map.

> The Bookmarks menu can also show you Recents, the places and directions you last searched for and the locations where you have dropped pins.

Using Maps to update your address book

The Maps app can help you keep your Contacts updated. Sometimes it's quicker to find an address in Maps than to type it – especially if you're already there.

Here's how. When you're at a friend's house, connect by using 4G/3G or ask your friend if you can use his Wi-Fi. In the Maps app, tap the arrow to find your current location, tap the blue pin, tap the Information button in the label that opens and choose Add to Contacts. Then you can add the address of where you are to an existing or new contact. Don't forget to edit the house number and postcode to make sure they're accurate, using the techniques we discuss in Chapter 5.

Summary

- To use Maps on your iPad, you need to have an Internet connection.

- You may have different Maps apps on your iPad, depending on which iPad model and version of its iOS software you're using. Both apps help you find and navigate to places of interest.

- To find your location on a map, you need to have Location Services enabled.

- You can use Google Maps via your web browser if you prefer its more detailed views.

- Tap the Arrow icon to see your current location. Tap it again to turn on the compass.

- The blue pin shows you where you are on the map.

- You can drag the map and double-tap or pinch to zoom.

- To choose the map type and turn on traffic settings, tap the bottom-right corner of the map in either Apple Maps or Google Maps.

- Use the search box to search for a place by name or type of business.

- Tap and hold the map to drop a pin.

- Tap the Bookmarks button to find your bookmarks and contacts on the map.

- Tap the Information button on a pin's label to plot a route to or from that location, create a bookmark or add an address to a contact.

Brain training

Find out whether you've mastered Maps by taking this short quiz.

1. Using the Maps app, you may be able to see:

(a) A friend's house, as seen from a taxi

(b) Your house, as viewed from space

(c) The Houses of Parliament, as seen from inside

(d) The terrain of the Alps

2. A yellow line along a road on the map means:

(a) It's a dirt track.

(b) The road is closed.

(c) Traffic is moving slowly.

(d) There's been a custard spillage following a lorry accident.

3. To see what a shop's front door looks like:

(a) Drop a pin and tap the Information button on its label.

(b) Drop a pin and tap the person icon on its label.

(c) Use the pinch gesture to zoom in.

(d) Change the map view to Satellite.

4. To choose between suggested routes:

(a) Tap the Next button.

(b) Tap the Start button.

(c) Tap the route lines on the map.

(d) Tap the Directions button.

5. To go back to some directions you recently searched for:

(a) Tap the Previous button.

(b) Tap the Bookmarks button.

(c) Tap Directions.

(d) Tap Reverse Trip.

Answers

Q1 – a, b and d   **Q2** – c   **Q3** – b (this view works in Google Maps but not in Apple Maps)

Q4 – c   **Q5** – b

Reading books and magazines

16

Equipment needed: An iPad with an Internet connection.

Skills needed: Experience installing apps (see Chapter 14). Experience using the iTunes Store (see Chapter 10) is helpful but not essential.

If you're an avid reader, you've probably noticed the publishing revolution that has taken place in the past few years: the ebook. This is a digital version of a book that has been created for reading on dedicated ebook reading devices like Amazon's Kindle or on multipurpose devices like your iPad.

Although more people still read paper books than ebooks, it tends to be the most passionate readers who have gone digital. Why? It's so convenient. You can buy a book anywhere you can get an Internet connection and start reading in a minute or two. In the summer, you can take 30 books on holiday without paying for excess baggage. You can increase the text size and enlarge photos, search an ebook for particular words or names and add bookmarks. Sometimes the content is enhanced with videos, audio recordings, or interactive animations.

Apple has an ebook-reading app called iBooks, which is supported by its own bookstore. There's also a part of the App Store for magazines called Newsstand, and you can use a Kindle app to read books from Amazon's store, too. In this chapter, we introduce you to the joy of reading on your iPad.

Alaska Airlines has ditched the heavy airline manuals pilots used to carry around in favour of the iPad. Instead of carrying 11kg of paper onto the plane, each pilot has a company-issued iPad with 41 flight, systems and performance manuals on it.

Installing iBooks on your iPad

The Newsstand app comes pre-installed on your iPad, but you have to go to the App Store and download iBooks for free. In practice, if you search for a book title in the iTunes Store and tap it, you get a message stating that you need iBooks to read it and are offered a link that lets you install it for free. (See Chapter 14 for more on finding and downloading apps.) If you're heading to the App Store, you may want to download the Kindle app too, which enables you to read ebooks from Amazon's store. Having both apps gives you a wider choice of books and enables you to shop for the keenest price.

The apps are free, but you have to pay to download many of the books. Publishers do sometimes make ebooks available for free or cheaper than printed books, so it's worth browsing your favourite authors and genres to see what's on offer. Classic works of literature are often available for free download because they're out of copyright.

When you first start the app, it asks whether you want to sync your bookmarks, notes and collections among devices. If you plan to use iBooks on several devices, this feature helps you keep all your information synchronised across them, so if you stop reading your latest mystery on page 57, you can open up to the same spot on any device. You can change your mind later, if you need to, by turning off this option in the Settings app.

Downloading books using iBooks

When the app starts, you see an empty bookshelf. When you have some books, it looks more like the shelf in Figure 16.1. To download your first books, tap Store in the top-left corner of the screen, and you enter the iBookstore, which looks and feels the same as the App Store (see Chapter 14) and the iTunes Store (see Chapter 10). As with apps and music, you tap the Price button to buy a book. You download a free ebook by tapping the Free button that replaces its price. If you want to weigh up a book before buying it, tap the Get Sample button.

To the iBookstore

Change library view

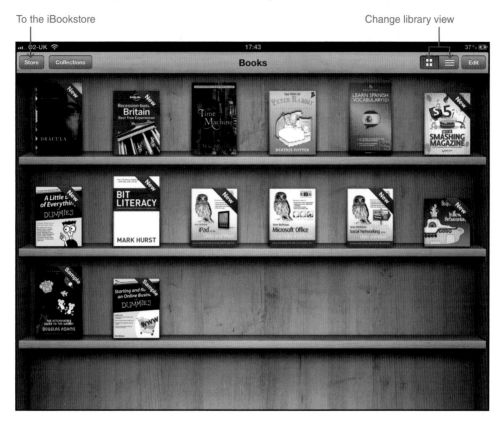

Figure 16.1

When you buy or download a book for free, you're taken back to your bookshelf automatically. If you decide to leave the store without getting a new book, tap Library in the top-left corner to return to your bookshelf.

When you have too many books to fit on the screen, you can scroll down bookshelves by dragging upwards. You can also drag down to reveal a search box above the top shelf so you can quickly find a specific title. We wish they'd invent something similar that works in our town libraries.

Reading books using iBooks

To start reading a book, tap its cover in your library on your bookshelf. You can read books in portrait orientation (where the pictures might be larger) or landscape orientation (which feels more like a real book).

You can often double-tap a picture to enlarge it and then use the pinch gesture on it to zoom in further. When you've finished, tap the picture and then tap Done in the top-right corner.

To turn to the next page, put your finger on the right side of the screen and flick it left. To go back a page, put your finger on the left side of the screen and flick it right. You can also slide the page chooser along the bottom of the screen.

Figure 16.2 shows iBooks in action, with its controls labelled.

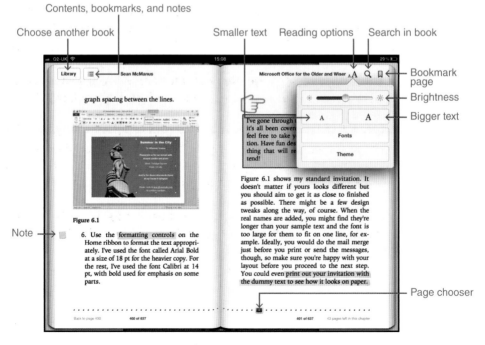

Figure 16.2

There's some clever stuff you can do with a digital book (ebook) that you can't do with a real book. Double-tap a word, for example, and you can adjust the grab points to select text (see Chapter 4). You can do several things to selected text: have it spoken aloud to you, copy it for pasting into other apps like Notes, search for it elsewhere in the book, look it up in the dictionary, highlight it in one of five colours or add a note about it.

Unlike when you scribble comments in the margin of a printed book, you can quickly see all your notes in one place by going to the Bookmarks page for your ebook. When you're reading a book, the notes appear in the margin. Just tap them to enlarge them, and tap outside them to hide them again. To see your notes and bookmarks, tap the icon in the top-left corner (refer to Figure 16.2).

If you find the iBooks controls distracting, you can tap the page to hide them. Tap again to bring them back when you need them.

If you struggle to read small print, you can change the text size. Just tap where indicated in Figure 16.2 to open the reading options; then tap the Bigger Text button until you can read comfortably. You can also change the text style used (the font) and the theme to something easier on the eyes. Try the Sepia theme if you find the white pages too dazzling. The Night theme uses white text on a black background, so there's less light glaring at you when you're reading in the dark.

Books can include links, too. If you tap an entry in the table of contents, for example, you jump to the relevant section of the book. You can see the table of contents by tapping the button in the top-left corner indicated in Figure 16.2. You can also tap a website link to open its web page in Safari.

When you're reading a free sample of a book, a Buy button appears in the top-left corner. Tap that button to skip to the last page in the sample, which has a price button you can tap to buy the book.

In the top-right corner are two basic but useful controls:

- **Bookmark button:** Use this button when you want to mark a page that you're interested in coming back to later. Tap the button in the top-left corner to see all your bookmarked pages at a glance.

- **Search:** A search option in the top-right corner lets you scan the whole book for a particular word or phrase.

When you've finished reading, tap Library in the top-left corner to return to your bookshelves.

Lots of great free books are available, so why not see what you can find? You can get free books by Beatrix Potter, Charles Dickens, HG Wells and many more. You can find a selection of free ebooks in the Books section of the App Store (see Figure 16.3), but there are plenty of other online sources too. It's also worth searching for 'free ePubs' and 'free PDFs' as these are formats that are often used to make ebooks.

Other types of ebooks

The books we've just described in Apple's iBookstore aren't the only kind of ebook you can get. In fact, ebooks have existed since 1971, when Michael Hart began digitising out-of-copyright publications. These are available as PDF (portable document format) and ePub downloads at **www.projectgutenberg.org**. Aside from PDF, which is often used to distribute marketing brochures and user manuals, for example, the most widely used ebook format is ePub. Apple's iBooks is a proprietary version of it. Other ebook formats include eReader, plain text (.txt) files, and AZW and KF8, for which you'll need to use the free Amazon Kindle app (see the following section). Less common are MOBI, which was used on small-screen portable devices that predate the iPhone and iPad, and variations of the Comic-Book Reader format, which combines text and images. Graphic novels often have .cbr or .cbc at the end of their filenames.

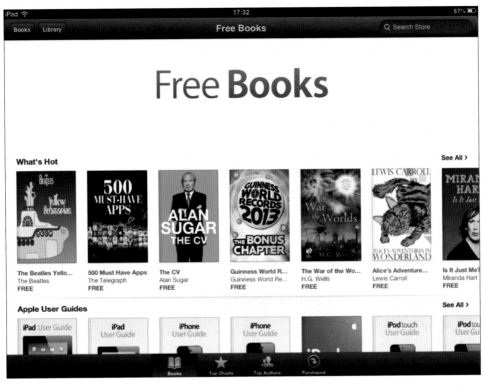

Figure 16.3

A more sophisticated form of ebook is the interactive storybook. For a glimpse into the future of storytelling, take a look at the free ebook based on *Yellow Submarine*, the film by The Beatles. You'll find it listed in the Books section of the iTunes Store. This interactive book includes sound effects, video and animations. Apple promises many more interactive books in future, and several interactive textbooks are already available, such as the Shakespearean study guides from Cambridge University Press. Navigating interactive books is often slightly different to how you progress through the essentially static pages of a standard digital book, so many of the tips in this section won't work as we describe.

It's not just Apple and Amazon that offer ebooks for download. Major book-shops such as Barnes & Noble, Waterstones and Foyles all offer their own digital download stores on their websites. Some public libraries offer digital book loans too; you still need a reading card, but it's much simpler than venturing out in the cold. For book recommendations, it's worth signing up to sites such as LoveReading (**www.lovereading.co.uk**), which offer you taster chapters of books. Sites such as Goodreads (**www.goodreads.com**) provide recommended reads and reviews from your friends. The best-known repository of free digital books is Project Gutenberg, which offers more than 40,000 titles across many genres. Turn your web browser to **www.gutenberg.org** to find out more.

Using the Amazon Kindle app

If you've already got iBooks, why would you want Amazon's rival ebook app too? First, books are sometimes cheaper at Amazon, and second, you can read the books you buy from Amazon on lots of other devices, including the Kindle. By comparison, books bought on iBooks can be read only on compatible Apple devices.

The main gotcha with the Kindle app (see Figure 16.4) is that there's no store built in and no hint about where you find it. To buy content or order free content, you have to visit the Amazon website at **www.amazon.co.uk**, using your web browser (see Chapter 9). Any orders you make are then sent to your Kindle app.

The Kindle app predates iBooks and has several features you may prefer. You can change the brightness levels, background page colour, text size, number of columns per page and space between lines, all by tapping the Aa icon in the top-right corner. There's also a useful Furthest Page tool that recognises that you might have read ahead on another device and takes you to the page at which you left off.

Both the Apple and Amazon ebook readers (and others such as Stanza that you may use instead) can act as viewers for PDFs and other electronic documents. When you're synchronising your iPad using iCloud, though, iBooks generally copies across only the items you've bought from the iTunes Store or the App Store.

Figure 16.4

Many publishers present their books and magazines as separate apps, rather than as digital books, so some will be installed on your iPad as apps rather than appearing in the iBooks library.

Using Newsstand to buy magazines

There's a part of the App Store you can use to find newspapers and magazines for your iPad, called Newsstand. It has a special folder on your Home screen. When you tap the folder, which looks just like an app icon, Newsstand shows you the magazines you've downloaded (if any) and displays a Store button you can tap to find more (see Figure 16.5). Typically, you download an app that's like a catalogue of issues; then you can choose to buy individual issues or subscribe to get each issue when it comes out. The latest copy of a publication automatically appears in your Newsstand library. Because each publication has created its own digital edition, there's much more variance in the designs than with ebooks.

It's also worth noting that many publications you can buy through the Newsstand are listed as free – but may not be without cost. Often, you'll be offered a free issue to see whether you enjoy reading your favourite magazine this way. The fine print that's easy to skip in your eagerness to download the publication, however, often states that while the first issue is free, you're actually signing up for a rolling subscription. Because your iPad account is authorised to debit your bank account, you may not even notice this catch at first. Ensure that you know whether you're making a one-off purchase or starting a subscription.

Figure 16.5

Summary

- To read books on your iPad, you can install Apple's iBooks app.

- The apps and many classic books are free, but you have to pay for other content.

- You can synchronise your iBooks bookmarks, notes and collections among different devices.

- Tap Store in the top-left corner of the iBooks app to browse and download books, both free and paid.

- You can read books in portrait or landscape orientation.

- Just flick a page to turn it.

- If you select text, you can copy it, look it up in the dictionary, highlight it or add a note to it.

- Tap the top-left corner to see the table of contents, bookmarks and notes.

- You can adjust the text style and size to your preference, and you can change the colour theme to something that's easier on the eyes too.

- Alternative ebook readers include Amazon's Kindle app. This app allows you to read ebooks bought from Amazon's website on the iPad too.

- The Newsstand app stores digital versions of magazines and newspapers that you download and to which you may subscribe.

Brain training

It's the end of the book, but we hope that this chapter has helped you discover your next read. We finish up as usual with a quiz.

1. To find a free book to read in iBooks, you have to:

(a) Tap Library.

(b) Tap Store.

(c) Use Newsstand.

(d) Use the Kindle app.

2. To see a picture in a book more clearly, you can:

(a) Tap the picture.

(b) Double-tap the picture.

(c) Rotate your iPad.

(d) Squint.

3. If you spot an interesting word in a book and double-tap it, you can:

(a) Find out what it means.

(b) Change its text colour.

(c) Find out where else in the book it appears.

(d) Email your friends about it.

4. If you select text in iBooks, you can:

(a) Have it read aloud.

(b) Enlarge it.

(c) Add a bookmark.

(d) Add a note to it.

5. To buy books to read in the Kindle app, you have to:

(a) Tap the Store button.

(b) Go into the Kindle app.

(c) Visit the Amazon website in your browser.

(d) Buy a Kindle reader device

Answers

Q1 – b   **Q2** – b and c   **Q3** – a and c

Q4 – a and d   **Q5** – c

PART V
Appendices and Index

Why are so many people reading books about apples these days?

Looking after your iPad

Equipment needed: Just your iPad.

Skills needed: An idea of what you want the iPad to do and what you need advice about.

There are times when the iPad won't behave as expected. That's what the next few pages cover. If the advice in this appendix doesn't help, the iPad User Guide bookmark in the Safari web browser may well lead you to the solution you need. And don't forget the power of the Internet. Now that you know how to get online and search for information, you can always hunt down the answer on Apple's website (**www.apple.com**) or on one of the many websites devoted to its products, such as **www.macworld.co.uk**.

Looking after my iPad's battery

Your iPad should operate for around ten hours before it needs to be recharged. This is how much active use you can expect, rather than the standby time. The iPad won't use much power while it's idle. The battery life also varies depending on what you use the iPad for. Watching documentaries on the BBC iPlayer may drain the battery faster than other activities.

You can always see how much battery life is left: The percentage of battery charge is displayed in the very top-right corner of the iPad's screen.

Minimise battery drain by switching off the Wi-Fi and Bluetooth connections when you aren't actively using them. The same applies to the 3G and 4G connections on a Wi-Fi + Cellular iPad model. Having a satnav app running all the time is a real battery drain, so if you've 50 miles to burn through on the motorway before your exit, quit the satnav until a few minutes before you next need guidance.

Switching off any apps you aren't using will also help. To do this, double-tap the Home button and then scroll along the list of running apps that appears across the bottom of the screen. Press the Home button twice to show the list; then tap and hold one of the icons. All the icons start to jiggle. Tap the minus sign in the top-left corner of the icon for an app you're not currently using, and it is closed and removed from the list. Although you can have music or a podcast playing while you surf the Internet, having several items running at the same time uses more power.

Location Services works by confirming your current whereabouts; to do so, it sends information to and from online servers. This potential battery drain can be deactivated when not needed. Go into the Settings app, tap Privacy and switch Location Services off across the whole device or deactivate it on an app-by-app basis by changing the settings for each app.

Email messages and Twitter alerts that pop up onscreen can also reduce battery life. You can switch off many of these power hogs by putting your iPad in Airplane Mode when it's not in use. Just switch it back on in the Settings app to get your Wi-Fi, email, iMessages and so on.

Trouble getting online

Unable to get at your emails or surf the web? Check these things first:

- **Does the 'fan' icon in the top-left corner of the screen show several bars?** If not, go into the Settings app, and check whether a Wi-Fi connection name is showing. If there's only a weak signal, another connection might allow you to get online. You need a password to access secured connections.

- **Switch off the existing Wi-Fi connection and log in again.** This process sometimes helps.

- **Restart the broadband Wi-Fi router.** Sometimes, computing equipment 'forgets' what it's supposed to be doing and absentmindedly stops doing anything useful – such as providing Wi-Fi to your iPad. Turn off the router for 30 seconds and then restart it. There's usually a button on the router itself; if not, power down the computer to which your router connects to the Internet and then start everything up again.

- **Is your iPad in Airplane Mode?** A single setting change that turns off your Internet connection, email and Wi-Fi, Airplane Mode can help preserve battery life. To switch on all these services again, go to the Settings app, and turn off Airplane Mode.

- **Power down and restart your iPad.** It's a cliché, but turning off the iPad and then starting it again can magically fix many issues. Switch it off using the power switch on the top right (when holding the iPad vertically). Swipe your finger across the screen to confirm the action. Switch it back on by pressing the power switch.

Issues using mobile Wi-Fi

Are you using your iPad when you're out and about? You may simply be out of range of a Wi-Fi connection. Basements and lifts often have no connectivity. Look out for the Wi-Fi 'fan' reappearing on your iPad when you emerge and then select the Wi-Fi service you want to connect to.

If you have a Wi-Fi + Cellular iPad, you should see a 3G or 4G/LTE label or the name of your mobile network provider (O2, Vodafone, Verizon, and so on) in the top-left corner of your iPad. If it's inactive, go into the Settings app, and switch the cellular service off and on again. If this doesn't work, try switching off the Wi-Fi connection and then turning it back on again. Enabling and disabling Airplane Mode, also in the Settings menu, may also help.

If none of these options help, it may be that your mobile provider is at fault and no service is currently available. Frustrating as that is, you'll need to use Wi-Fi until the cellular service is active again.

If you're travelling overseas or are out of range of the coverage that your mobile provider offers, it could simply be that there's no service in the area. Use Wi-Fi instead, where available.

Error messages relating to a particular Wi-Fi hotspot can be caused by too many people trying to use the connection at the same time; by a weak signal because you're not very close to the connection point; or by interference from another, stronger Wi-Fi service in the area. Your iPad naturally tries to connect you to the strongest available connection.

Getting music from my computer on to my iPad

Apple allows you to link as many as seven devices to your Apple ID account. These devices could be your iPad, an iPhone or iPod touch, a Windows or Mac computer or laptop, and so on. The restrictions are there to satisfy copyright issues relating to the music, books, films and TV programmes you can enjoy on your iPad and other iOS devices. Occasionally, you get a message such as the one in Figure A.1, telling you that there's music or other content on another device that is not on your iPad. Turn on Automatic Downloads in the Settings, iTunes & App Stores menu for your iPad, and your computer will resolve this.

Figure A.1

Issues connecting to the iTunes Store while downloading

The very large amounts of data in a video file mean that as well as taking a long time to copy to your iPad, films and TV programmes can stumble in the process. If you see the message shown in Figure A.2, tap Retry and be patient. Assuming that you're still in a Wi-Fi area, the iPad will resume the download of its own accord.

Figure A.2

I've forgotten my password

You need to enter your Apple ID whenever you want to buy something from the App Store or the iTunes Store. If you've forgotten your password, go into the Settings app, choose iTunes & App Stores. Tap Apple ID followed by the iForgot option below the Apple ID and password fields, and you'll be taken to a web page where you can answer the secret questions you filled out when you set up your account. A link to reset your password will be emailed to you. Look out for it, as the link will expire after a day or two. Note that you can't use the same password again, so you need to think of another memorable letter-and-numeral combination.

Securing my iPad

We strongly encourage you to use the four-digit passcode on your iPad to prevent someone casually picking it up and taking a look through your email messages and more. Go into the Settings app, tap General and turn on Passcode Lock. For greater security, you might prefer to use a password instead. In this case, switch off the Simple Passcode (four-digit keypad) option and tap the Turn Passcode On option above it. Now you can choose a password using a combination of numbers and letters. If you're fairly paranoid about someone flicking through the contents of your iPad, you may want to enable the Erase Data feature, which erases your iPad's contents after ten failed passcode entry attempts. Just be very sure that you've got a backup before enabling this feature. In most cases, we recommend using the passcode or password to prevent access and using the remote wipe feature of Find My iPad to erase the device's contents should you be unfortunate enough to have it stolen. Find My iPad can be enabled in the Settings, iCloud menu. For it to work, you also need Location Services to be active. This option is in the Settings, Privacy menu.

Be careful with Bluetooth

Bluetooth is a form of wireless connection that lets your iPad talk directly to your Mac (if it's in the same room) and share files with it. It can also be used to connect wireless speakers and wireless keyboards. It works by pairing devices, with each device accepting an invitation to connect. Bluetooth also poses a mild security risk, because people who have Bluetooth on their smartphones, laptops and iPads can see that your Bluetooth connection is active and may try to connect to it.

Your best bet is to ensure that Bluetooth is switched off except when you're using it. Never have Bluetooth switched on when you're at an Internet café or another Wi-Fi hotspot.

Stumped by Siri

Siri is the name of the built-in assistant available on the third-generation iPad or later that's running iOS6. Siri has voice-recognition capabilities but doesn't understand every accent or every command. You can invoke Siri by pressing down and holding the iPad's Home button. You can have a more personal relationship with Siri by telling her/him who you are: Go into the Settings app, tap General, select Siri and tap My Info. Your Contacts list appears. Choose your name from the list, and Siri will address you by your first name from now on.

Siri can be useful for setting reminders and alarms, and for finding out the weather forecast, sports scores and restaurant recommendations (see Figure A.3). You can also dictate notes (see Chapter 4) and emails to Siri. If you have a 3G/4G iPad, you can also use Siri for turn-by-turn navigation with your Maps app (see Chapter 15).

Figure A.3

Call up Siri by pressing the Home button. Tap the microphone button to begin talking to Siri. Unless you change the Passcode Lock settings in the Settings app, you can use Siri without having to swipe to unlock the iPad. Note that Siri works only when the iPad has access to an Internet connection.

If you want to disable Siri (so you don't accidentally invoke her when pressing the Home button), go to Settings, General, and deselect Siri.

How can I protect my iPad's screen?

We don't recommend many iPad accessories, but an iPad case is definitely worth considering. A folio-style case with a protective screen cover that folds back and becomes a stand for your iPad probably is ideal. Some cases also come with acetate screen protectors, but these protectors are fiddly to apply; they also spoil the look of your iPad and make the touchscreen less responsive.

I'm finding the keyboard hard to type on

Using a touchscreen keyboard is certainly different to using a computer keyboard or typewriter. The tips we provide in Chapter 4 should help. If you've persevered and still don't like typing emails or Notes this way, a separate keyboard, such as the one shown in Figure A.4, may help. This type of keyboard uses the wireless Bluetooth technology to send information to your iPad, such as the letters you've just typed. Several companies, including Apple, sell wireless keyboards for iPad use.

Copyright © Apple Inc.

Figure A.4

Stop the annoying email alerts

Whenever a new email arrives, your iPad 'dings'. If you also have an iPhone, it 'dings', too. You can change all this in the Notification Centre by choosing Mail, selecting the type of email account (such as iCloud or Gmail) and then selecting None in the New Mail Sound options. To be totally interruption-free, simply enable Do Not Disturb in the Settings app.

I'm worried about my credit card information

It's good to be cautious about entering credit-card information on electronic devices and the Internet. When you first set up your iPad, you should do so from the comfort of home, or at least somewhere where no one can peer over your shoulder to watch you type your name and address details and your credit card information. The Apple ID and password you set up for use with your iPad are there to prevent anyone else using your iPad to purchase books, music or anything else. That's why you have a lot of personal questions to answer at the start – and why you can't simply use the same password again if you forget yours and ask Apple for a reminder to help you log in.

You should be just as cautious when using the Internet on your computer or iPad to buy items online. A Wi-Fi hotspot, such as an Internet café or coffee shop, isn't a good place to make purchases from Amazon.com. Do so from the privacy and security of home (or at least from your hotel room). Also, you should only ever shop at a site that has a padlock displayed in the top-left corner, showing that it uses a secure server to process payments. You should never give out your credit card details by email.

Should I worry about viruses on my iPad?

Windows PCs users have spent years being told of the dangers that viruses and other security issues pose. The iPad is far less vulnerable to attack, simply because of the amount of control Apple exercises over every element of it. Rather than a virus, your biggest danger when using your iPad is being tricked into giving out personal information that someone could use against you. Date of birth, full address details, mother's maiden name, credit card information and National Insurance numbers are all valuable to other people.

Phishing email concerns

Be very wary of emails purporting to be from your bank or another well-known organization such as Amazon, PayPal or eBay. Scammers often use the look and logos of well-known companies to spoof their email addresses and send out seemingly legitimate requests asking the recipient to confirm bank account numbers or passwords. *Never, ever* respond to such requests. It's almost certainly from a scammer and is what's known as a 'phishing' email (because it's fishing for information).

Pick up the phone and talk to your bank or credit card company directly and explain that you've received an unexpected email from them. They will assure you they'd never request your password, account of credit card numbers or other personal or financial information by email.

It's also important that you don't click on a link in an email that comes out of the blue. Even if the email is from your son or daughter or someone else you completely trust, or the email was sent to you as a direct response to an email you sent to someone, be ultra-cautious. Email links are easily forged and may take you to an undesirable website run by hackers. Be especially wary of an email coming from a trusted source that contains only a link – no other text. Delete it without clicking the link.

Can I use my iPad abroad?

If yours is a Wi-Fi–only iPad, you can pay to access wireless Internet at hotels, cafés and other secure hotspots in the same way as you would in your own country. All the content stored on your iPad will be available to you.

If you've got a 3G or 4G iPad, overseas use is likely to be very expensive and may involve activation several days before you go. Consult your mobile operator (or the company from which you bought your iPad) in good time.

Can I safely allow others to use my iPad?

Yes. You can set up multiple accounts on your iPad so that everyone has his or her own iPad experience, with personal settings and access to personal email accounts, Safari bookmarks, music and other apps. Go to the Settings app, tap iTunes & App Stores, tap your Apple ID and sign out. Now choose Create New Apple ID, or have the other person sign in to the iPad with his or her own existing Apple ID.

If you simply want to be able to allow another family member to use your iPad for an hour or so, ignore this advice and use Restrictions instead. To access the Restrictions settings, go to the Settings app, tap General and then tap Restrictions.

Can I use my iPad with speakers and headphones?

If you want to enjoy your music, audiobook or a movie privately, almost any earphones or headphones will be fine. The iPad uses a standard 3.5mm jack.

A huge range of iPad and iPhone speakers is available – but not many so far work directly with the latest iPad model or the iPad mini. We think that the iPad's built-in speaker is quite loud anyway, but if you want to have a party, using a speaker may be a good idea.

You can buy a separate 30-pin–to–Lightning adapter to allow speakers designed for previous generations of iPads to connect to the latest iPad or iPad mini, but this solution may not be suitable for a docking speaker. Some such speakers are moulded to fit around the iPad itself. Either buy a speaker with a Lightning connector or ask advice in-store before handing over your credit card.

How do I watch movies I've downloaded to my iPad on a bigger screen?

You can watch anything you've downloaded to your iPad on your computer or laptop screen. You can also connect your iPad to your TV if you buy the necessary Digital AV Adapter, which is available from the Apple Store and other Apple stockists. Make sure to choose the right adapter for your iPad model, though. The latest iPad (October 2012) and the iPad mini use the thinner Lightning connector. Previous iPad models use the flat, wide 30-pin connector.

My iPad is full

You can find out what's hogging all the space by going to the Settings app, tapping General and then tapping Usage. Then, to free space, back up your music and downloaded books and films to your computer (if you have one). You can do this by plugging the iPad into the computer and allowing iTunes to synchronise the contents. Make sure you choose the Full backup option. It will then be safe to delete from your iPad albums you rarely listen to or films you won't watch immediately. They'll still be stored on your computer. If you use iCloud, backups happen automatically, but don't cover everything. Music is managed through iTunes, for example. Also note that any photos or videos you've just taken on your iPad, may not yet have been saved to iCloud. If you've been using an app extensively and saved files within it, check for a backup or export option within that app, or an option in the Settings app to active backups for it.

My iPad freezes or crashes

This behaviour can be symptomatic of a battery that will soon need to be recharged, too many apps being active at once or a badly designed app faltering. Your iPad may also be full or nearly full, or a download taking place may be making other things run slowly. Satnav apps can use up large proportions of your iPad's processing resources, as they constantly update the maps you see as well as the instructions about where to go next.

To switch off (but not delete) any apps that are running, double-click the Home button. Any apps that are currently running appear in a bar at the bottom of the screen. Swipe your finger back and forth along this list to see what's running (see Figure A.5). Press and hold any app's icon to make all the icons jiggle. Now tap the red 'no entry' sign to switch off any apps that you'd sooner weren't active. Press the Home button to stop the app icons jiggling about.

Figure A.5

An app I've bought doesn't work

Apple checks all the apps that appear in the App Store to ensure that they don't violate any security, decency, copyright or other international laws. But Apple doesn't make most of the apps, and some are simply better written than others. There are reviews of apps in the App Store and elsewhere on the Internet. Customers aren't shy about telling the developers that their app crashes a lot or doesn't work as it should.

Often, updating the app fixes the issues that customers have raised. If there's a number next to the App Store icon on your Home screen, it denotes the number of apps you've bought that have updates available. These updates are free. Tap the App Store icon, and choose Updates at the bottom of the screen. You see a page listing which apps are offering updates and possible performance improvements. Read what the developer says has changed; then click the Update lozenge to the right to install the update.

If the app still performs badly or doesn't do what you want, you can uninstall it by pressing and holding its icon and then tapping the X button to banish it. Other customers might like to know why you did so, so add a quick review or select a star rating in the App Store when you get a chance.

Will iPhone apps work on my iPad?

iPhone apps can be used on your iPad and can be useful if no equivalent app has been written for the iPad. iPhone apps launch the same way as iPad apps but appear smaller on your screen.

Go to the App Store, tap the iPhone apps lozenge at the top of the screen and enter the app's name in the Search box. After the app installs, you see a 2x button in the bottom-right corner of the screen. Tap this button to double the size at which the app is displayed. At the 2x size, the app is a little fuzzy because it's being shown in zoomed-in view. At this point, the indicator in the corner shows 1x again. Tap that to revert to the smaller size.

Getting a new iPad

Follow our advice about keeping everything backed up, and make sure that you complete a full backup of everything on your current iPad. You'll need your Apple ID and password, and your iPad must be connected to main power so it doesn't run out of juice while copying everything to your new device.

Once you've got the new iPad up and running and have checked that all your photos, files, music, apps and iBooks are present and correct, you may want to pass on your old iPad to a family member. To erase everything from your iPad, tap the Reset option at the very bottom of the Settings screen. Alternatively, you could just sign out of your account and have the iPad's new owner create his or her own Apple ID and user account.

4G or 3G A mobile Internet connection that works in a similar way to a mobile phone connection. It's also referred to as mobile broadband. iPads that support 4G or 3G are referred to as 'Wi-Fi + Cellular' by Apple. They cost more than Wi-Fi only iPads. You pay a subscription to use 4G or 3G, and you must have a 4G or 3G signal available wherever you are when you want to use it. You will probably be subject to a monthly data usage limit. A 3G signal is available in most places in urban areas, most of the time. In the U.S., 4G is supported only by fourth-generation iPads and the iPad mini. In the UK, 4G is available through Everything Everywhere (also known as 'EE') and on the 3 network. In 2013, other mobile operators will begin offering 4G services, but coverage will still be very limited. Where a 4G signal is not available, your iPad will use the best signal available, which is generally 3G, but may be Wi-Fi.

app Short for *application*. An app is a program on your iPad, such as Notes or Mail. The iPad comes with many apps, and you can download additional paid and free apps from the App Store.

App Store Apple's online store that enables you to download new apps for your iPad, many of which are free. You can access the store through the App Store icon on your iPad's Home screen or through the iTunes software on your computer.

Apple ID A personal ID that you use to access various services provided by Apple, including FaceTime, Find My iPad, the iTunes Store (for buying music and video) and the App Store. Your ID is a combination of your email address and a password you set up when you create your Apple ID.

Apple Maps Digital maps used to pinpoint addresses and photos and provide navigation directions. In October 2012, Apple replaced the Google Maps app found on previous iPad models with its own, currently less-detailed Apple Maps. Users who update their iPad software to iOS6 will find this change to Apple Maps.

arrangement mode Refers to a setting in which apps on the iPad's screen are freed from their locations and can be moved to new positions, including other screens. You enter arrangement mode by pressing and holding your finger on an app. To move an app, you select it by pressing and holding the icon and then dragging it to the desired location. Press the Home button to exit arrangement mode.

Bluetooth A wireless technology used to connect electronic devices in fairly close proximity (30 feet or less). If you buy a wireless keyboard for your iPad, it uses Bluetooth to send information to the iPad. Bluetooth is also ideal if you want to use speakers to play your iTunes music out loud.

bookmark Used to keep note of web pages, ebook pages or map locations you may want to refer to later.

Contacts An app that provides a single place to store information about your friends – information that is then shared with the Mail, Messages, Maps and FaceTime apps to ensure that those apps have postal addresses, phone numbers and email addresses available to use whenever they're needed.

Do Not Disturb A useful setting to invoke when you don't want to be reminded of incoming emails and iMessages, or to have people try to call you using FaceTime. You'll find it in the Settings screen if your iPad is running iOS6.

Dock The shelf at the bottom of the iPad's screen, showing several important apps. The Dock's apps are the same on all your screens, so you can always find these important apps quickly.

The term 'dock' also refers to a device you can buy to charge your iPad that may also function as a speaker system or stand.

double-tap To briefly touch something on the screen twice in quick succession.

drag A gesture used to scroll around the screen so you can see different content on it. Touch the screen and move your finger up, down, left or right. If a web page spills off the bottom of the screen, for example, you need to drag the web page up to see more.

ebook Short for *electronic book,* a book you can read on your iPad or another electronic device. There are around a dozen ebook formats, not all of which can be read by the Apple iBooks app. However, ebook reader apps are usually free, so you can install as many as you need.

FaceTime Apple's app for videoconferencing with other iPad users and friends who have the right models of iPhone, iPod touch, or any Mac computer that has a camera and is running OS X Lion or Mountain Lion. FaceTime can be used on all iPads except the original model of iPad (which has no cameras). FaceTime needs an Internet connection to work.

Find My iPad An app that tracks down your iPad to the nearest few metres – or closer! – should you ever mislay it (as if you'd let your iPad out your sight!). Find My iPad also lets you remotely lock or wipe the device so the person who finds your iPad can't access the contents. You need to have Location Services switched on for it to work.

flick A gesture for moving through content quickly. Touch the screen and move your finger left, right, up or down quickly, lifting your finger partway through.

gestures Ways to control the iPad by touching its screen in different ways, such as by briefly touching an icon (tapping it) or by moving your fingers closer together or farther apart while they're on the screen's surface (the pinch gesture).

high definition (HD) A term for high-quality video, also used to indicate films and TV programmes designed for the iPad's large screen.

Home button The round button on the front of the iPad at the bottom. Press it to exit apps, cancel actions and return to the Home screen. This button also invokes Siri – a voice-based assistant.

Home screen A bit like a main menu, the screen that's shown whenever you start using your iPad or tap the Home button twice to go back to the main menu.

iBooks The Apple app for reading ebooks on your iPad. You can download iBooks for free from the App Store and use it to read PDF files. You can buy ebooks from the iBookstore by using your Apple ID.

iCloud Apple's service for storing your files on its computers in its vast data centre and making them available to you over the Internet. You can use iCloud to copy content among your devices and to back up your iPad. You also need iCloud to share some sorts of content with friends.

icon A small picture used to represent an app on the Home screen. Tap an app's icon to start the app. An icon can also be a symbol inside an app that's used as a button, such as the magnifying glass you tap to search in iBooks.

iMessage The Apple service for sending instant messages between people who are using iPads, iPhones or other Apple devices. You can send and receive iMessage for free, but you do need an Internet connection.

iOS The software the iPad uses. The same software is also used on iPhones and the iPod touch. Free updates that add new features are often released around the same time as new iPad and iPhone models.

iPhone Apple's mobile phone, which also runs apps but has a much smaller screen than the iPad. Since they both run on iOS software, you can use iPhone apps on your iPad. However, they use only a small part of the screen by default and can become 'blocky' when you enlarge them.

iPod Apple music and video players, including the iPod touch, that can run apps but have a much smaller screen than the iPad.

iTunes Apple software that runs on your computer and is used to manage your iPad and the content on it. The iTunes Store is where you buy and download music, video and other content. You access the iTunes Store on your iPad by tapping the iTunes icon on the Home screen. You can also access the iTunes Store on your computer by using the iTunes software.

iTunes Match A subscription service that enables you to download and play all your music on your iPad.

iTunes Store Apple's online store where you can buy music, TV programmes and films, as well as find free podcasts and iTunes U lectures.

iTunes U Short for *iTunes University*, a section of the iTunes Store that provides free educational programmes for download. Before downloading and watching these programmes, you must download the free iTunes U app from the App Store.

landscape orientation A way of holding your iPad so that it's wider than it is tall, like a landscape painting.

Lightning connector Plugs in to your iPad to power it or connect other devices such as speakers. With the iPad and iPad mini introduced in October 2012, Apple changed from the familiar 30-pin connector to a tiny, much more powerful, all-digital connector known as Lightning. Its equivalent on Apple Mac computers is called Thunderbolt. (Do you think someone at Apple is a Queen fan?) Older iPad accessories may not be compatible with this latest-generation iPad as a result.

Location Services Used for displaying maps, tagging photos and finding a mislaid iPad. Location Services can affect battery use, so don't have it active if you aren't able to charge your iPad until tomorrow.

Lock Used to prevent other people using your iPad without your permission. When your iPad is locked, the screen is off, and it doesn't respond to your touch. The device can continue to play music and show slideshows from your Photos collection. To unlock the iPad, press the Home button and slide the onscreen switch. Alternatively, open your iPad's Smart Cover or Smart Case, if it has one.

Newsstand Stores your digital magazine collection. You can buy individual issues of digital magazines or sign up for ongoing subscriptions. Subscription issues are delivered to your iPad automatically so you can read them at your leisure.

Notification Centre A single panel you can use to see recent alerts from all your apps. You reveal it by dragging down from the top of the screen.

passcode A four-digit number you must enter to unlock your iPad or an alphanumeric password you set for the same purpose. One of the first things you should do when you get your iPad is secure it with a passcode.

Picture Frame A slide show consisting of photos stored on your iPad. To display it, tap the flower icon next to the Slide to Unlock bar on your iPad's Home screen. It's a nice touch, but you may not want the world to be able to see all your photos so easily.

pinch A gesture used to enlarge content on the screen (zoom in) or reduce its size (zoom out). Put two fingers on the screen and move them farther apart to zoom in. Close your fingers together to zoom out again.

phishing email The term for a fraudulent email message sent for the purpose of getting information from the recipient that can then be used illegally to obtain financial or personal information, such as credit card numbers, or to make electronic purchases.

Photo Booth A fun app that comes with your iPad that lets you take zany photos of yourself with the iPad's front-facing camera.

Photo Stream Displays photos from one Apple device on another Apple device. To use this feature and automatically copy photos between Apple devices, each one must be using the same Apple ID. Photos taken on your iPhone can magically appear on your iPad, for example.

podcast A free video or audio programme you can download from the iTunes Store. Lots of radio stations make their programmes available as podcasts, but anyone can publish a podcast. So lots of inventive amateur productions are available. Podcasts is the name of the free app you can download to listen to these shows.

portrait orientation A way of holding your iPad so that it's taller than it is wide, like a portrait painting.

Retina display Apple term for high-resolution screen on third- and fourth-generation iPads and on iPhone 4 onwards. So-called because detail is so finely rendered that the pixels that make up the image are invisible to the naked eye.

Safari The name of the software (known as a *web browser*) provided on the iPad that you use to explore the Internet. It has a compass icon. (Is the browser called *Safari* because it's a jungle out there?)

Settings app App used to manage almost everything on your iPad. You can change permissions and get an overview of what's happening on your iPad.

Sleep/Wake button The button on your iPad that locks the device or switches it off. If you hold your iPad with the round Home button at the bottom, the Sleep/Wake button is in the top-right corner.

Siri The voice-recognition assistant that lives in the iPad with Retina display (third- and fourth-generation devices) and the iPad mini. To call up Siri and ask what the weather will be like or to set an alarm, press and hold down the Home button. Tap the microphone to start telling Siri what you'd like help with. You can use Siri to dictate emails and messages, too.

Spotlight search The search feature built into the iPad that you can use to find notes, emails, contacts, videos and audio content stored on your iPad.

status bar The black bar across the top of the iPad's screen, which shows the time and the status of the battery and Internet connection. In many apps, you can tap the status bar to jump to the top of the page content.

streaming The process of playing music or videos or showing photos, directly from the Internet (generally using Wi-Fi), rather than downloading the content to your iPad first. The advantage is that streaming doesn't fill up your iPad with TV programmes, music and films. Instead, you can rent them and play them over Wi-Fi.

synchronising The process of connecting your iPad to your computer and copying content between them. Your contacts and web browser bookmarks, for example, are synchronised (synched) so that the same information is stored on your iPad and your computer. You can choose which audio, video, podcasts, photos and other content are copied from your computer to your iPad. Any content you create or download on your iPad is automatically backed up to your computer when you connect to it. You can synchronise with your computer by using Wi-Fi instead of physically connecting it to your iPad, or you can use iCloud so that you don't need to connect your iPad to your computer at all. Note that iCloud only synchronises some types of content.

tap Briefly touching something onscreen. You start an app by tapping its icon.

tap and hold Touching something on the screen and keeping your finger on it. You tap and hold an image or a link in the web browser to open additional options, for example, and you tap and hold an app icon on the Home screen to enter *arrangement mode*.

touchscreen The screen on the iPad. It not only displays information, but it also recognises where and when you touch it so that you can control the iPad.

unlock The state your iPad is in when it responds to your touch, and the screen is on and ready to use. To unlock a locked iPad, press the Home button and slide the slider to the right.

wallpaper The image that appears behind your icons on your Home and lock screens. You can change your wallpaper in the Settings app.

web browser The program used to view and interact with web pages. On the iPad, this program is the Safari app.

web clip Bookmark for a web page; appears on your Home screen like an app icon.

Wi-Fi A wireless Internet connection that you can use on your iPad to access the Internet, the App Store and the iTunes Store. Wi-Fi hotspots are often provided at cafés, holiday resorts and hotels, and you can set up your own hotspot at home.

YouTube A website that anyone can use to publish and view videos. On your iPad, the YouTube app enables you to search and view videos from the YouTube website. With the latest iPad models, YouTube is no longer preinstalled, so you must download it from the App Store, for free.

Index